HALFWAY HOME

Halfway Home

Race, Punishment, and the Afterlife of Mass Incarceration

REUBEN JONATHAN MILLER

Little, Brown and Company

New York Boston London

Little, Brown and Company
Hachette Book Group
1290 Avenue of the Americas, New York, NY 10104
littlebrown.com

First Edition: February 2021

Little, Brown and Company is a division of Hachette Book Group, Inc. The Little, Brown name and logo are trademarks of Hachette Book Group, Inc.

The publisher is not responsible for websites (or their content) that are not owned by the publisher.

The Hachette Speakers Bureau provides a wide range of authors for speaking events. To find out more, go to hachettespeakersbureau.com or call (866) 376-6591.

ISBN 978-0-316-45151-2
LCCN 2020938872

10 9 8 7 6 5 4 3 2 1

THOMSON REUTERS

Printed in the United States of America

For Dorothy Jean and Tommy.

For George Walter, and all our saints.

And for Kyle, who slept too early.

For Hyacinth and Mary, and for Michele,
for all that they have done.

For Janice and for our children, with all the
love that I have.

Contents

HALFWAY HOME

SOMETHING LIKE AN INTRODUCTION

I'd grown accustomed to the sounds of buzzers and gray steel doors shutting and locking behind me. It's not like in the movies. The men who live there don't flinch when the gates close. The smell of must, instant coffee, hastily brushed teeth, unwashed jumpsuits, and stomach flu tells you precisely where you are. But learning how to get around a place like this is an altogether different question. Underground passageways, some narrower and dingier than others, connect ten divisions sprawled across a ninety-six-acre compound. The campus feels stitched together. Red-brick, whitewashed, and gray stone buildings, each built at a different architectural moment, stretch up several stories before stretching out a full square mile; they're connected by sidewalk trails, "the yard," and hints of green space. Lines leading into the main dormitories wrap around the block-long brick-and-concrete walls that separate men and women in cages from their loved ones. The pace inside is slow but dizzying. A Frankenstein of a jail complex, Cook County is a patchwork of construction projects and racial poli-

3

tics lurching from the eighteenth century into the twenty-first.

In 1779, Chicago's black immigrant founder, trapper and fur trader Jean Baptiste Point du Sable, was arrested by the British under suspicion of "intercourse with the enemy."[1] He was Chicago's first "permanent non-indigenous resident"[2]—that is to say, he was the land's first colonial settler.[3] Du Sable must have stood out in a world of colonists at war with the "savages" and the elements and their own beasts of burden. And the colonists were at war with themselves—the French against the British and the British against the newly formed United States, asserting its right to be free. They warred over the right to take native lands, though all of them owned black slaves.[4] In the middle of the American Revolution, eighty-four years before the Great Emancipator ordered black freedom in the rogue states,[5] a free Haitian, son of a Frenchman and a formerly enslaved African woman, established a farm and trading post in the not yet settled marshland of Eschecagou (Chicago).[6] Du Sable raised two "quadroon" children on the bank of the Chicago River with his Potawatomi wife, Kittahawa.[7] In a sign of things to come, historians first encounter du Sable through the account of his jailer.[8] Arent Schuyler de Peyster, the British commandant of Fort Michilimackinac, wrote that du Sable was a "handsome negro, (well-educated and settled in Eschecagou) but much in the French interest,"[9] and that he sent him to Detroit, the coming symbol of American progress and decline. Du Sable would manage trade between the Brits, his captors; the French, who used to occupy that land; and the "Indians," with whom he found family.[10] Having built the first home and established the first trading post in what would become a global city, du Sable amassed some wealth.[11] Yet he died like many formerly incarcerated black men—penniless in his final years, his very American story almost lost to history.[12]

Two centuries later, the psychologist Winston Moore, a "bear of a man" nicknamed "Buddha" by his colleagues, was appointed "America's first black Warden." Presiding over the notorious and poorly run Cook County Jail, Moore was given the task of reforming and expanding it.[13] He was a tough-on-crime kind of guy, working in the shadow of Nixon's many wars—on hippies, on the poor, on drug addicts, on black protesters mourning the murders of their leaders.[14] Moore once penned an essay, published in *Ebony,* faulting black people for their "extraordinary tolerance" of "the growing army of black criminals." The black community, he wrote, needed "a massive re-education campaign" to "expose black criminals for what they are, not heroes but deadly enemies."[15] Despite Moore's law-and-order politics and identification with "hard working black people" who just "wanted their ghettos back," his tough demeanor backfired. Blamed for the jail's many failures, including the escape of thirty-eight people, he was shamed, arrested, and fired from his job under allegations that he beat three prisoners, a political move that esteemed black journalist Vernon Jarrett called the return of "dunk the darkie."[16] Moore was subjected to a very public trial and considerable public scorn. And while the charges were dropped, the damage had been done. The city founded by a black "ex-convict" tried to convict its first black jailer.[17]

That Moore was tried in the courthouse he helped to fill reveals much about American so-called race relations and the uneven administration of what we've misrecognized as justice. The word *justice* suggests some harm repaired or some truth revealed, but 95 percent of all court cases end in a plea deal after a person has spent anywhere from several weeks to several years in a cage. Of the 2.3 million people who are incarcerated, 40 percent are black, 84 percent are poor, and half have no income at all.[18] The 2,626 people who have been exonerated since 1989 spent an average of nine years in prison for crimes they did not commit.[19] Nearly half are black, and almost all of them are poor. It is clear to anyone paying attention that the legal system does not administer anything resembling justice but instead manages the nation's problemed populations.[20]

This is the weight and history of punishment in the United States, which poor people encounter before their arrests. To live through mass incarceration is to take part in a lineage of control that can be traced from the slave ships, through the Jim Crow South, to the ghettos of the North, and to the many millions of almost-always-filled bunk beds in jails and prison cells that make the United States the world's leading jailer.[21]

Neither Moore nor du Sable fully rebounded from their encounters with the law. This is because a history of arrest, whether it leads to a conviction or not, whether the conviction is overturned or not, is just like any other history, especially those told inaccurately.[22] It need not be well understood, or even true, to exercise power. The history of punishment and black incarceration, of racism and the production of race, the whole history of crime and criminality haunt the people we've accused of crimes. It whispers into the ears of prospective employers and landlords, urging them to reject applications. And it whispers into the ears of grandmothers and girlfriends as they make life-or-death decisions on behalf of their loved ones, forcing them to withhold a couch to sleep on or risk eviction to help them because the state has labeled the people they care for most criminals. Mass incarceration has changed the social life of the city. It has filtered into the most intimate relationships and deformed the contours of American democracy, one poor (and most often) black family at a time.

Winston Moore was a member of the political elite, a man who, through his long list of connections, could avoid getting caught in the leviathan's teeth. He was arrested and fired twice, once under scandal and once for criticizing his employer. But Moore, who could hire an attorney, did not spend a single night in jail. And while you can ask any Illinois governor if the occupant of that office can survive a brush with the law,[23] the experiences of the political class, like those of the economic elite, are far from typical. Rod Blagojevich, who was an attorney and the most recent governor in Illinois to be convicted, went to federal prison for trying to sell President Barack Obama's vacant Senate seat in 2008. He was caught on tape soliciting bribes and was convicted in federal court,[24] but he somehow found the time between his trial and incarceration to appear on Donald Trump's reality-TV show *Celebrity Apprentice*. Trump granted Blagojevich clemency in the third year of his presidency. "If we really wish to know how justice is administered," James Baldwin tells us in *No Name in the Street*, we must "go to the unprotected—those, precisely, who need the law's protection most!—and listen to their testimony.... Ask the wretched how they fare in the halls of justice," he writes, "and then you will know, not whether or not the country is just, but whether or not it has any love for justice, or any concept of it."

Let us go, then, to hear the stories that only the people we've labeled criminals can tell us about their lives. But we should not just go to the obvious places where the poor come into contact with the law, like the jails and prisons where they languish or the street corners where police detain them. To fully understand mass incarceration, we must go to the neighbor-hoods that hemmed them in long before they occupied cages, the same places that serve as their confines for years after they return. We must wait with them for a space to open in the halfway house or in the shelter, because the laws and policies that the U.S. government has enacted ensure there is no place for them to go. We must sit in the homes of the parents, lovers, and children who share their burdens. And we must march with the formerly incarcerated as they resist the slow death of hunger and cold.

The story of mass incarceration in America is bigger than American jails and prisons, even with their two million captives. And it's bigger than probation and parole, even with the five million people held in the prison of their homes through ankle bracelets, weekly drug tests, and GPS technology. This is because mass incarceration has an afterlife, and that afterlife is a supervised society—a hidden social world and an alternate legal reality. The prison lives on through the people who've been convicted long after they complete their sentences, and it lives on through the grandmothers, lovers, and children forced to share their burdens because they are never really allowed to pay their so-called debt to society.

Today, 19.6 million people live with a felony record,[25] four times the size of the population on probation and parole, and ten times the size of the American prison census. Almost all of these people lived in dire poverty before they entered a cage, and they return to these same conditions on the day of their release. One-third are black; one in three currently living black American men have felony records. And while the number of black women held behind bars is eight times higher today than it was in 1980, the reach of the carceral state does not stop at the threshold of the black family.

Forty-five thousand federal and state laws regulate the lives of the accused. They dictate where and with whom they may live and what they may do with their days. The greatest harms are concentrated at the state level, reaching into their neighborhoods. In Michigan, there are 789 of these laws. In Illinois, there are over 1,400, including more than 1,000 employment regulations, 186 policies that limit political participation, 54 laws restricting family rights, and 21 housing statutes. In most states, this means that people with criminal records may not hold public office or live in public housing. They can be fired from their jobs on the whim of their employers or have their applications for apartments denied, even when they have the jobs, the credit scores, and the references to qualify otherwise. In some states, they may not be allowed to vote. With few places to work or live and fewer ways to change the circumstances they face, they still may not qualify for food stamps or student loans to go back to school and improve their living conditions. They may have to give up their parental rights. They certainly may not adopt children or even live in a home with a foster child. They may not be able to leave the country, and, for some crimes, they can't even leave the state. It doesn't matter that they've finished probation or that their incarceration was decades ago. They can still be rejected, and there's nothing that anyone can do.

If all politics are local, law-and-order politics are hyper-local. Over half of the thirty-five thousand people released from Illinois prisons annually return to Chicago, and half of them, about nine thousand people, to just six of the city's poorest neighborhoods. All six areas have crime, arrest, and unemployment rates triple the national average, with black Americans accounting for 90 percent of their residents, save one neighborhood that is over 90 percent black and Latinx.[26]

No other marginalized group—not poor black people without criminal records, not mothers on welfare, not even undocumented immigrants—experience this profound level of legal exclusion. No other group shoulders the burdens of social policy in quite the same way. The laws and statutes our elected officials enacted at the federal and local level, most of them passed in the 1980s and 1990s during the so-called tough-on-crime era, have altered, fundamentally, the public and private lives of millions of Americans. The supervised society has produced a new form of citizenship through practices of punishment and exclusion that target our nation's poorest families.

Criminal justice reform has focused on the near-term goals of building better prisons and providing more services for the people who are eventually released. We've failed to see, or perhaps we've ignored, how the ways we've chosen to punish the poor extend far beyond the prison's walls and start long before an arrest occurs. This, too, is part of the afterlife of mass incarceration and a condition we have not yet reckoned with. An entire class of people are presumed guilty of some unspecified crime long before they break a law.

Were we to better understand the living conditions of the people we've labeled criminals, we might not wonder what they did to deserve poverty, prison, or the police officer's bullet. Were we to aim our gaze at the everyday routines of arrest, incarceration, and release or at what it takes to piece together a life after being branded *ex-convict, ex-offender,* or *ex-felon,* we might be curious about how such practices abide in the land of the free. We might ask what it means to carry the weight of being already accused as we weather life's predictable tragedies—caring for the sick or burying the dead and dealing with the adversities that come.

Halfway Home is an invitation to go with the nation's castaways as they gather their belongings, spend time with their loved ones, and try to make lives for themselves. The book travels back in time to show the beginnings of the supervised society, which started in 1972, although its roots run much deeper. And it travels forward through the lives of the people you will meet in its pages, beginning with their earliest encounters with the law. I went where the action is—to the social-service centers and food pantries where people with records struggle to find ways to feed themselves and fill the bellies of their hungry and embarrassed children. And I went to the church basements where men slept when they had nowhere else to go. I went to the corners where poor black kids smiled awkwardly in staged video clips as police officers, who are filmed every day killing people just like them, bring gifts of potato chips, blue juice, bottled water, fruit chews, and prayer. We've erected a supervised society where these kinds of experiences are justified because they happen so often that we've learned to take them for granted. To grasp the inner workings of this alternate legal reality requires us to pay attention to people we've learned not to see. And it requires us to get close to people we've learned to fear and dismiss.

When I arrived at the Cook County Jail in the fall of 2003, a twenty-something religious volunteer, ethical commitments on my sleeve, the first black warden had long since accomplished his task of "reform" by expanding the jail. Winston Moore's administration tripled the jail's daily capacity, going from thirteen hundred inmates in 1969 to four thousand by the time he was fired under scandal. Twenty-five years and several construction projects later, there were ten thousand almost-always-filled jail beds. Millions of people had passed through the courthouse, and millions more did time. Today, one hundred thousand men, women, and teenagers, nearly half of whom are awaiting their trials, circulate between the Cook County Jail and some poor black neighborhood on the South Side or West Side of Chicago each year.[27]

Long lines of visitors snake around corners outside the entrances to each of the main dormitories. Once visitors get inside the first gate, longer lines mark the pilgrimage of overworked public defenders, parents and grandparents, social workers, wives, husbands, and partners, some with strollers, others holding the hands of their little ones, huddled together under the elements. They fix shirts, braid hair, discipline children, forget to hide cell phones, lose and regain their place in line, all while being herded single file into the lobbies and waiting areas of the buildings that cage their loved ones.

The line moves through a second gate that leads out to a sidewalk and, eventually, to the main entrance. Family members make their way to the front desk. One line is for visitation, another is to post bail, a third is to retrieve property. Visitors wait at the head of their line, ignored for several beats before some administrator, peering over her glasses, acknowledges their turn. Having barely answered their questions—about property, about visiting hours, about what might or might not be considered contraband—the administrator reminds them that the rules are posted online and then directs them to hard plastic chairs. The visitors take seats, wait their turn to be metal-detected and patted down, then sit again, passing the time in relative silence. Twenty minutes later, they are led through a doorway into another waiting area, where they sit for their half-hour visits, guards monitoring their affections.

These lines are not the only ones. Behind the walls and Plexiglas and locked, sallow, whitewashed cinder-block corridors, men, sometimes chained, shuffle single file down the hallways. Even those who walk freely do so in rows.

The jargon thrown around in this jail doesn't seem to describe the things men do. *Movement, meds,* and *yard* seem best fit for herding cattle. When "feeding time" is announced, some man in oversize khakis hauling an industrial-strength black garbage bag filled with bologna or ham sandwiches on white bread, sometimes with oranges and cartons of milk, makes his way to the front of the wing to pass out his goods.

I was a volunteer chaplain, Bible tucked under my arm. I used a pass that allowed me to move to the front of the line. I was greeted on the way by requests from grandmothers with loved ones behind bars. They would ask for me to see about their sons or pray for pending court cases or talk about evictions or pains in their legs or being tired or having lost a job. I was struck by their kindness. I was also glad for the fraternity among service staff. Social workers and clergy depend on one another. The chaplains visit sick family members; they grieve and pray with the men. Social workers give referrals to drug-treatment programs and food pantries. They lend chaplains their offices to decompress, to tell a man his mother died, to have a cup of weak coffee, or to talk about something other than the jail. The nurses are always kind to the chaplains, and most seem kind to the men. The guards, some of them friendly, most ambivalent, a few unwelcoming, sometimes exchanged pleasantries with me and sometimes made requests. "You got an extra Bible?"

or "God bless you, brother. Pray for me," they would say; occasionally they made conversation about their calling, the church they went to, or their wayward kids. Chaplains prayed for their upcoming surgeries or for their loved ones who'd died. When their children wound up in the jail, we went to sit with them quietly.

I became fast friends with many of these folks. At twenty-seven, I was one of the youngest of the visiting helping professionals. Besides the guards, there were few black men of any age helping, and the ones that visited regularly were in their sixties. I visited three of the jail's ten divisions, four to six hours per day, two to three days per week, for just over five years. I worked in the minimum-, medium-, and maximum-security wings of the jail, and I grew accustomed to the men's stories: Someone had shot someone else. Someone's mother was about to be evicted. Someone's grandfather died. Someone beat his girlfriend. Someone was framed. Someone was sick with the flu or diabetes or was suffering from withdrawal. Someone had lots of cash from selling dope. A few people asked about my life and motivations. A few called me a fraud. Some tried to convert me to their religions. Others were preachers themselves, men who swore they were different from their cell mates. Most were friendly, but from time to time I met some who were angry and not so orderly, who were dissatisfied with some aspect of how they were caged. Some complained about the guards that abused or mistreated them. Others yelled at me for interrupting their card games.

Once in a while, someone would threaten another man, like the one who would not tell me his name or shake my hand. He paced around the stainless-steel table where we held Bible study mouthing quiet, inaudible hostilities. He stopped behind a frail, graying, flamboyant man who attended our services who was rumored to have AIDS. We held hands and prayed while the cross-eyed, six-foot, three-hundred-pounder loomed over his shoulder, repeatedly clenching his fists. It's striking that the guards never noticed these kinds of things. They would leave me locked in a cell while they ran their errands. I grew accustomed to this neglect of my own safety and the safety of the men.

By the spring of 2006, I worked exclusively in division 10, the maximum-security dorm. The men sat at the benches in the common area, some playing cards but most watching Jerry Springer on the television set suspended high in the right corner of the wing. I arrived and gave the call for chapel, which was their cue to turn the TV down or off. A few men straggled over, some coming from the shower or from movement. I greeted them as they came forward. When about twenty men had arrived, we stood in a circle, held hands, and prayed for the service, for our families, and for God to "use us." One time, one of the men, whose name I never learned and who I would never see again, asked if he could sing a song. He left the circle and stood with his back toward his cell. He pounded his foot against the steel door to keep rhythm and led the clapping men in a rendition of the gospel song "Wait on the Lord."

Waiting was one of few things the men could depend on. Learning *how* to wait would come in handy. I heard countless stories of languishing. For one man, Lorenzo, it took nine continuances and nearly a year for the drug dealer he robbed to show up to court and testify against him, and Philip's story sticks with me. It had been three weeks since his booking and three weeks since he'd met with his public defender. We didn't discuss much about his case—I don't believe he trusted me—but the circumstances had something to do with a murder and the possibility of a seventy-nine-year prison sentence. Seventy-nine seemed like such an odd and arbitrary number. He was twenty-six, and I was twenty-eight. I had a young family and a job, and I had started graduate school. He had a young family and was unemployed, and he had not finished high school. Philip was preparing for trial, his fate in the hands of a judge and jury who had more in common with the prosecutor than with him and a public defender who was too busy to meet with him before his day in court. The world of prosecution, with its legalese and court routines, was as alien to Philip as the white, middle-aged jurist who would decide where he'd spend the next eight decades of his life. I identified with his predicament because of my own experience with the courts and my own feelings of powerlessness.

In the early 1980s, my grandmother, whom we called Ma Ma (pronounced "Mah-Ma"), took me to court with my two brothers, Joseph and Jeremiah. Our mother had left us at a police station. This was right before the crack era but after Reagan made a scandal out of the "welfare queen." The police station was one of the few places that a poor, drug-addicted, or mentally ill woman could leave the children she couldn't raise, or simply did not want to raise, without risking a charge of child neglect. The first custody hearing took place a few weeks after Ma Ma rescued us from the last of a series of foster homes. I was five. We had been in foster care for four years, and she was asking the family courts to name her our legal guardian. (The four of us would go to a hearing every few years after that.) I was the youngest of the boys, holding her hand as she stood before a judge who looked nothing like her, whose brief words we could hardly understand although they would determine the course of our lives together. I remember her face, which was animated with a slight sense of urgency, juxtaposed with his—stoic, silent. Then the judge made some brief pronouncement and she carried me away, Joseph and Jeremiah struggling to keep pace with her. Years later I would think about the many foster kids who wound up in prison—nearly half of them in some states. My family was no exception.

My brother Jeremiah was handed an eighteen-month sentence in the state of Michigan, where I lived and worked as a professor. My father's eldest son, Stephen, whom I didn't know growing up, went to prison while I was a teenager for reasons I never knew. My father had five sons, three of whom I never met, two of whom had been to prison. Years after I'd volunteered at the jail and after I had already started my research on the lives of people who leave prison, I met my father. I was twenty-eight and had never seen his face. He said he'd been locked up off and on for two decades.

These events are unsurprising in the age of mass incarceration. Like the men I met at the county jail, my father, my brothers, myself, and so many of my friends have been subjected to the decisions of others by forces far beyond our control. Some judge or underpaid hearing officer got to decide whether or not my family stayed together or if my brothers and I would be sent back to the foster homes where the other kids did not know us, where we could not play with the toys, where as a toddler I once sat in shit for an entire day. As we grew up, my brothers and I got into trouble. We got into fights and dropped out of school. My brothers cycled between different kinds of confinement—group homes and foster care and jails and prison cells and treatment facilities and electronic monitors. At various points in our lives we've all slept on park benches or stayed in shelters and lived in neighborhoods that none of us felt were safe.

It occurred to me while I was visiting that jail that neither Philip nor I had much control over our lives growing up. On a hearing officer's whim, I was spared the worst parts of the system and left in the care of my grandmother. I'm fortunate never to have done time. My brothers weren't so lucky. I'm not sure what happened to Philip. I never saw him again. But I learned in that encounter that our lives were shaped by the laws and the many different kinds of cages we learned to occupy over time. Men in power made decisions about where we would live and whether or not we could see our families.[28]

The vulnerability to surveillance and arrest, to frequent rounds and types of incarceration, extends far beyond jails, courts, and prison yards. It moves in and through families and workplaces and the institutions black and poor families turn to for help. This is a new kind of prison. It's one that has no bars, and sometimes it has no formal connection to the police or criminal courts.

This was a reality I couldn't quite grasp as a young man. I knew that something was wrong. Almost everyone I visited at that jail looked like me, and they would come back over and over again. I went to graduate school in hopes of becoming a better chaplain, enrolling in a social work program at the University of Chicago, where I now teach. I thought the people I encountered needed counseling or a social-service agency to support them, but no matter how many therapy sessions or drug-treatment programs I referred them to and no matter how many Bible-study groups they attended, the coffle of men making their way down those hallways never got any shorter.

James Baldwin says one writes only from experience. Nina Simone tells us that it is the artist's obligation to address the times in which she lives. It seems to me that sitting with history, allowing myself to be moved by it, and finding myself within it is the only way to capture what it means to be alive. To write this book in a way that is faithful to my own life and the lives of the men and women I followed and to the sacrifices of my family, especially my grandmother who gave me so much, I have taken James and Nina as muses. I write from my experience as a scholar, as an advocate, and as a man with loved ones who have spent time in prison.

I was born poor and black after 1972, the year that mass incarceration began in earnest. Incarceration is a subject that I cannot shake. It haunts me like it haunts the men and women whom I've followed. I simply could not write this as some detached observer because I am close to this book, and I am close to the people in it. Being close allows me to see things the detached observers miss and move in spaces where the policy makers rarely care to look. I've found no easy answers; a five-point plan for policy reform can't save us from the society we've made. But I have found people making lives for themselves in the wake of a conviction. We must understand their lives if we hope to bring about meaningful change. It is from this vantage point that I tell the stories of the people that I've encountered, and it is from this vantage that I interpret what I found.

— I —

DEBT

CHAPTER 1

CONFESSION

I'd never seen Ronald so upset. He'd worked in criminal justice reform for years and had been to dozens of hearings. "But today was different," he wrote to his social media followers. "Today I returned to the court that handed down my wrongful conviction to advocate for a loved one."

Ronald described himself as "triggered." Confronted with the "stark realities," the "apathetic disdain," the "failure of the courts to recognize the humanity of the accused, the unfairness of it all hurt...in an unexpected way," he said.

It was the spring of 2018. Ronald had been out of prison for nearly six years. He was on his way back to a Flint courthouse to be there for his nephew. Johnny, the little boy he watched "grow up through family pictures" while he was in prison, was now a man about to enter a guilty plea. The charge was second-degree murder. Johnny would stand in front of a judge who would decide the course of his life. Ronald understood this position all too well. He knew it from his flesh after spending decades in a Michigan penitentiary for a crime he did not commit.[1]

*   *   *

Ronald grew up in a different Flint, one that existed before white flight cut the city's population in half and before the auto plants closed their doors in the recessions of the 1980s. It was before a crime wave in the 1990s saw Flint ranked among the nation's most dangerous cities,[2] before the first emergency manager was appointed in 2002, threatening city pensions and slashing government salaries by nearly 80 percent. This was before the two most recent emergency managers were charged in federal court for making the cost-cutting decision that poisoned a generation of Flint's children, reminding the world what happens when a city doesn't matter to the rest of the nation.[3]

Ronald's Flint, the city of the late 1960s, was vibrant and filled with possibility. "People sleep on Flint," he said when I asked what it was like to grow up there. "Everybody had new cars. Everybody had two cars. Flint was a hell of a town." There were clubs, restaurants, movie theaters, and four top-ranked high schools that made Flint the state's "sports mecca," surpassing even Detroit. And Ronald was a multisport athlete, excelling in school and winning state championships in track, basketball, and football. But it was clear to Ronald even then that manufacturing was the city's lifeblood. "General Motors was everywhere," he said.

GM traced its origin back to the carriage makers that put Flint on the map, so the company set down roots there, building its largest plant within city limits. GM was the biggest game in town when Ronald's father, Ronald Simpson Sr., worked in the factories, and it was still the biggest game in 1980 when Ronald took a job there as a tool-and-die maker. The auto industry had ten times the number of workers it has today, and at one point, GM employed 45 percent of Flint's residents. The city was booming, flush with jobs and cash, a place where working-class people earned good wages, bought homes, and raised their children.

Ronald's mother, Cassandra, moved from Biloxi, Mississippi, to Grand Rapids in the 1940s. As a teenager, she and her family moved to Flint. She met Ronald Sr. a few years later, got married, and had Ronald, the oldest of their five children. Ronald Sr. was a pillar of the community. He played French horn in high school and went on to play in the air force and then in a local band. After a shoulder injury took him off the factory floor he went back to school and earned a master's degree at Michigan State University. He took a job as a middle-school teacher and worked there the remaining years of his life.

Ronald Jr. was a performer like his father. He played drums throughout middle and high school, and he was the floor captain of a local roller-skating crew. "I used to travel all over the Midwest, bro. Me and my buddies," he said. "We'd come to Chicago, Toledo, and we'd just travel all over."

"So you used to dance?" I asked.

"Oh yeah. I enjoyed it," he said, seeming satisfied with the memory. "I was good, but I was an athlete too, so it was hard to do both. And I was more focused on football and track and basketball. But I still love music, though."

I asked Ronald about his home. "My dad was old-school," he said. He was the provider, the family patriarch, and he took his role seriously. Cassandra was mild-mannered, and Ronald Sr. was a micromanager. "He didn't believe women should be working, so [my mother] grew up in that era. She was stuck being the homemaker, taking care of the kids. And she did a good job of it. That's my girl," Ronald said fondly.

"We was like the Jeffersons in our neighborhood," Ronald told me, holding back a laugh. "We had this big-ass motor home. You know, didn't nobody in the black neighborhood have no thirty-foot motor home back in the seventies, shoot," he said. They took road trips in the summer, spending weeks traveling from campground to campground, the only black family at the campsites. "So, yeah, we were upwardly mobile," he said. "We weren't well off or nothing." Ronald looked at me directly, a mischievous smile on his face. "He was cheap as hell, but we didn't go without nothing." *Cheap* was an understatement.

"When he shopped," Ronald said, laughing, "he would buy all this shit out the bargain basket. Cans and all that stuff. He would buy all the off-brand stuff, but he wouldn't buy nothing name brand.

"And you know, back then, when I was growing up," he said, "the Converse All Stars were the shoes to have when you were an athlete. And they were like ten dollars and thirty-one cents a pair. He would not buy them damn shoes!" Ronald was laughing harder now. "He would buy the dollar Kmarts." The soles were slippery. "You slide across the floor at all times to stop."

His father's thrift didn't stop at not buying name-brand gear. "He counted the squares on the toilet paper. Who the fuck does that?" Ronald said. "And it's funny because he would steal the toilet paper from the school! And back then, they had this cheap-ass toilet paper. It looked like tissue paper." We were both laughing. Ronald was crying, wiping tears from the side of his face. "You could see little pieces of bark in the toilet tissue. It was so cheap, it still had sticks and shit!"

We sat in my living room laughing together about what seemed like good times, but then the mood turned, slowly. I started to realize that this wasn't just eccentric behavior from a strange, if cheap, man.

"Like I told you, my dad, he was old-school. He ruled with an iron hand," Ronald said, his tone now somber. "His motto was 'I'm right even when I'm wrong in my house.' And he treated us like that. He didn't let my mother have opinions. He was just..." Ronald paused, looking at me squarely. "He was just tyrannical."

Ronald walked me through the many ways his father controlled his family. Ronald Sr. not only counted the squares of tissue that he stole from the school but handed out one square of toilet tissue at a time to the kids and his wife. He told them what and when to eat. He managed their every move, and he had the last word on every decision.

"Who the fuck does that, man?" he asked again, not laughing anymore. "And, I mean, it was crazy. It was just all kinds of crazy stuff."

"Was he abusive? Did he hurt you?" I asked.

"Yeah, he was abusive," Ronald said flatly. "He would hit us. He would spank us, beat us with extension cords, all kind of stuff. He was physically abusive. He was emotionally and verbally abusive. You know, he would hit my mom, and sometimes even in front of us. That kind of stuff happened. You don't realize it's not normal."

I asked Ronald how old he was when he first experienced the abuse.

"From my earliest memories on," he told me. "That's why I said you don't realize this is not normal when you live like that your whole life, [not] until you not in it anymore. That happened from my earliest memories as a child up to my adulthood—till he passed, I guess."

Their relationship was complicated. "I loved my father to death," Ronald said, tears falling down his cheeks. "He taught me a lot and showed me a lot. He took us traveling around the country. And, you know, it wasn't like it was just a totally bad situation. Even after he died, I tried to make sense of it."

I've heard similar stories from many men who have spent time in cages, but I've heard variations on the same theme from people who have never been to prison. They loved their parents despite their flaws.

"I was a good student. A hell of an athlete," Ronald said. "I did all kinds of stuff, and I never got recognition from him for it." Ronald Sr. didn't attend games, and he didn't let Cassandra attend either. Coaches were there. Teachers were there. Ronald was featured in the local newspaper. People respected Ronald Sr. in part because of how much they liked his affable and accomplished son. Once, Ronald told me, his father had a barbecue for his colleagues. "The principal said, 'Hey, Ronald, you know Ronnie was the regional champion for the hurdles, and he won a quarter-mile in the state.'" Ronald looked at me. "This man knew everything about me. My father didn't know shit." We sat there together in my living room, Ronald remembering his father, thinking through the things he might regret most were he still alive.

Ronald tried to get over his anger and disappointment toward this hard and violent man. He moved out after his high-school graduation, took a job at the factory, and went to school part-time on a track scholarship at the local community college.

The last time he spoke to his father was in 1980. Ronald Sr. had gotten into an argument with Ronald's younger brother. The middle boy had cursed in his house, and Ronald Sr. felt disrespected. He pulled a gun and threatened to kill the boy.

The boy called Ronald, his big brother, who tried to broker peace between the two.

"I go over there trying to be a moderator," he said, "and I'm like, 'Okay, Dad, it's not the end of the world,'" trying to calm his father. "You know what? He got mad at me!" Ronald said. The two men got in a pushing match. Ronald Sr. threatened to shoot Ronald Jr. right there in the Simpson family home while his wife and children looked on, afraid. But Ronald was no longer a child. He carried a gun of his own.

"I said, 'Look, Dad. Don't pull no gun on me.'" His father could tell he was serious. "I had a shoulder holster," he said. "If he would [have pulled that gun], I would have shot him right there." Ronald took his brother and left. They never spoke again.

Three weeks later, Ronald Sr.'s mild-mannered wife of twenty-three years shot her husband in the head, killing him, in the bedroom of the Simpson family home.

There was no time to grieve. Ronald had to clean the house, bury his father, and keep his mother out of prison.

"I spent all that weekend in Detroit trying to find an attorney for my mom," he said. He wanted to hire Ken Cockrel, a prominent black civil rights attorney who famously sued the city of Detroit for police abuse during the '67 riots. Cockrel was on the city council, and rumor had it he was running for mayor. He wasn't taking new cases. Cockrel referred Ronald to Jean Bishop, a whip-smart young attorney, who took Cassandra's case. But securing Bishop's help was just the beginning. Someone had to clean up "the blood and brains and shit that was on the floor," he said. "I had to move my mom and my youngest brother and sister into my marital home." He put down new carpet at the old house and prepared it so the family could one day return.

It was Ronald's job to identify the body. "You walk in this cold sterile room with a real odd odor to it. You never forget it," he said. "When I think about it, I can just smell it. I can smell it right now. A cross between death and disinfectant," he said. "It's the craziest smell you ever want."

The mortician slid the body out of a stainless-steel shelf in the preparation room. There was Ronald's father. "He had been shot in the head, so his eye was out, out hanging," Ronald said. "And you know what, it was a pretty gruesome scene." But there was no time to think about it. His mother would soon have a bond hearing and Ronald's wife was very pregnant, and their relationship was strained. "Trying to process it all," he said. "My dad dying, trying to keep my mom out of jail, trying to go to school. My marriage is crumbling. It was just too much." Ronald needed a way out. "The drug scene just kind of gave me an escape. I started smoking cocaine, snorting it and stuff. I enjoyed it."

Ronald cried when he shared this story with me, sitting in my living room nearly forty years later. "It was a painful chapter in my life," he said. "How do you emotionally justify or rectify or know within yourself? You're burying your father while trying to keep your mother out of prison. And you love both of your parents. I never realized we were dysfunctional."

Ronald never talked about these kinds of things with his mother. "She apologized," he said. "She told me, 'I didn't mean to kill your dad. He was being abusive,' and blah-blah-blah." She didn't need to explain herself to him; Ronald had grown up in that house. But there were rumblings among other members of the family.

Ronald Sr. had brothers. They were angry, and they were talking; their brother had been shot in the head. It got back to Ronald, and he confronted them. That's just who he was, and by now everyone knew it. "I said, 'Look, I respect you because you my dad's brothers, but if you say anything out of the way about my mother to anybody again, next time you see me it's going to be gunshots. That ain't going to be the only funeral going on. I will be back, and you know it.'"

By that time, Ronald was wild. "I'm running with guys doing stickups and shootings, and, you know, I was just in the lifestyle." And if there's anything I've learned about Ronald Simpson Jr., or Ronald Simpson-Bey as he would come to be known after joining the Moorish Science Temple of America in prison, it's that whatever he does, he embraces fully. "If I'll be a fool," he once told me, "I'm gonna be a damn fool. And I was a damn fool."

In the meantime, Jean Bishop, the attorney Ronald hired, was busy working on Cassandra's case. She secured bail and pushed for a bench trial, avoiding the problems associated with a jury in a state like Michigan.[4] "Jean was a whiz," Ronald said. "She cultivated the battered-woman syndrome before it even became a recognized defense in Michigan." She arranged for psychological testing and drew on Cassandra's history of being abused as well as many of Ronald's memories—of Cassandra's two nervous breakdowns, of Ronald Sr.'s controlling and obsessive behavior, of the beatings over all the years that he could remember. The stakes were high. This was 1980; many women had gone to prison for killing their abusive husbands, and many of them had gotten life sentences. But Bishop was good at her job.

"She gave just enough depth to make the judge sympathetic," Ronald said. Cassandra was offered a plea deal. In exchange for a confession of guilt, she would be given five years of probation. If Cassandra had had a different, less skillful attorney and a less resourceful son, Ronald would have been visiting his mother at Women's Huron Valley Correctional Facility. Ronald's mother took the plea, confessing to killing her husband after twenty-three years of abuse. Her confession saved her life.

A confession is a strange and powerful thing. What began as a religious ritual about a set of secret and taboo acts has become the chief process through which we, as a society, think we learn the truth. And not just any truth; confession is believed to reveal the deep truths of who people are, a moral litmus test that shapes Western thought and culture. Michel Foucault once wrote that we live in a "confessional society." By this he meant that the act of bearing witness against oneself has gone from the confessional to the courtroom to the psychiatrist's couch to the realms of education and parenting. "Western man," Foucault wrote, "has become a confessing animal."[5] A few hundred philosophers and social scientists have picked up this thread, noting that all of us are expected to tell our darkest secrets to strangers. We tell on ourselves through every tweet and Facebook post. And there are so many places and so many people who specialize in hearing confessions. Churches and AA groups and NA groups and groups for sexual addictions. Weight-loss camps. Personal trainers and life coaches. And we lose ourselves in the confessions of others through talk shows and memoirs detailing the "real lives" of the people we admire or learn to loathe. But confessions were not originally about fact-finding, nor were they meant to entertain. Confession began as a search for absolution.

The confession of sin in the Catholic Church and the confession of guilt in the court came to prominence together.[6] During confessions, the confessants would tell their sins to their God, or priests whom their God had appointed, in hopes of being forgiven, revealing their secrets from a place of guilt. They bared their souls to the confessor, the one whom they hoped, in the words of Saint Augustine, had "the keys to the church." The presumption is that the confessor has the confessant's best interests at heart, that he is kind and benevolent and will offer forgiveness. According to 1 John 1:9, "If we confess our sins, He"—meaning God—"is faithful and just to forgive our sins and cleanse us from all unrighteousness."

In the court, confessions were brought about first through torture and then through torturous examination during which an inquisitor extracted the "truth." But guilt admitted due to force may not be truth at all. The confession must be voluntary, in the same way that the heart of the sinner must be repentant. Without guilt and sorrow and the rejection of sin, what theologians call *contrition*,[7] a person cannot be forgiven by God or a priest. The Fifth Amendment to the U.S. Constitution established this "truth"—that confession must be voluntary—as law. The notion of due process hangs on the idea of fair treatment, that the accused may not be coerced into confession.[8] But confessions have been extracted with fists, whips, or whatever objects torturers could get their hands on, forcing the courts to go further to regulate the practice.

One of the most important Supreme Court decisions on criminal confessions happened in 1936 in the case of *Brown v. Mississippi*. Raymond Stewart, a white planter, was killed in Kempton County, Mississippi, on March 30, 1934. Arthur "Yank" Ellington, Ed Brown, and Henry Shields, three black tenant farmers, were accused of the crime. Mr. Ellington, who lived on and worked Raymond's land—"Raymond's nigger," according to locals—was taken from his home and brought to the scene of the crime by the police and a mob of twenty white men. They demanded a confession, but Mr. Ellington proclaimed his innocence.[9] They stripped him, whipped him, and hung him by his neck from a tree, twice. He maintained his innocence. The mob finally released him and, according to court records, he returned "with some difficulty to his home, suffering intense pain and agony."[10] The next day the deputy and one other white man drove Mr. Ellington across state lines into neighboring Alabama. The historian Neil McMillen writes, "The officer and another white flogged him nearly to death with a metal-tipped strap until he cried: 'Tell me what you want me to say and I will say it.'"[11]

Mr. Brown and Mr. Shields, the two other tenant farmers, were taken into custody and held overnight for the same crime. They were stripped and laid across chairs, their backs "cut to pieces with a leather strap with buckles on it," according to court records.[12] They were told by the police that the beatings would continue until they confessed to the crime. And, like Mr. Ellington, the farmers were beaten until the content of their confessions satisfied their torturers.

Four local attorneys were appointed to defend the men. Three pushed for a "swift conviction," but the fourth, state senator John Clark, became sympathetic to their case in the eleventh hour. At trial, the men recanted their confessions, telling the judge and jury that the police had tortured them. And the deputies admitted as much in court. The rope burns on Mr. Ellington's neck were still visible, and he reportedly walked with a limp and stood while he was questioned.[13] When asked how severely he whipped Mr. Ellington, one deputy testified, "Not too much for a negro" and "Not as much as I would have done if it were left to me." When asked about the rope burns the same deputy said, "They pulled him up, but didn't hang him."[14] Not a single deputy accused by the defense denied that they had tortured the men, yet their trial took less than one day and the all-white jury deliberated for less than thirty minutes.[15] The men were convicted and sentenced to death by hanging.

State senator John Clark filed for an appeal but the appeals court upheld the conviction, twice. Senator Clark then petitioned the state's supreme court, but that court also upheld the conviction, stating that while the deputies whipped "all three ignorant negroes" and that these "apparently coerced" confessions were the only evidence presented at trial, the confessions were "properly entered." The "rules of procedure" had been followed.[16] Clark took the case to the U.S. Supreme Court. "Torturing a suspect until they confessed was barbaric and unconstitutional," wrote Chief Justice Hughes in the majority opinion in this now famous case.[17] "The transcript reads more like pages torn from some medieval account than a record made within the confines of a modern civilization," he continued. "The rack and torture chamber may not be substituted for the witness stand...It would be difficult to conceive of methods more revolting to the sense of justice than those taken to procure the confessions." The U.S. Supreme Court, for the first time, reversed a criminal conviction based on a coerced confession.[18]

It's illegal for a confession to be whipped or beaten from a confessant. And while the justices acknowledged that everyone involved knew about the torture and ruled in no uncertain terms that confessions obtained under these circumstances were unconstitutional and flatly wrong, there was little to no accountability for those who broke the rules. John Stennis, the district attorney on the case, was promoted, appointed by the governor to the bench of Mississippi's Sixteenth Judicial District Circuit Court. A decade later, he was elected to the U.S. Senate; he was reelected twelve consecutive times and served for forty-two years. Stennis held the second-longest tenure on record when he retired. This was the same John Stennis who voted against the Civil Rights Act of 1964, the Voting Rights Act of 1965, the Civil Rights Act of 1968, and the recognition of Dr. King's birthday as a national holiday in 1983, the year that Ronald's mother took her plea deal.[19]

By all indications, Stennis lived a long and happy life. Colleagues on both sides of the aisle remembered him as a statesman despite his history as a staunch segregationist. John Clark, the men's defense attorney, did not meet a similar end. He lost his seat in the state senate. The "object of intense personal abuse," he "suffered a physical and mental collapse and retired from the law in 1938 at the age of fifty-four."[20] The black tenant farmers Stennis tried to send to the hangman have been all but lost to history. This may be because while the Supreme Court reversed the men's initial conviction, Stennis introduced "new evidence" and the men were taken back into custody. Afraid to be tried in "Bloody Kemper," the men pleaded no contest to manslaughter. All three went to prison, Mr. Shields for two and a half years, Mr. Brown for seven and a half years, and Mr. Ellington for six months. While the men weren't hanged, they were convicted of a lesser crime on a plea deal, admitting their guilt—that is to say, they confessed to a crime they likely did not commit.

*   *   *

The plea deal is a perverse kind of a confession. It is an abdication of the inquisitorial process. Fact-finding is unnecessary. No deep truths are revealed through plea deals. They are negotiations between a prosecutor with the power of incarceration and death at his or her disposal, whether or not there is evidence, and a defendant who just wants to go home. And despite images from courtroom dramas seared in the public's imagination, 95 percent of all convictions are resolved through plea deals.[21] The people who take these pleas are typically stuck in cells and live under the threat of long prison sentences. They've been separated from their families. They confess guilt to a judge and to their accusers in open court, giving up their right to a trial that they likely couldn't afford. They do this whether or not they believe that they are guilty because copping a plea is the fastest way to get home, but almost everyone I met who took a plea regretted it.

You cannot undo a guilty plea. Once it's entered, the defendant gives up the right to an appeal. And you can never do enough to erase it. A conviction follows you through news clippings, mug-shot databases, and cheap electronic background checks easily accessible to employers, landlords, licensing officials, and anyone with thirty dollars, a credit card, and enough curiosity to look. There are whole industries built around disseminating criminal records and storing files in digital databases. Sometimes, companies make records publicly available and charge a fee to take them down. Most times, they compile the data and charge a fee for people who want to use the information to investigate others.[22] And while a plea deal saved Ronald's mother from a lifetime of incarceration, this was an atypical outcome. Nearly two thousand women are doing time today in Michigan penitentiaries; two hundred and twenty-six are serving life sentences. Almost all of them have been abused. Many women are there for killing their abusers.[23] And while Ronald's mother was safe, the circumstances inside that home would continue to take their toll on Ronald.

It was 1980. Ronald's father was killed in July. Ronald's son was born in September. His wife filed for divorce in October. By December, he was selling dope.

"I had already been paying child support before I started selling cocaine, but, you know, once the divorce got filed, fuck it. I'm all in," Ronald said. He needed the extra money. His new child-support obligations cut his take-home pay to just a hundred and fifty dollars a week. A family, a mortgage, and a couple of car notes with the divorce—he had to start over. He took up DJing at a local nightclub, hosting cocaine parties in what he called "an immaculate crack house." Ronald knew his clients from the factory and met his suppliers through connections at the club. He wasn't rich, but he made good money. This went on for five years.

By October of 1985, Ronald had a crew. One day, they were making rounds to collect debts, money he'd fronted to local dope dealers who needed an advance. They stopped by a partner's place to pick up some cash, but Ronald's partner wasn't there. His partner's girlfriend was, so they relaxed for an hour before they left; they didn't know the housing complex was under surveillance.

Ronald noticed a red Ford Thunderbird following them. He stopped the car and got out, thinking it might be his partner looking to drop off the cash. "We all had Jheri curls. The driver had a Jheri curl too!" Ronald told me, laughing. He sat on the hood, sipping from a forty, as the Thunderbird pulled up, but no one recognized the driver.

"He didn't say, 'Police, Stop!' He didn't put no light in the window, on the hood, nothing," Ronald said. "He [just] got out [and] crouched down behind the door with a gun."

"So I'm out in the open," Ronald said. "No gun, with a forty-ounce in my hand. And the guys in my car started shooting at him. And he returned fire. This was the craziest situation," he said. "Bullets whizzing by within inches, so close you can feel it. You can feel the vibration," he said. "So I got out of the line of fire."

Ronald ducked and ran, trying to get out of the way, doing his best not to get hit. The cars took off, the officer chasing Ronald's friends. A second gunfight ensued two miles away from the housing complex where they had been. A bullet grazed the officer's arm. By this time, Ronald was far from the scene.

"We had a pickup spot in case we got separated, because we were in that bullshit," Ronald said. He called one of his partner's girlfriends and learned his crew had been arrested. The men were driving Ronald's car, so he knew it was just a matter of time before the police came for him.

Ronald lived with his second wife in a town house in an affluent, mostly white suburb of Flint. The police showed up with dogs and helicopters. "Man, they made a scene," Ronald said.

His crew was held in the county jail. Interrogators tried to get them to flip, working to persuade each man to testify against the others, but no one talked.

"We got arraigned a couple of days later," Ronald said. "They made a big spectacle out of that, man. They chained us all together like we came off an African slave ship. No soap and no water for three days. Our hair is all wild. We look like animals and shit," he said. It took a few weeks, but Ronald posted a sixty-thousand-dollar bond and went home. His attorney called six months later and told him his partners had turned state's evidence. Ronald and his codefendants were charged with attempted murder.

There were many reasons to throw out the case. The first was a conflict of interests—the judge hated Ronald's father. Ronald Sr. had been a process server in the 1960s; his job was to serve subpoenas to Flint residents, and he'd gotten into arguments with the judge over matters that were never explained to Ronald. Ronald had his father's name. To make matters worse, the judge also hated Ronald's attorney, a recent retiree who had been the first black judge to sit on the bench in Genesee County. "I thought this was the perfect person to hire," Ronald said. But Ronald's defense attorney and the judge had a long history. They fought about admitting evidence and they fought about how they addressed each other in court, and they did this in front of the all-white jury.

"My attorney laid out a whole laundry list of incidents that him and this judge had with each other when he was on the bench. In a document!" Ronald said. "Of course the judge wouldn't recuse himself," and the appeals court wouldn't grant a new venue, meaning they couldn't try the matter in a different court. And this mattered for the defense.

"We filed a motion for a separate trial," Ronald said, since he wasn't at the scene where the police officer had been shot. Being tried separately from his codefendants, even with the same judge, might keep him from being convicted for the crimes his codefendants committed. The judge granted that motion, but he didn't separate the juries. This meant the juries from what were supposed to be two separate cases sat in the courtroom together. They heard all the same evidence despite the judge granting Ronald what should have been a second and separate trial. And the prosecutor submitted evidence the judge said was inadmissible.

"We objected every time, but the judge would just say, 'I'll allow it.' He contradicted his own rulings," Ronald said. Ronald learned, years later, that the judge and the prosecutor had worked together in this way before. "There was a whole string of cases that had similar convictions under similar circumstances. They ended up getting overturned," Ronald said.

Beyond the conflicts of interest and what seemed like a biased courtroom dynamic, there was the fact that Ronald wasn't the shooter. He hadn't even been at the scene when the officer was shot. The undercover police officer said as much in his first sworn statement, but changed his testimony at trial. He admitted that he did not see Ronald shoot at him but said that he believed Ronald was the culprit because he was holding a literal smoking gun.

"We tore that up on defense. A smoking gun in 1985? Is this Davy Crockett or Daniel Boone or something? Did I have a musket or some shit? *He's* smoking some shit," Ronald said, laughing. A firearms expert reproduced the scene, shooting a similar gun, and gave a statement saying guns no longer smoked, but none of that mattered. The jury convicted Ronald of assault with attempt to commit murder. The judge, who hated Ronald's father and attorney and who would later have many of his rulings overturned, sentenced Ronald to fifty years in a Michigan penitentiary.

*   *   *

Ronald's sentence began on July of 1986, almost six years to the date that his father died. His attorney said this was the most unjust trial he'd ever seen.

"That haunted him up to his death," Ronald said. "'Cause after he died in the late nineties, his son or his nephew...somebody contacted my mother and gave her a file. He was still trying to figure out a way to help me." He had even written letters to the appellate court laying out why the case should be overturned. Ronald didn't stop fighting either, but he had spent nearly thirty thousand dollars on his legal defense and still wound up in prison. "I told my mother don't spend another quarter on a lawyer." He decided to take matters into his own hands.

Ronald filed his first appeal in 1986, just a few weeks after he began his sentence. The appeal was dismissed by the same judge who had convicted him. He filed with the Michigan court of appeals in 1987, and while the justices seemed to agree on five of the six issues he raised, they did not grant relief, saying they would view the case in the most favorable light to the prosecution. "I'm, like, the fuck you mean, the most favorable light of the prosecution?" Ronald said. "They agreed I got it right, but they just dismissed it to give the prosecutor the benefit of the doubt? I knew I was onto something."

He began to do legal research even more seriously, and his motions grew more sophisticated. In 1992 he filed a motion for relief from judgment. He explained the process.

"In Michigan, this is court rule MCR six point five hundred. In prison jargon, it's a sixty-five-hundred motion. This is the way that you ask for the evidence in your case to be reconsidered." The judge who sentenced Ronald was still on the bench, and he dismissed the motion again, saying his request had no merit.

A few years later, when Ronald was in solitary confinement for a reason he could no longer remember, he got a letter from an old friend. Laila Stewart, one of Ronald's coworkers from the GM factory, reached out to him. They hadn't dated, but they were close.

"I didn't forget about you," she wrote. "I went back to school and eventually entered politics." She had been elected to the city council and now, years later, was a commissioner for Genesee County. She asked Ronald if there was anything she could do.

"I said, 'Man.' I went back to work on my second sixty-five hundred motion," Ronald said. "And during this time, I had been trying to get some evidence that the court kept saying wasn't there." He wanted the original police report, the one where the officer admitted that Ronald wasn't on the scene when the other officer was shot. They had never provided the official statement to Ronald's attorney. When Ronald asked the county administrators for a copy, they claimed there had been a flood in the basement of the records room and the file had been destroyed.

"They were lying," Ronald said. "I filed a Freedom of Information Act Request, and back then they had to pay you five hundred dollars if they didn't [fulfill the request]." This was before the Supreme Court stopped allowing people in prison to receive the money. "Instead of giving me the document, they gave me five hundred dollars." He asked his friend to see if she could get her hands on the officer's statement, the one supposedly destroyed in the flood. Within thirty days, she sent him a copy.

Ronald filed a new 6500 motion, this time with the officer's sworn statement. There was now enough evidence to exonerate him—evidence that had always been there. But an officer had been shot. Ronald knew he needed political support. And he was hopeful.

He had been incarcerated for nearly fifteen years, but things were finally starting to work in his favor. The old trial judge retired, and the campaign manager for the new judge had once worked with Ronald's father.[24] By now, Ronald was a skilled jailhouse lawyer, working on other people's cases. He said he got "more than a few" convictions overturned. He met an organizer from Operation Push in Chicago while working on her brother's case. Operation Push launched a campaign for Ronald's release, gathering five thousand signatures from people in and around Flint and getting letters of support from Jesse Jackson and Flint's mayor and local community leaders. After reviewing the new evidence submitted and seeing the outpouring of community support, the new trial judge wrote a thirty-page opinion overturning Ronald's conviction.

"A thirty-page opinion is unheard of on motions of release from judgment," Ronald said. It's usually a one-paragraph denial. But while the opinion outlined in great detail why Ronald should be released, the judge noted he didn't have the jurisdiction to release him. It would take three years to get a final decision. The court of appeals disagreed with the merits of Ronald's motion. He took it to the Supreme Court of Michigan, but they also denied the motion. Ronald had to take his motion to federal court. In 2006, the federal courts reversed Ronald's conviction, using the trial judge's decision as the basis for their ruling.

What happened next? I asked Ronald, hanging on every word.

"Oh, they sat on it for three [more] years. The judicial system slow as hell!" He laughed.

Ronald filed a memorandum for habeas corpus, which

literally means "bring the body." With this filing, Ronald was asking for his day in court.

"I filed that in October 2006, and by September 2009 they ruled on it. And they ruled in my favor...[ordering] me to either be released or to have a new trial." But this wasn't the end of the ordeal. "I couldn't get a bond! I was back in pretrial status," Ronald said, emphasizing each word. "I didn't have a conviction anymore. I was constitutionally entitled to a bond. Constitutionally entitled!" he repeated. "I wasn't asking for a privilege!"

I wondered how a judge could justify withholding a constitutional right. These were stalling tactics. The federal court that reversed the decision said the local court should issue the bond. The local court said it was the federal court's jurisdiction.

"They sent me around the horn," Ronald said. He filed a dozen motions over the next three years, but the outcomes were always the same. "No one took responsibility," he said. "They finally brought me back to court in June. The case had been gutted, and they offered me a plea deal."

Ronald could walk out of prison that day if he agreed to the conviction, but this time it was a conviction with time served. In other words, he would still be considered guilty, but the years he'd spent in prison would satisfy his sentence. There would be no more court dates. No more continuances. He would not have to be on probation.

"By that time, I was like, Great! I mean, that's it. If I can walk out of court today, I'll take it," Ronald said. "But if you make me wait one more day, I'll fight you motherfuckers until the cows come home."

After serving all that time for a crime he did not commit,

Ronald Simpson-Bey stood before the judge, satisfied. He raised his right hand to take the plea and walked out of court a free man. He had been in prison for twenty-seven years.

I met Ronald in 2013. Finn Bell, my first PhD student and my research manager, introduced us. I had defended my dissertation in June and started my first job as a professor at the University of Michigan a few weeks later. By September, I was launching the Detroit Reentry Study, a research project that would follow ninety newly released prisoners for two years. I would meet them on the day of their release from jails, prisons, and police lockup facilities nearby and observe them as they tried to put their lives back together. Finn helped lead my research team. We followed men and women as they looked for work or places to live and as they did their best to reconnect with their families. Some had been locked up for just a few days; others had been incarcerated for decades.

Ronald was an organizer and a jailhouse lawyer in prison, well known for working on and winning some of the largest class-action lawsuits against the Michigan Department of Corrections. Now a free man, Ronald was launching the Good Neighbors Project, an initiative to connect lifers in the Michigan penitentiary with people living in the outside world. He'd heard about my work through Finn, who volunteered at a prisoner-advocacy organization. He asked me to join his board. I couldn't say no.

I needed research assistants to help me conduct interviews and a consultant who understood the landscape of mass incarceration in Michigan. I asked Ronald to join as a research associate and a consultant. As my team grew and the work got more intense, I frequently drew on his leadership. We worked together for years, collecting data in Detroit and the surrounding suburbs.

Ronald worked part-time for the project, attending meetings, conducting interviews, and providing consultation, all while his career as an advocate took off. He joined Just Leadership USA, a national criminal justice–advocacy network, traveling frequently as a fellow. He pushed for change in the statehouse and in Congress through organizing campaigns, at community-based organizations, and with anyone who would listen. When the founder, Glenn Martin, hired him full-time, Ronald began traveling every week, doing his part to help build a national movement that aimed to cut the prison population in half by 2030. Over the next three years, Ronald earned enough frequent-flyer miles for an upgrade to first class whenever he traveled. He bought a house in Detroit in 2017 and got engaged to a woman he'd worked with back at GM. He reconnected with his family, who now know him as a devoted son, father, grandfather, and uncle.

We've become close over the years. I wrapped up my project in 2016 and left Detroit but I checked in on my friend whenever I came to town. Ronald was a success by any measure: A house. A new fiancée. A career he loved. A professional reputation that preceded him. He'd had most of those things before he went to prison, but that was thirty years ago. Few people manage to get back on their feet after spending so long in a cage.

During one of my visits, we ate and drank in his new home, toasting our success. Life was good. "I tell people all the time," Ronald said, leaning over his plate to take a bite of a shrimp skewer, "I wouldn't change where I ended up, but I sure as hell would change what I went through to get here."

Less than a week after my visit, Ronald had to return to the site of much harder times—the courthouse where he had been sentenced for a crime he didn't commit, the same place where he'd fought for his mother's freedom. Now, a third generation's lives were hanging in the balance of some judge's decision. Ronald's nephew Little Johnny was in the very same courthouse to confess that he'd killed a man.

Little Johnny was now an adult. His mug shot had been posted to local news websites for over a year. In the photo, the twenty-three-year-old wore an orange jumpsuit. His face was puffy, his neck thick, his hair in an unkempt and matted Afro. His mouth was twisted to the right as if he were pouting. If this mug shot resembled the kid in real life and the camera hadn't just caught him at a bad angle on a bad day, it should have been clear to anyone paying attention that Johnny was in need of help.

Little Johnny had been hearing voices since he was a child. These same voices might have whispered to him as he beat his roommate to death with a hammer. Johnny had a severe psychiatric illness. The prosecutor knew this and offered a plea. In exchange for a lighter sentence, Johnny could confess that he was "guilty but mentally ill" to the crime of second-degree murder.[25] Everything but the murder charge made sense. There are certainly carve-outs in the criminal law for defendants with "diminished capacity." And the boy was not taking his meds when he'd gotten into the altercation with his roommate. He had never been arrested and was already on disability for his condition. He even called the police himself and requested that they do a "welfare check" on the man he'd killed. Perhaps he did not comprehend what had transpired. None of that mattered. Little Johnny confessed to the crime when the police questioned him. And while he was found to have been in a psychotic state when he committed the crime, having not taken his meds, and then held in a cage for five hundred and sixty-eight days before his day in court, the boy who had heard voices since he was a child was deemed competent enough to offer a confession.

Ronald knew the stakes of his nephew's encounter. A white man was dead and a big black defendant—mentally ill or not, with "diminished capacity" or not—had confessed to it; there was no jury in Flint, and perhaps none in the country, that would set him free. And even though in 1847, the State of Michigan had become the first government in the English-speaking world to abolish the death penalty, in 2017, 5,711 people were serving life sentences in Michigan prisons, 3,804 of them without the possibility of parole.[26] They would never go home, and if Johnny went to trial, he would never leave prison alive. He had to confess. He had to take the plea.

Ronald arrived early to observe the judge's other rulings that day. In one case, a slim white man who the judge said was a known gang member violated his probation, again. This time he was caught with "numerous guns." The prosecutor offered a sentence that Ronald felt was reasonable, but the judge ignored the recommendation. He asked the man if he felt "large enough to survive prison," which seemed like a strange and inappropriate question. Of course the thin white man said no. The judge put a man whom the courts classified as a "repeat violent offender" back on probation. The thin white man went home.[27]

What Ronald witnessed was an all too common occurrence. White women across the country who have sexually assaulted boys have famously been given light sentences after being deemed too dainty or too beautiful to survive behind bars.[28] White men have been spared the worst parts of the system too. Brock Turner, for example, a member of Stanford's swim team, was given a "moderate jail sentence" after being caught raping a woman behind a dumpster at a local bar. The judge said, "A prison sentence would have a severe impact" on the boy, citing a character reference from Turner's father and his request of lenience for his son's "20 minutes of action."[29] But Johnny was not Brock Turner. He was a six-foot-one, two-hundred-seventy-five-pound mentally ill black man. The judge did not ask whether the disabled boy would be able to survive in prison. The prosecutor did not ask if a man in the midst of a psychotic episode could be held accountable for a crime. And there was no discussion of what it meant for someone with a developmental disability to plead guilty in open court.

Johnny had spent five hundred and sixty-eight days in jail, but what sociologist Michael Walker calls the "courtroom ordeal"[30] played out in just a few minutes. The prosecutors offered Johnny a plea bargain of fifteen to twenty years, which may have been reasonable, given the severity of the crime. But the judge disregarded even those guidelines and sentenced Johnny to spend the next fifteen to fifty years in a Michigan penitentiary.

I'll never forget my brother's hearing. It was July 12, 2016. I was preparing to move to Princeton, New Jersey, for a fellowship. I'd been to court dozens of times, and Ann Arbor, where the hearing was being held, was a progressive town, so we thought we had less to worry about. The judge and the defense attorneys seemed pleasant. Even the prosecutors seemed friendly, but this time it was my brother who was about to be sentenced for a crime he said he did not commit.

Jeremiah has always been popular. He's always cracking

jokes, and it's been like this since we were little. I don't know why it annoyed me that so many people knew him at court. I suppose I was angry and sad. He could go to jail for the next decade and a half, but he wanted to laugh and joke with friends in the gallery. What would the judge think? I wondered, worrying we'd be kicked out of the courtroom. I was nervous, but he didn't seem much bothered.

"What's up, Chi-Town!" said some thinnish white man in a short-sleeved shirt that showed the tattoos running up his fore-arm. "Chi-Town!" said the woman sitting with the man, giving Jeremiah a hug like this was some reunion. They were waiting, like we were, for their cases to be called, chatting loudly enough to annoy me but quietly enough to avoid the bailiff's attention. I felt more like the mothers and grandmothers who were there pleading for mercy for their wayward children than like the forty-something-year-old defendants my brother was sitting with, all of them catching up like they were on a park bench.

"This is my baby bro," he said, smiling as he introduced me to the pair. He told them, as he always told people, that I was a professor at the University of Michigan. He was proud of me. I was his little brother. I had a good job and a family who loved me, and him. We were close. He'd always been supportive. I gave dap and remained pleasant, but I couldn't help wondering if they'd been in my house.

Jeremiah had lived with me and my family for less than a year when he'd caught his case by throwing a crack party in my basement while I was away. I was doing research in Europe; my wife, Janice, and my son, Jonathan, were with me. Like a scene from a bad movie, nearly a dozen people had partied in our home. I would never have found out if it had been up to him, but it wasn't.

I always got up early on the days that I taught, leaving the house at six a.m. to grab a spot at a local coffee shop. I'd have a dark roast and a croissant if I went to Starbucks, or a toasted almond tea with foamed milk if I posted up at Espresso Royale. Sometimes I'd read the news to pull relevant clips, go over my lecture notes, or listen to music, but mostly I'd just clear my head. Ann Arbor was a small city. There's a safety in the kinds of routines you can establish in a place like that, and that's what I miss most when I think of my time there.

It had been a few months since we'd returned from Europe and I was back in the swing of fall classes. I had barely made it to my office when Janice called and told me to come home. The police had banged on the door, and Jonathan, who was eight, answered. He saw men wearing badges standing there on our porch. He ran upstairs to his mother. She flew downstairs to see what was going on. The officer showed her a warrant and said, "We were just about to break down the door." Then they proceeded to raid our home.

I canceled class and headed back to my house. There was one police car parked crookedly in our driveway, two more in the driveway of a building one door down. I went in and asked the officers why they hadn't just called. "We had no way to know who you were," said the officer who'd threatened to break down the door of the home we rented. "I'm faculty," I said. "You could have Googled me." I was upset but careful to watch my tone. Black people have been killed for much less.

Later that day, Jeremiah called collect from the Washtenaw County Jail and said "they on some bullshit." He denied he'd done anything wrong, but nonetheless, he'd brought the police to my home. Ownership of the house had just changed hands from people we knew to an investor who did not know my family. Using drugs in a rental unit is a violation of the lease. We could have been evicted. My brother had to go, and he had to leave right away.

Jeremiah was released two days later. I bought him a ticket for the Megabus, gathered his things, and met him at the county jail. I drove him to the bus station; no words were exchanged between us. We hugged. He got on the bus and headed back to Chicago.

Months went by. We stayed in touch. There were no hard feelings. He just couldn't live in my house. He'd moved back in with his wife in Chicago and gotten a job at a car wash, but he continued to party with his friends. He was pulled over one day, and the officers found he was driving without a license; it had been suspended after his last DUI. When they ran his name, they saw he had an open warrant in Michigan. They took him into custody. He was processed, shackled, and put on a transport van to Ann Arbor, where he would face his day in court.

Jeremiah told me the trip took three days even though Chicago to Ann Arbor is only a four-and-a-half-hour drive, five hours if you stop for coffee and bathroom breaks. The van, which was privately owned, took a detour to the East Coast to pick up additional passengers. After three days in a van and three days in jail, Jeremiah was released on his own recognizance. A judge ordered him to check in with a probation officer and submit to weekly drug tests, even though he had not (yet) been convicted of a crime.

It didn't matter that he had a wife and a job back in Chicago. He could not leave Michigan. He could not go back to my home, which was, after all, the scene of the crime. It would have been hard for me to let him stay anyway. He had put my family in danger, crossing lines most people didn't cross.

While he awaited trial, no one in liberal Ann Arbor would hire him. He did not have an address, which made it nearly impossible for him to find steady work, and he knew landlords rejected applicants with records. With no job, he couldn't have afforded an apartment anyway. Jeremiah couch-surfed with people he barely knew or slept in a moving truck. He eventually found a community—a local priest allowed the homeless to erect a tent city in the church parking lot, and he slept outside on the asphalt on a makeshift cot. I brought him food and washed his clothes. We moved to a new house when my lease expired, and he stayed with us from time to time. This went on for a year.

Here we were in court again, and for forty minutes, until his public defender arrived, he sat there cracking jokes with his two friends like nothing was hanging in the balance. This attorney was new. Jeremiah had only spoken on the phone with him for ten minutes the day before.

His previous public defender was a graduate of Michigan Law. He was young and confident, ordering psychiatric evaluations and arranging mock lie-detector tests for Jeremiah. He put in regular requests with the prosecutor to review evidence. The few times the plaintiff failed to show up in court, Jeremiah's lawyer had pressed the judge to drop the charges. He explained the steps he planned to take clearly to my brother and walked him through his defense strategy. Even the prosecutor knew he was a good attorney and that he was mounting a strong defense, so he offered my brother a plea deal for a twelve-month sentence. It was still a felony conviction, but he would get credit for time served and would spend maybe six months in the local jail. Jeremiah said he didn't commit the crime. He bet on how sharp his attorney was, refused the plea, and pushed for a trial date.

After many months and many continuances and several periods for document review, Jeremiah's sharp public defender took a job at a law firm and moved out of town. Jeremiah learned this the day before court from the new guy, who sounded like he was distracted or uninterested.

We showed up early, in part to watch the new guy work. When the lawyer arrived, my brother walked over to get his attention. The seemingly checked-out public defender shooed him away and walked out of the courtroom through a different exit. He returned a half an hour later, but this time with a client from the county jail.

"Well, Your Honor," the public defender said, standing before the bench, "it's obvious my client didn't consult with me. I honestly don't know what he's trying to accomplish."

I couldn't hear much else. All I knew was his client, a black man with braids wearing a khaki jumpsuit, looked angry. A few minutes later, the man stood before the bench struggling to raise his right hand. He swore that his admission of guilt was voluntary.

Jeremiah's ease faded. He sat quietly until it was his turn to go into a back office and consult with the public defender. His two friends were just as pensive, no longer chatty the way they'd been an hour before. It was clear to all of us that we needed to pay attention.

In the very next case, a black man in his twenties stood before the judge, charged with failure to pay child support. Why wasn't he in family court, the place designated to handle these matters? Why was a felony on the table? The judge and the prosecutor discussed the complicated arrangement they'd made for his plea deal. He would pay roughly half his income until he caught up with what he owed, at which point he'd pay a third of what he brought home. He started to protest. I supposed he couldn't afford to do that, but then he thanked the judge for not sending him back to jail. He had already missed two days' work. The man raised his right hand, attested to the voluntary nature of the plea, and left the court without speaking to the public defender.

In the next case, an eighteen-year-old white boy stood before the judge. He wore an ill-fitting suit and was flanked by a team of attorneys, all three of whom were white, one of whom had been appointed by the court. The boy had a history of assault and property damage. The judge nodded as his team presented his repeat offenses. "An expression of mental illness," one attorney said in reference to his crime. "Obvious self-medication," said another. The prosecutor offered a plea deal. The boy would complete treatment in the community following the guidelines of the Holmes Youthful Trainee Act (HYTA), a special designation for "youthful offenders" in Michigan. If he stayed clean and sober for the next three months, the court would drop the charges against him. He raised his hand and took the plea, then left the court abruptly without saying a word to the judge or his defense team.

A black boy in khakis who looked younger than eighteen was next. He had no prior criminal record but had been caught with enough drugs to sell. He stood with my brother's apathetic public defender, raised his right hand, and entered his guilty plea. For his misdemeanor conviction for drug possession, he was sentenced to six months of community supervision. While he was not convicted of a felony and perhaps could have been, he was not offered treatment through the HYTA program. He went home a free man with a charge that he could probably explain if he was asked about it in an interview, but he had a conviction. He would be considered a "habitual offender" should he ever be arrested again, and "habitual offenders" got "sentence enhancements"—legalese that meant a judge could give a longer sentence.

Jeremiah's public defender called us back into an office to discuss my brother's case. The prosecutor was offering a plea deal: eighteen months to ten years.

"Eighteen months to ten years? What happened to the twelve months he offered last time?" Jeremiah asked.

"That's not what's on the table," the lawyer responded.

"What would you do?" Jeremiah asked him, signaling he wanted to fight.

"I can't presume to make that decision for you," said the man representing my brother.

I was angry. What did he mean? What was his job if not to give legal advice? Jeremiah asked me what I thought. I thought he should have taken the plea from a year ago; he would be back home by now. But this was not the time for *I told you so*s.

I turned to the attorney and asked, "What if we fought and lost?" He said that if Jeremiah was convicted, he would do ten to fifteen years. Plus, the judge could add an additional ten to fifteen years because he was a "repeat offender." Jeremiah had been caught shoplifting a cart full of goods worth more than five hundred dollars from a Target in Ohio. He had been convicted of grand larceny, making him a "habitual offender."

"Shit!" Jeremiah said. He took a breath before again asking me what I thought.

I had seen this go so wrong so many times. His lawyer was

bad at his job, and we were in Michigan, a state known to hand out long sentences. And I had just watched a judge in this very progressive city spend the day giving people who looked like us lots and lots of time, even if he was pleasant while he did it. The public defender, having offered no legal advice, nodded his head in agreement as we talked about racism in the Michigan prisons. He was black too. I suppose he wanted us to feel like he was sympathetic to our case, but we'd watched him throw a client under the bus not an hour before. It broke my heart. I was angry that we were in this situation at all, but I told my brother what I thought he should do.

"I think you should take the plea," I said, knowing that he was tired. He had just spent a year on the streets. As soon as he heard this, the lawyer headed to the courtroom, not giving us time to mull it over.

About an hour later, Jeremiah was standing with his right hand raised before the judge, the public defender at his side. The judge went through his script. "How old are you?"

Jeremiah gave his age.

"How far did you go in school?"

"Eleventh grade," Jeremiah said.

He went on: "Have you discussed this case completely with your attorney?" and "Are you confident you understood your attorney's advice?" and "Have you listened carefully to your attorney and made this decision?" and "Do you know that you're giving up your constitutional rights?" Those were his right to a trial, his right to an appeal, his right to be presumed innocent, and his right to have the government prove his guilt beyond a reasonable doubt before locking him away.

"Yes," Jeremiah replied to everything he was asked.

The judge had posed the last question to half a dozen

men while I sat in that courtroom: "Are you entering this plea voluntarily?"

But how could this be voluntary? That word presumes a choice: take the plea or do fifteen years in a Michigan penitentiary. Jeremiah was considered a repeat offender; he might do thirty years. And where would he live while he fought his case? Should he sleep outdoors during another Michigan winter? Jeremiah was from Chicago. His family and friends were there. And I was moving out of the state the very next day.

"Yes," my brother said, making his confession.

CHAPTER 2

GUILT

A video taken in Grand Rapids, Michigan, surfaces on March 24, 2017. There is a blurred image of an officer talking to a man on a street.[1] It's hard to make out what they're saying. Kids, a basketball game, and a gun. The media reports the incident this way: A "boy in black" pulls a black revolver from his book bag. "Hundreds of boys" get into a fight at a Salvation Army Kroc Community Center. The boys disperse before the police arrive. The screen fades to black.

The video shows another scene. This time, the view is from an officer's chest cam. We see down the barrel of an already drawn gun that there are five black boys in the distance.

"Guys, get on the ground. Keep your hands up," the officer says. The orders are calm but come quickly.

The footage reveals the boys' personalities. One is obedient but shaken, lying facedown during most of the ordeal. Another fidgets, unsure of whether to stay on his belly or walk toward the officer. "What did we do, bro?" asks a third prone boy, his head and arms raised awkwardly. The fourth boy whimpers, "I don't want to die." Was this the youngest child? The boys are reportedly between twelve and fourteen years old. The fifth boy, the one in black, is noticeably angry. "Can you please put your gun away?" He stands, repeating his request.

"Ay!" shouts the officer. "Don't come over here!"

The murmuring twelve-year-old begins to wail. "I don't want to die," he says again.

"Okay," the officer says. "It will be all right." His voice is now soothing, as if he knows he's talking to children, but his gun is still drawn.

The boy in black tries to quiet the crying boy.

"Just follow our directions," says the officer, and then he calls in some code. "They're being compliant. How do you want to do this?" he says into the radio.

Seeing the action from her stoop, the mother of one of the boys moves toward the fray.

"Ma'am! Can you go back in your house for me?" the officer says firmly. Impossible. A gun is drawn on her child. "Ma'am! Ma'am!" shouts the officer as she approaches. Again, the scene fades to black.

The officer is speaking to the mother when the video fades back in. He says, "He just happened to be at the wrong place at the wrong time. No one was hurt…everything's okay." He says it twice.

A final scene. An officer talks to two parents. "We're just doing our job, because a lot of people out here have guns."

The father says, "You're saying they didn't have guns, but y'all pulled y'all guns?"

"We don't know that," the officer replies firmly.

A mother, the same one as before, chimes in. "Exactly! They didn't have a gun. But y'all pulled guns on my kid."

The officer responds politely, "Do you understand where we're coming from? Matching description. We're not just gonna walk up on someone and say, 'Hey, do you have a gun?' No one got hurt in this... Wrong place at the wrong time, obviously, for these kids," says the officer.

"Right place at the wrong time. They were in the right place," says the father. The footage ends.

There was, of course, no weapon. The mother's impulse to go to her child being held at gunpoint and the confusion, fear, and frustration of the boys should make sense to most observers. Why would a mother stand by and watch while police officers point guns at her child? Why wouldn't a twelve-year-old fear for his life? Why wouldn't a fourteen-year-old be angry? I suppose the families should have been thankful that "no one was hurt."[2] Much worse had happened under hauntingly similar circumstances.[3]

The boys' parents were familiar with the cruel and remarkable history that confronted their children each time they left home. Like many other American cities, Grand Rapids had recently commissioned a stop-and-frisk study that found racial disparities in police procedures. Black people were stopped at twice the rate of whites but were less likely to carry guns or drugs.[4]

The wrong place at the wrong time. At a park, a playground, or a street outside their home. There is no right place for these children. Innocence and childhood may be synonymous in the American imagination, but our children—that is to say, black children—are presumed guilty.

I'm sure that it was surprising when the police chief apologized to the boys' families in his public statement. Within the hour, two police officers' unions issued a joint statement of their own. The officers followed protocol, they said, and the protocol would not change. But how did we get here, and why is this the protocol?

In some ways, this is an old story. It would be tempting to start with the war on drugs or the advent of modern policing, but our presumptions of black guilt and the collective sin that renders black people criminal emerges with the concept of race itself.[5] This is because the idea of a black people, uniform and constituted as black, is a child of racial slavery. Before that, neither European aristocrats calling for unfree labor, nor the raiders they sent to plunder the African continent, nor the network of merchants, nor "middlemen and brokers," nor the "warrior aristocracies that captured people and supplied slaves to the coast" thought of "black people" as a "people" at all. They were outsiders, foreigners, like the Eastern Europeans and the classes of so-called barbarians who were traded by warring empires. Saidiya Hartman, the eminent scholar of transatlantic slavery, put it best: "Africans did not sell their brothers and sisters into slavery. They sold strangers: those outside the web of kin and clan relationships...foreigners and barbarians...lawbreakers expelled from society. In order to betray your race, you had to first imagine yourself as one."[6]

In the social hierarchy that existed, slaves were at the bottom, but the exclusive trade in Africans as slaves wasn't established until the fifteenth century.[7] Before then, most captives were Eastern Europeans; in fact, the word *slave* comes from *Slav*. "Envious of Muslim riches"—that is, envious of their "gold and black captives"—King John of Portugal sent forces to capture the chief trading post in Morocco. The historian Ibram X. Kendi writes that the European trade in Slavs diminished and new trade lines stretched to sub-Saharan Africa; "Europeans began to see the natural Slav(e) not as White, but Black."[8]

But it was the salvation of "lost black souls" that drew King John to western Africa, or at least that's what his biographer said in the first written defense of the European slave trade.[9] King John was a grand master in the Military Order of Christ. His mission in Africa and, by extension, the purpose of slavery itself was to save the lost African who was considered dark, beastly, naked, and undifferentiated. An entire people guilty of sin—shiftless, lawless, godless.

The European empires stretching into the New World were met with resistance. African captives fought back in their villages, in ports, in shipyards, and at sea.[10] And they rebelled in the New World colonies, sometimes joining with indigenous people who died by the thousands resisting captivity. Many more would succumb to Old World plagues or fall in the fields, coal mines, or gold mines. While the threat of black insurrection was real, black slaves, who had been exposed to European disease, didn't die as often as Indian slaves. It would take two hundred years for the narrative on black captivity to take hold. By the seventeenth century, the people represented by the "20 and odd negroes" to the governor of the fledgling Jamestown Colony in 1619 were transfigured into the "cursed sons of Ham," the mass of African captives who were not just in need of slavery's salvation but who were "naturally" fit to be chattel. They were industrious and sturdy, the colonists learned to say, better suited for slavery than the Indians and the European indentured servants they would replace.[11]

An indentured servant's quality of life wasn't much better than a slave's. Indentured servants could not marry, have children, or travel without permission. They were sold and whipped, and the women were raped by their masters and made the subject of public scorn.[12] These servants found common cause and joined ranks with their chained compatriots. They drank and ran away together, made love, and raised children who would now be called biracial. They even rebelled together, which was a colonist's nightmare.[13]

England had been in a series of wars, and war had reached the colonies.[14] And while slave rebellions were common in the century before the American Revolution, a rebellion led by a wealthy white landowner wielding the muscle of slaves and indentured servants would cement the fiction of race and establish the collective guilt of the nation's so-called black residents.

Governor Berkeley of Jamestown hoped to avoid war. He was not sympathetic to the plight of the Indians, but he sought peace with cooperative tribes. Nathaniel Bacon, a young landowning colonist, wanted Native land and sought to wipe out his Indian neighbors. He requested permission to build a militia. Governor Berkeley refused and accused Bacon of treason. After promising freedom to the slaves and indentured servants who took up his cause, Bacon led a rebellion of some five hundred men. They burned down Jamestown and ignited revolts across the colonies. The rebellion was put down quickly, thanks to Bacon's untimely death from dysentery and the force of a thousand-troop army regiment, but the wealthier colonists took note: poor Europeans would work in concert with African slaves if need be. To prevent this from happening, indentured servants and slaves had to be kept separate, their social distance absolute.

The separation of black and white people took place across law and in everyday life. The slave codes outlawed the vestiges of black freedom. Miscegenation was a crime. Reading was a crime. Traveling without papers was a crime. Work shortages were crimes. Escape was certainly a crime—the crime of stealing oneself.[15] All of these crimes were associated with Negro insurrection. To combat solidarity across racial lines, white servants were given new freedoms. They were allowed to settle Indian land and permitted to punish enslaved and free black people. The word *white* was used for the first time in print to describe people of European descent, and these newly white people began to identify with the masters they had once opposed.[16] While these sharp lines separated the so-called races, they also separated black people, including black children, from any presumption of innocence.[17]

While the fear of black insurrection was always palpable, and white slave patrols, constables, and, eventually, the police stood at the ready to beat back black rebellion, the way that black people were depicted in popular culture wouldn't change until emancipation, more than two centuries later. In the words of historian David Levering Lewis, "The African American becomes demonized, a threat, a lascivious beast roaming the countryside of the South, people loosed by the end of slavery and now upon us like locusts."[18] The idea of black criminality preoccupied American minds. Police in the South rounded up thousands of black people for failing to work, for attempting to leave, for the so-called crime of "being idle." The convict leasing system ballooned as newly freed slaves and their children were recaptured and used to rebuild the South. This was an early form of mass incarceration. The number of black "convicts" more than tripled in southern states between 1865 and 1890.[19] And there was overincarceration in the North as black workers fled racial terror to arrive in the slums of Chicago, Philadelphia, St. Louis, and New York.[20] From the tabulating of black crime in ways that erased the criminality of white immigrants to the many wars on the poor—the war on crime, the war on drugs, and, to some extent, the war on poverty—black people were overincarcerated and increasingly treated like criminals.[21]

By the time the Grand Rapids police held those five unarmed boys at gunpoint, the collective guilt of black people had long been established. Psychologist Phillip Atiba Goff found that black boys were viewed as less innocent and assumed to be much older than white children of the same age—four and a half years older, on average.[22] And psychologists Rebecca Hetey and Jennifer Eberhardt found that as white Americans became more aware of racial disparities in U.S. jails and prisons, they increasingly favored the kinds of criminal justice policies that led to the overincarceration of black people.[23] The work was complete. Black boys and girls were not just seen as guilty—they were separated from their innocence.

The 1990s brought us visions of wayward black children as super-predators marauding across a dystopian urban landscape. The most recent progressive explanation for black dysfunction and black guilt is that black youth are "disconnected" from school and work. In any case, black children are viewed as a problem. No wonder black people are twice as likely to be arrested than whites and five times more likely to be incarcerated. No wonder they serve longer sentences. No wonder unarmed black boys are twenty-one times more likely to be killed by the police than unarmed white boys. One study found that over a third of black boys will be arrested by the time they turn eighteen, and nearly half will be arrested before they turn twenty-three.[24] The same study found that 39 percent of white boys will be arrested by the same age, but they haven't been separated from their innocence, so their crimes aren't discussed as often.[25]

Everyone I knew growing up understood these statistics, and we knew them "from our flesh."[26] Prisons were bulging. We had a sense that our neighborhoods fed them.

The factories left and black businesses folded—the candy lady first and then every other black-owned grocery, gas station, and hardware store. The liquor store where Ma Ma sent me with a note to pick up her cigarettes was among the last holdouts. And our neighborhoods began looking like prisons.[27] We ordered chicken wings with mild sauce through bulletproof glass.[28] Our buildings were wrapped in steel—wire-mesh cages for those of us in public housing and wrought-iron fencing for the multigenerational families who pooled their money for rent on the private market. We saw more of the Chicago Police than I like to remember. They patrolled our playgrounds, but never on foot. But who were they looking for? Our brothers? Our cousins? Us? The killers we all knew but avoided? Resource officers were installed in our schools a decade before Columbine. This was Chicago in the late 1980s. The jail and the courthouse and the prison yard closed in. I would soon have my own police encounter.

A freight car was parked on the train tracks by the Thirty-First Street Beach. It was 1987. I was second in command and second eldest of our group, the Ultimate Protectors. Like most eleven-year-olds hopped up on cereal, comic books, and

Saturday-morning cartoons, we thought we were wrestlers or superheroes. My crew would sneak off to the beach on the really hot days for a swim or to practice holding our breath or to climb the wall that separated the Thirty-First Street exit on Lake Shore Drive from the beachfront proper. I don't know exactly when we saw the freight train parked in the rail yard, but we had to know what was inside. BMX bikes. Of course.

The BMX was the luxury we hoped for but couldn't afford. And we knew there would be dangers. Railway police. Dogs. Homeless men who slept nearby. Where did we get these ideas? We didn't know anyone who had successfully busted a freight car; we didn't even know anyone who'd tried. This was the crack era, before the gentrifiers discovered our neighborhood and made it their own. As we walked down the hill to the wall that separated the tracks from the Thirty-First Street overpass, we reviewed our plans to break in. But the car door was open when we got there. The boxcar was empty. We ran back up the hill and climbed the wall, laughing, before the police showed up.

We were kids doing what kids do. We couldn't know exactly how, but we knew that getting caught could change our lives forever. Our brothers, friends, and fathers had already been shipped away to group homes, to job corps, to juvenile detention, to prison facilities downstate. I wouldn't be arrested for another three years.

I was fourteen when I got caught trying to bomb a wall in a train yard. It was the early 1990s. I wasn't really a graffiti artist, but my crew, binge-watching VHS tapes of 1980s movies and knee-deep in the Chicago backpack scene, knew that we'd found a good spot. We were arrested before we got our cans out of the bag.

I spent the night handcuffed to a bench in the back of a

police station. The charges were dropped, but the police called my grandmother. When I got home the next morning, Ma Ma said, "Go back to where you came from." I walked the streets all day, tired but grateful for the outcome. Jeremiah had been arrested a few years before, and the consequences were much worse.

In 1987, when he was thirteen, Jeremiah lost a fight to a boy twice his size. He was always willing to fight. We slept in the same bed until I was ten, when Ma Ma blew what must have been a whole paycheck on a solid oak bunk bed. We played Snoopy and Woodstock and something involving rocket ships at night. I'd kick his bunk. He'd jump down and kick me. All this to say that we were close. If he was fighting, I was too.

In anger and frustration, Jeremiah smashed the car window of a Porsche 911 parked close to our apartment building. The owner was the boyfriend of the big kid's mother. He said the window would cost fifteen hundred dollars to fix, which we couldn't afford.

The building manager and two police officers knocked on our door. Jeremiah had been in too many fights, and the manager told us that either he went or we all did. And we knew the pattern. My oldest brother, Joseph, got into fights. He drank and smoked weed and had sex on the staircase. The building manager and the police had knocked on our door for him one too many times, and they'd given the same ultimatum: if Joseph didn't go, we would be evicted.

Ma Ma must have thought about what eviction would mean for our family. She would be out of an apartment, a place she couldn't really afford. This was the home that her husband, Tommy, had worked two jobs to provide—night shifts as a painter and day shifts in the smokestack of an Indiana steel mill, where he developed the cancer that killed him. It was their home still, though he had been gone for ten years. His chair, an old tweed recliner that Ma Ma kept covered with a quilt, was still in the corner of our living room. Nobody was allowed to sit on Grumpy's chair. But she knew we jumped on it when she went next door to drink Crown Royal with her best friend, Voryce.

What could it mean for Dorothy Jean Miller to be put outdoors after her long journey from Baton Rouge? For a police officer, two movers, and the building manager to put her things on the sidewalk? This was a woman who pressed her two work outfits and starched our Sunday clothes. She arranged the remaining wisps of her gray hair by pulling them out in front of her wig, and she was a breast cancer survivor before anyone used that term. I knew this because once, as a child, I walked past her room and saw the scar where her breast used to be. How could she be evicted after putting herself through secretarial school in the Deep South and after raising my mother, her only child, in that very same apartment?

I was the youngest and the last child she would raise. She must have thought about me when the police came for Jeremiah. She'd made us read a book a week and lip-synch Michael Jackson. She enrolled me in academic programs, though she worried every time I left the four-block radius where she was sure her little black boys were safe. There was a crime wave then, nearly nine hundred murders in Chicago in 1987 alone. The murder of Benji Wilson, Simeon High School's star shooting guard, was fresh on the evening news. And a cashier at a pizza joint in Bridgeport called a customer the N-word, and a black boy was beaten and another one killed within walking distance from our apartment complex. She worried when I got into fights with the kids from the projects a few blocks away. And she worried when they stole the bike that Brother French from the little church I attended gave me as a Christmas gift. We brought her all these worries. Now both of my brothers were in group homes, and I felt profoundly alone.

Is this the afterlife of incarceration, the threat of being put outdoors or the lingering stain of arrests that jeopardizes the well-being of everyone you know? Is it the fact that your good deeds work against you, the way Ma Ma nearly lost everything because she took us in? Is it the loneliness? Or is it that you can't be innocent, no matter how young you are or how much life you have left to live?

A few months after Jeremiah's arrest, I got my ass beat by a boy twice my size. When Jeremiah found out, he took two buses and two trains from his group home to make sure I was okay. "Let's beat his ass together," he said when he arrived after the nearly two-hour trip. This was my brother. That was how he'd always been. But he was in another neighborhood, and it might as well have been another country.

The group home had a token economy, meaning you had to earn your privileges. He could come home only on a weekend pass and only if he played by their rules. But he did not. He got tickets and demerits and lost his liberty, often. It would be months between his visits. Jeremiah couldn't be there to help me the next time I got my ass beat.

I talked shit and got into fights and missed more and more of my classes. I eventually dropped out of school like my two big brothers and like the 60 percent of black boys who find themselves in cages.[29] But I was lucky. The police weren't there when my friends bought liquor and drank Mad Dog in the school parking lot. And they weren't there when I cut class or joined a gang or when Domonique's father choked the shit out of me because he'd thought I ridiculed his daughter. It was broad daylight. I was thirteen. He was a grown man, and everyone saw it. Had my brothers been there, we would have beat his old ass together. But they weren't. They were in group homes on the North Side. I was alone.

Later, the man knocked on Ma Ma's door and apologized. Domonique had told him it wasn't me. My grandmother, her face like stone, demanded that he leave. I imagined stomping him out. I was angry. I hadn't bothered his daughter. Mostly, I was embarrassed to be put in such a vulnerable position in front of so many people. I was too small to do anything about it.

My brothers were gone. So was my best friend's brother, whom I would visit first in a group home and then at a prison. They were all like me and almost every one of my friends. All of us had been arrested. Some were sent away—to foster care, to job corps, to jail. None of us had yet turned fifteen.

This, too, is the afterlife of slavery, which is to say it is the afterlife of mass incarceration. It is the arrests and poverty and premature death that follow the sons of Ham.[30] It's the separation from our homes and our families. It is the precarious lives we live with too few people to come to our aid. It's the profound sense of loneliness and the embarrassment and guilt that comes with knowing that you're alone.

Two of my brothers were shipped away, as were at least one of the brothers, cousins, fathers, or sons of almost every one of my friends. Every other black person I meet and every one of us who grew up poor has firsthand experience of this predicament. We understand quite well this level of precariousness.[31]

It followed us into adulthood. We've all struggled to keep the lights on. Every one of us has a story about the time we almost lost our lives to a bullet or depression or disease or incarceration. Almost all of us have. This, too, is black life, or at least life for the black and poor. You know you will probably be arrested, since everyone you know has been, but you don't know when or for what. And you know that there will be consequences for that arrest, but you can't predict what they will be. This is what James Baldwin called the "bloody catalog of oppression."[32] There's simply no time to process it all. You spend your days picking up pieces and stitching together what you find. These were the reasons why I didn't flinch when I asked a man about the first time he had been arrested.

Timothy's first arrest happened when he was twelve. "They caught me up on some bullshit," he said. It was shoplifting and riding in a stolen car. He was arrested again at fifteen. He was eighteen when he went to prison. His landlord had a habit of letting himself into Timothy's mother's apartment. The last time—and the last straw—his mother was taking a bath. "I don't know much about landlords," he said, "but that's not very landlord-like." Timothy and the landlord got into an argument. "He upped a gun," Timothy said. "He put it in my face. [But] while he was talking, I pulled my gun and I used it. You pull a gun, you use it," Timothy said. He was charged with attempted murder.

Timothy and I were meeting at a McDonald's not far from the halfway house where he lived. It had been a decade since he'd shot that landlord. He had been out of prison less than a month. Timothy's story was like that of so many other people I'd interviewed. I would ask, "How old were you when you were first arrested?" They would tell me ten or twelve or sixteen. I would ask, "How many times?" They would say ten or fifteen or, sometimes, they'd laugh and say something like "Shit, too many times to count."

Chicago, Detroit, New York, LA, Ann Arbor or Ypsilanti, Michigan, even Harvey, Illinois. It didn't matter what city. Boys got in trouble. Boys got into fights. Boys cut class. Boys got arrested. And their trials were so similar: A boy or his mother or his brother or his friend was assaulted. The police were called, and they either came too late or didn't come at all. In Detroit, in 2013 the average response time for a 911 call was fifty-eight minutes, and that was for "high-priority calls" like robberies, sexual assault, or active shooters.[33] And the homicide clearance rate in Chicago in 2017 was just 17 percent.[34] This meant that 83 percent of the city's murderers were never brought to "justice." Why would anyone call the police?[35]

The girls' stories were similar, but there were important distinctions. They were sixteen on average when they were first arrested. Almost all of them had children. They leaned on their mothers or sisters or friends when they were locked up, rarely on their lovers. Almost all of them had been sex-ually assaulted—by babysitters, by parents, by boyfriends, by strangers. (Some of the boys were sexually assaulted too, but it took many, many interviews and sometimes a number of years before they shared those stories with me.) New York City had something like seventeen thousand untested rape kits; Detroit and Chicago and every other major city in the country were about the same.

The people I met told me without fail that the police didn't come when they needed them, but they were there when they smoked a joint or sold a few rocks or turned a trick to get out of a bad situation. This, too, is the afterlife of slavery—that is to say, the afterlife of mass incarceration. You are overpoliced and under-protected. The police don't come when you call them, and when they do show up, they beat your ass, because they come only when you're being arrested.

By the time I met Lorenzo, whom everyone called Zo, I was used to the script.[36] I asked, "How old were you when you were first arrested?"

"Ten," he said.

"How many times were you arrested?"

"Fifteen or sixteen times," he told me.

"What led to your first arrest?" I asked.

Zo was thirty-four years old when we met. He'd grown up in K-Town, a neighborhood on Chicago's West Side where all the street names begin with the letter *K*. "I was up every morning at the gas station, pumping gas. Going on back porches, taking pop bottles, selling them to the store, stealing clothes. We was doing that seven, eight years old," Zo said.

We sat across a table at Emmaus Road, a faith-based halfway house on Chicago's West Side. He was the intake coordinator, responsible for screening men who applied for an open bed. He told me that his father was murdered when he was just a few months old and his mother was charged with involuntary manslaughter. She was "strung out" on drugs. He thought she'd set him up. "I still don't know whether or not she did it," he said. He had tried to get her to talk to him about it over the years, but she wouldn't. "I learned to let it be," he said.

Zo's father was a dope dealer, and dope dealers in K-Town took care of things. "They made certain we had school clothes; we went to school. They made certain we had food [and] clean clothing. They would help out with rent, lights, gas." Zo said that the dope dealers gave money to the mothers of all the boys in the neighborhood. But the boys had an enterprise of their own. "I would steal cars and sell them to older guys for fifty, sixty, a hundred bucks," he said. "They would sell them to the chop shops for twenty times that. It was just a little pocket money for me to get an outfit."

Zo was eleven when the police pulled him over in one of those cars. He did four months at the Illinois Youth Center in St. Charles. He was pulled over in another car a year later, and he did time at the youth center's branch on Chicago's West Side, not far from Emmaus Road. A year later and another car, and this time he was sent to the Arthur J. Audy Home—a facility for kids who had committed serious crimes but who were too young to be tried as adults. By the time he was fifteen, his hustle changed. Zo started robbing dope dealers.

Everyone Zo ran with carried a gun, and he started carrying all the time. "I kid you not," he told me. "I would walk to the laundromat with my laundry bag with a shoe on top with my pistol. And that was an everyday thing, because we were all doing the same things." His crew went from making a couple hundred dollars a month stealing and selling cars to making nearly a thousand dollars a week as drug robbers. He learned to take care of things in K-Town, like his father did before he was murdered.

"If I had a thousand dollars," Zo said, "I would take two, three hundred off. I would go pay rent to my aunt, probably go give my mama a couple dollars. Make sure my little brother was taken care of... Whatever he wanted, I did. I used it for every-day life. To make sure we had a place to stay... even though I knew what [my mother] was doing with the money. I wanted to help her," he said.

They all knew where the money was coming from. His aunt knew. His mother. The mothers of his friends. The landlords. The drug addicts, whom dope boys called hypes, who rented stolen cars. The police who arrested the boys who stole cars along with the dope boys who sat on their corners for hours at a time. That's how the economy worked. The more drugs, the more hypes. The more hypes, the more dealers. The more dealers, the more police. The more police, the more arrests, and the more the drugs cost. The bigger the margins for the bigger dealers, the more dope boys they put on the street. Zo was waiting to pick the dope boys' pockets. But Zo's choice of trade wasn't due solely to the financial rewards. "I thought I wouldn't get too much flak [from police]. No drug dealer is going to report somebody just robbed him for ten thousand dollars." Zo would sometimes need to work in a crew, and that work was often dangerous — dope spots had security; dope dealers carried guns. But the benefits outweighed the risks. A dope dealer "would most likely take it out in the streets," Zo said. "And if he found out [it was me who robbed them], he would already know I'm out here. If he tries to shoot, I was already into shooting."

But there was something else that led Zo to his trade: he didn't like dope dealers. Zo wouldn't even sell dope on the side, unlike most of his friends. His mother was on crack. He'd lost his father to some drug-related act of jealousy or greed. "For me, it was the best choice, morally," he said. Zo robbed drug dealers, and he was good at it. "They sold it. I copped it." He laughed.

Zo paid a hype fifty dollars to sign the lease on a studio apartment, and another fifty dollars each month to take his two-hundred-thirty-five-dollar rent payment downstairs to the real estate office. He was sixteen and hardly ever there, but he had his own place to take a girl or for his friends to crash or to get off the block when he needed to. It would be two full years before he caught his next case, but this time he was an adult.

Zo had a cousin who robbed a dope boy. A week later, the dope boy retaliated, fatally shooting Zo's cousin from behind. Zo got the call from his aunt, confirmed the shooter's identity, and went to work. He robbed the man who'd killed his cousin later that evening, then shot the dope boy from behind and left him in the street. But he didn't kill him. He was sending a message: "I'm out here. I see you," Zo said. He was arrested a week later, not for that but as a suspect in a different armed robbery.

"They call it a blood hit," Zo told me, sipping from his oversize coffee mug.

"What's a blood hit?" I asked.

"Say the police have ten burglaries unsolved, and they catch me for a burglary," he said, "and when they catch me for the burglary, it's in the same area—[same] geographic location, [or the robber] probably used the same type of tools, took the same type of stuff, and at the same time. They can match that because they have ten others that haven't been solved that fit the same criteria."

"You might not have done [the robbery]?" I asked, for some reason surprised that black people could be arrested and charged with crimes they might not have committed.

"More than likely I *didn't* do it," he said, some exasperation in his voice. "It's just they don't have anybody [in custody], and now, the way that I did mine *matches* the way that those [other crimes were] committed. That's what they call a blood hit."

"The cops call it a blood hit?" I asked with some disbelief.

"It's called a blood hit," he said. This was the second time that I'd annoyed him, but he was patient. "It has nothing to do with blood," he explained in a tone that meant *Look, man, I'm trying to tell you but you're not listening.* "It just means it matches, like a DNA structure. It's a great possibility that you *were* the person," he said. "I actually took four convictions for that—four armed robberies that I had nothing to do with. And you know, the funny part is," he said, "when they brought the people in, it was people that I had *never* seen before. And then again, they was white. Not to sound racial." Zo laughed.

"They were white?" I repeated. Thinking, *How could this* not *be racial?*

Zo was laughing louder now; he seemed like he was getting more and more comfortable. "They're saying, 'Yeah, that was him.' I was looking like, *I know I haven't took nothing from them, 'cause they white! I haven't been in any white neighborhoods.* There is no white neighborhood in my community," Zo said.

"Did any of your boys rob white folks?" I asked, the social scientist in me getting in the way. Social scientists are trained not to believe the people they interview. They're taught to test what people say—that is, to look for what's called "disconfirming evidence."

"Huh?" Zo said, annoyed, looking like he was thinking I hadn't heard him the whole time, like I hadn't gotten a single thing he'd told me over the three years I'd known him. I followed my research protocol, even though I knew that black people can be arrested for nothing.

"Any of *your* people rob white folks?" I asked again, now annoyed with myself.

"Nah," he said, "we robbed drug dealers. When are white people selling drugs in my community? They were from, like, Naperville or Evanston...areas that I had *never* been to."

"No North Side neighborhoods? No western suburbs, like Oak Park?" I asked.

"My first time ever going to downtown Chicago was after I got released [from prison], and I've been in Chicago *all my life!*" Zo said. "I had never been to the lake. I had never been to the beach. I had never been to Great America. I had never been to a baseball game or a football game or a softball game. I had never been to any of that. I went to the beach for the first time just last year," Zo said, laughing again. "I didn't go where I didn't feel like I fit," he said. "The way I dressed, the way I talked, the way I looked—People would automatically know. *He's either up there committing a crime or he new to the country or something.* But I didn't go where I didn't feel comfortable."

Zo was caught with three pistols on the day of his arrest, but he hadn't left his neighborhood. He did not rob those white suburbanites, despite what the police and the prosecutor claimed, and he knew his cousin's murderer would never come to court. The state had a weak case. Zo rejected the plea deals they offered, choosing to bide his time in the Cook County Jail. Every month, Zo was called to court, and every month, the state requested a continuance. "There was no police. No witness. No nobody," Zo said. "I was sitting in the bullpen waiting for two hours to go to court. When they called me in, I would be in there less than two minutes. That's how it was."

But after ten months of Zo waiting in the county jail, the man who'd shot Zo's cousin showed up to testify against him. Zo was convicted on the word of his cousin's murderer and of the four white suburbanites he had never seen. He was found guilty on seven counts—one count for armed violence, four counts of armed robbery, and two counts of attempted armed robbery. The judge cited his "pattern of criminality" as he rendered his decision. Zo, who was nineteen years old, was sentenced to twenty years in prison. His public defender assured him he would do "just nine years." He had been at Cook County for nearly a year and would get credit for time served, and he could earn "good time" if he "kept his nose clean" while he was inside.[37]

We sat at a white plastic folding table, my hands gripping a Styrofoam cup of lukewarm coffee. He lifted his mug and took another sip.

Zo had committed many crimes. He was guilty of many things, but he was arrested for something he did not do and was incarcerated for it for many years of his relatively young life. Why was I surprised that this happened?

I've sat across many tables from many different people, sometimes when they were in prison, most times after they were released. Most had been locked away for years. We'd have coffee or break bread or share a bench during cigarette breaks at their AA meetings or their anger-management sessions. I'd meet them at the unemployment office or a library or when they filled out applications for public aid. I'd go to their homes and sit with their families, doing my best to learn what it was like to live in a supervised society. I spent hours talking with some and years talking with others. It didn't matter if they were convicted of killing a man or robbing a store or getting high. There was a pattern: An arrest. A series of incarcerations. A sense of guilt. A feeling of shame. A struggle to find their way.

I met Martin in the summer of 2003. We worshipped together under a parking-lot revival tent at a Pentecostal church on the West Side. I was there when he finished a workforce-development program for veterans at a local university. We celebrated when he graduated from community college and when he started doing street outreach ministry, offering sandwiches and coffee to men and women who slept on the street. I was there when he launched the nonprofit organization he named after his late father. And he was there when I got married and when my youngest son was born and when I finished graduate school. And he was there when I got the job that finally broke me into the middle class. We've been to each other's homes dozens of times, and we've celebrated our accomplishments together. We've also mourned losses. He's had more than I've had. Two of his sisters and his brother died. He's lost apartments in a few bouts with addiction, though he eventually won that fight. He's lost many, many friends.

Martin was much older than Zo, and Zo was older than me. I was a teenager in the 1990s, and in the South Side neighborhood where I grew up, my world was black on all sides. Black teachers and black parents; black friends and black churches; black gangsters and black classmates who went to all-black schools. White social workers, white firemen, and white police officers, usually, though some of them were black. There was one kid we called White Dennis growing up, but he was black too, or at least both of his parents were.

Martin was a teenager in the 1960s. His Chicago was filled with immigrants—Greek deli owners, Italian barkeeps, and Irish kids who threw rocks when he walked under the viaduct. They worked together selling newspapers, delivering groceries, or packing meat at the stockyards. The city was certainly segregated, but factory work brought people into contact, even if just for their shifts. This happened much less for people who grew up after the factories closed, like me.

Martin lived in a housing project two miles west of the university where I now teach. His mother was fifteen when he was born, and his father was fifty-eight.

"The thing was," Martin explained, sitting in my living room, "girls were taught, 'Get you an older man, so when you need something, he'll take care of you.'"

Martin's mother came up from a small mining town in Caldwell Parish, Louisiana, during the second wave of the Great Migration. Her parents had separated. "She was passed around by her kinfolk" from her grandmother to her great-grandmother to her cousin, who accompanied her north. She met Martin's father, a former sharecropper from the Mississippi Delta. He worked in the factories, fixed cars, and did electrical work on the side. They had Martin a short time later, the first of their seven children.

It was hard being a mother at fifteen and harder being married to Martin's father. "You got a forty-some-odd-year difference," Martin said. "And my mother wanted certain things. Her cousin from down south would tell her, 'You ought to get this from him...my man doing this for me.' So that caused a lot of friction." The friction turned into arguments. Arguments turned into fights. Martin's father misplaced money and blamed his wife. He threatened her. Sometimes he beat her.

"I won't say he wasn't wrong," Martin told me, remembering the time he saw his father standing over his mother and raining down blows. But most times, Martin said, "he just tried to hold her down." Martin said his mother "talked to [my father] like a john, and, quite naturally, you talk to me like that, I'm going to have an adverse reaction." He told me about the "little things" she did to provoke his anger, like the time she smashed his father's hand in a doorway.

Martin and his mother had "friction" too. She would use Martin as a shield to avoid beatings, placing her boy between her body and the body of her charging husband. He refused to take her side. "I told her, 'Look, that's your man, but he's only my daddy. I ain't have nothing to do with that!'"

Martin said that his father never beat him save for once—when Martin hit a girl. "He punched me so hard, I was like, *Whoa.*" And there was the time that his father pulled his pistol when Martin talked back to his mother. "That's my woman," he told Martin. "Don't you never put your hands on your mother."

Martin felt safe with his father. He said his father would never have shot him. "In his era, a gun was a credible threat," he said. "All you had to do was pull it out." His mother, however, beat Martin frequently. She punched him in the head until he was woozy. She beat him when he got the answers wrong on his homework. She beat him when he talked back or got into trouble at school. She beat him when he forgot to do chores. She beat him when he stayed out late to get away from all of the beatings. And she beat him when she found out that he had been sexually abused.

Martin was five. The girl was eight. The girl's mother "had a lot of guys," Martin said, perhaps trying to explain how a child could be abusive, but I'd worked for years in social services; I was used to these kinds of stories. Martin said, "She molested me behind a truck that was parked in the yard behind our building." He told his aunt Caroline. "She called me Master Martin when I was in trouble," he said, laughing. Aunt Caroline loved her Martin, and he loved her. She made him feel safe. His aunt promised to break the news to his mother to keep Martin from getting in trouble.

But Martin's mother beat him anyway and blamed him for having sex.

Martin was abused again, this time by the fourteen-year-old his mother hired to babysit her children while she went to work. "I thought I was enjoying something," he said. "She rode me so hard, I blacked out." The girl's father walked in, found Martin in bed, beat his daughter, and sent Martin home. His mother beat him when he returned. Martin was six years old.

He started spending more and more time outside, walking the streets for hours, visiting friends who lived in Cabrini Green, a housing project that was miles away. He'd stay outside as long as he could. He'd do anything to get out of the house, even brave Chicago winters. He found work with a man who delivered newspapers for the *Chicago Defender,* once considered the "most important paper" of the Associated Negro Press. He would leave early in the morning, deliver the papers, go to school, then go home for dinner and to get some rest.

When Martin was ten and "they were still building parts of the Dan Ryan," an expressway along the east/west dividing line on the south side of the city, Martin often visited a friend who lived on the other side of the construction site. One time, three men followed him. They dragged him into an empty garage and "did what they wanted to do." He told me with some regret that he went straight home, not stopping to first tell his aunt. When his mother saw blood in his underwear, she beat him and ridiculed him in front of his siblings. "He's a boy," she said. "Look what he did now!"

It was at that moment, Martin said, that he felt like everyone in the world was against him except for his father, whom Martin still deified, and his aunt, who loved him but could not protect him. He felt guilty of some ambiguous sin before he encountered, in any meaningful way, the laws of God or man. He told me once, "That moment kind of reinforced for me I was the problem." But how does it feel to be a problem?[38] And how does a person respond to being told by the world that they are the source of their own misery? Martin ran away from home. He had just turned eleven years old.

Martin picked up odd jobs to support himself. His day went something like this: In the early mornings, before most people got up, Martin delivered the *Defender* or the *Sun-Times/Daily News*. After his last delivery, he would go to a friend's apartment, wash up, then hit the streets. He walked around for the rest of the day and returned to the *Sun-Times* at night, where he met up with two friends, Jason and Stevie the Greek. The boys stuffed inserts for the *Bulldog*, the *Sun-Times'* evening edition, and holed up in the mailroom until their shifts started again the next day.

Martin would go off in the mornings with a driver named Tommy who, like Stevie, was Greek. There was also a kid named John who didn't much care for Martin. "John was a big teenager," he said. "He was huge. He had to weigh about three hundred pounds. And I think the Greek was his family. So John used to always pick at me."

Martin was twelve by then, small even for a twelve-year-old boy. He would run errands with Tommy, who worked the downtown hotels. He would pay Martin three dollars for the day and buy him breakfast. One morning Martin missed his pickup, but he knew the route, so he went to meet Tommy at the delivery dock of one of the hotels. The maintenance men on his delivery route all knew him as "little Tommy." "When you worked for the Greeks and Italians, they would give you their name," he said.

When Martin got to the dock, a maintenance man asked if he wanted to make some extra cash. There was work in the ballroom. "The guy said, 'Well, come on, little Tommy.' So I went in the back of the ballroom," Martin told me. "When I got halfway through, something hit me up here," Martin said, pointing to his head. "I said, 'This ain't good.' As soon as that came to mind, [the maintenance man] said, 'Hey, you know what it is? Nobody can hear you. Ain't no need in you screaming or doing anything.'" Martin said he "went along with it," doing "enough to survive," because he had been through it all before. This was the fourth time Martin was raped.

Martin finally came out of the ballroom and made his way back to the dock. As the truck pulled out, big John noticed something was wrong. "I wasn't saying nothing. I wasn't joking like I usually do." John grabbed Martin by the collar and demanded he tell him what had happened. Martin told them. Tommy turned the truck around, and John stormed inside. "He beat that man stupid," Martin told me, sounding, in some way, proud. Martin was shocked. "I had never seen anybody standing up for me," he said. But when the police arrived, they arrested John for assault. They dropped the charges when they learned he assaulted Martin's rapist.

"The Greeks, they didn't believe in the victim suffering no more than they already did," Martin said. "They told me not to worry. 'We got this from now on.'" But when I asked Martin what had happened to the maintenance man after John "beat him stupid," he didn't know. He just knew that his rapist was never arrested.

Martin went on for a year delivering the morning news. Then one night his friend Jason, one of the three runaways who slept in that mailroom, didn't come back. "I don't know what happened," Martin said, "but he stayed a few days on Forty-Eighth and Dearborn." Martin lowered his voice and his head. "And then we found out...yeah." He paused. We sat together in silence for a moment while Martin regained his composure. "When we found out that Jason got killed, we were hurt, man." Martin knew it was time to go home.

It was 1969. Martin was thirteen years old and he started drinking, heavily. He went from alcohol to weed and then to pills in short order. "[I used] whatever I could get my hands on at the time," he said. He roamed the streets, worked odd jobs, and got into arguments with his mother, but he stayed home until he turned eighteen and left to join the navy.

Martin had always been smart. He scored high enough on the military entrance exam to sit for the engineer's test. But his white shipmates weren't interested in him being more than a custodian or a handyman working the boiler room. One petty officer told him he'd better *not* take the test. He told me he was "manhandled" and bullied by the older and higher-ranking white shipmates. They knew he was alone. There were a few black petty officers aboard the ship, and fewer still that knew him. None liked him very much. "I was younger than those guys," he told me. "They had problems of their own to deal with."

One group of white petty officers locked Martin in the engine room for a full ninety minutes. They warned him that the next time they might not let him out, and he'd be like the black navy man whose body had been found in a boiler room on a different ship just a few weeks before. In retaliation and to "get somebody's attention," when they reached the next duty station Martin stole one of their cars. He didn't know how to drive a stick shift and ended up crashing it into a gate.

Martin was court-martialed immediately. At captain's mast, the ship's chief officer said that despite the recommendation from Martin's superiors to give him a dishonorable discharge, Martin could stay in the service if he wanted to. The captain said he believed Martin's story, or at least he believed that Martin was young and afraid. But how could Martin stay? The white petty officers had threatened his life, and a man like him had been killed on another boat just a few weeks before. Martin declined the offer, he told me with some regret.

"There wasn't no name for it back then," he said. "In the seventies they called it shell shock." Martin said he suffered from PTSD but wished he hadn't gotten out of the navy. "A lot of things would have been [different] because I could have gotten help," he said. "I was still out there alone." Martin packed his seabag and headed home.

When Martin got back to the States, he became a truck driver, found his own place, and started a family, but his drug use escalated. He went from pills to PCP to "whatever means of escape" he could find. And while he used drugs for years, he wasn't arrested until he was well into his thirties. The mother of Martin's youngest child introduced him to crack. From that point until I met him, his life story was familiar. He became addicted, blew all his money, and suffered many losses. He was homeless off and on for years. I saw him once at Caring Hands Ministries, a shelter for homeless veterans, most of whom had been in trouble with the law, and once at the Cook County Jail, where he attended a chapel service that I led. He was caught in a drug sweep at a public-housing complex on the near South Side. He didn't have an ID, which was reason enough for the police to search him.

Martin was in jail two weeks awaiting a hearing on a plea deal for a charge of felony drug possession with intent to distribute. If he took the plea, the judge would release him on two years' probation. If he decided to fight the case, he would have to do so from his cell. This would cost him his veteran's benefits. He had been awarded disability for his PTSD diagnosis, but there was a rule: His benefits would be suspended if he spent more than thirty days in jail. And he would certainly lose his place on the waiting list to stay at Caring Hands.

At Martin's plea hearing, the judge said she thought a felony charge was "excessive," but the prosecutor said it was fair, given his record—fourteen charges for trespassing, a charge for having "burglary equipment," and many, many charges of possession of drugs or drug paraphernalia. Now he had been caught with three crack rocks in his pocket, which was enough for him to sell, according to the prosecutor. He couldn't afford the two-thousand-dollar bail. His father had died long ago, and his mother told him to take the plea. If people helped him with bail, they might hold it over his head. He would "owe them" and would need to repay the favor.

One of the brothers at church had already been "testifying" about him at service. "God is good," he would say. "I remember when I saw Brother Martin pushing a cart. Martin, do you remember that?"—as if Martin could ever forget. As if the brother would ever let him. "God is good!" he'd say to the congregation, reminding us all of Martin's past. I would smile awkwardly at Martin in support, but hearing that brother made me cringe.

In fear of losing his benefits and weary from his stay in jail, Martin took the plea.

*   *   *

In hindsight, I suppose Lorenzo and Martin were fortunate. Lorenzo became a social-service provider at the halfway house where we'd met. Martin has been sober for fifteen years. He's volunteered at food pantries and started an outreach organization that he named after his late father. He now delivers meals to Chicago's homeless population on some of the same streets and park benches where he once slept. He even got his commercial driver's license reinstated and drives trucks again for a living. After three years on a waiting list, he was selected for an apartment in a building for homeless veterans. Martin had a key to his own apartment for the first time in over a decade. "Praise God," that rude minister said from the pulpit one too many times. "Brother Martin has come a long way."

But Martin is sixty-five. He lived on and off the street for most of his life. And Lorenzo, who is now forty-six, spent a third of his life in a cage. There was no treatment center for Lorenzo's mother and no program for him to go to when he was a child stealing from his neighbors' back porches. The police did not arrest the hypes that bought the cars that he stole, and they didn't arrest his cousin's murderer. They arrested him when he retaliated and they sent him to prison for four armed robberies that occurred in places he had never been.

The courts labeled these men "repeat offenders," separating them, because of their histories, from the presumption of legal innocence—a right of citizenship in the United States. But where were the police when Martin needed them? They did not confront the petty officers who locked him in an engine room. They did not find the person who murdered his friend. They didn't look for any of Martin's many rapists, one of whom they knew, but they arrested big John for coming to Martin's aid and they arrested Martin for trespassing. Martin's prosecutor said his rap sheet revealed a "pattern of criminality," his guilt established by a steady cascade of arrests. But what precisely was Martin guilty of? His fourteen arrests for trespassing happened during the decade that Martin was homeless, and he was arrested once more for drug possession, which almost cost him his livelihood, for the crime of coping with his problems in the best way he knew how.

CHAPTER 3

SINNERMAN

It's 1962. Nina Simone sits at her piano for a live recording of "Sinnerman" at the Village Gate nightclub in New York City. She moans in the break; the drum and hand clap drive the beat; each keystroke expresses the urgency of the moment. Simone is slender and striking in a white sleeveless gown. Her features are pronounced, her gaze focused and sometimes intense. Her voice is full, deep, a complement to the jangling but precise chords she plays.

"Oh yeah," she sings. *"Oh yeah."* Her voice trails off now, accompanying the melody with an intensity that's directed toward all of us and no one in particular. She begins again, her audience on edge. This time the pitch is a bit higher. *"Oh yeah!"* she sings. The sound and tempo build and then diminish.

> *Oh, sinnerman, where you gonna run to?*
> *On that day?*

Simone recorded the song three years before the passage of the Civil Rights Act. Medgar Evers had not yet been assassinated in his driveway after coming home from an NAACP meeting. Fourteen-year-old Cynthia Wesley, eleven-year-old Carol Denise McNair, fourteen-year-old Carole Rosamond Robertson, and fourteen-year-old Addie Mae Collins had yet to be murdered by the white supremacists who bombed Birmingham's Sixteenth Street Baptist Church, and twelve-year-old Sarah Collins had not yet lost her big sister or the sight in her right eye.[1] But black life was no easier in 1962, when the song was recorded, than it was in 1963, when more people paid attention. And it was no easier in Harlem than it was in Birmingham or Bronzeville in Chicago.

Where will Sinnerman run and hide to escape the judgment that is all around him? Les Baxter recorded a show-tune cover a decade before Simone in which Sinnerman runs to the moon. But this is a Negro spiritual, one that has been sung in black churches since the beginning of the twentieth century and whose roots run much deeper. It is a song that should be sung with a tambourine. It is a warning and a call to "get right" so the church can "go home." The man has sinned, which is to say he has incurred a debt. And the debt is a real one. He must repay it.

The philosopher and polemicist Friedrich Nietzsche tells us in *The Genealogy of Morals* that the origin of guilt, what he calls "bad conscience," comes from the financial relationship between a debtor and his lender. Should the debtor fail to pay what he owes, he offers his very flesh to the lender. It is a sign of the debtor's free will to offer his body, the one thing over which he has mastery. The lender takes pleasure in torturing his debtor, which sears his debtor's conscience. The pain he inflicts will never be forgotten by the debtor or by anyone who sees his pain. This is not far from a theological tradition in which the sin-sick souls of a sin-sick world owes debts to their God. In sinning, they've broken a contract, and the debt must be repaid. The debtors must pay with their flesh.

"Sinnerman" was sung at the tail end of the nineteenth century. The survivors of the lash sang it, and they would continue to sing through the coming Great Depression. Slavery was punishing, but the hunger and disrespect that followed was nearly as bad. Ms. Simone's version was like the one our great-grandmothers and great-aunts sang. It was a song of fire and smoke, strummed on bass guitars and well-tuned pianos, but the hand clap was reminiscent of the washboard and their moans of redlines, cotton thorns, and slum clearance. The Sinnerman runs and hides on Earth. His punishment comes from this world. It is the *Southern Horrors* Ida B. Wells famously chronicled, and the scars of the long trek north, and the crack of the police baton in New York's Harlem and Detroit's Black Bottom. It is suffering the sting of eviction and hunger from unemployment and unsolved rapes and murders while preachers, politicians, social scientists, journalists, and do-gooders, their best intentions in tow, descend on your neighborhood to say this is really all your fault.[2] It's your refusal to snitch or to keep a man happy, to raise your children or to "delay gratification," or it's the deficits of your culture that put you in this position. It's your social disorganization or your disbelief in the legitimacy of the law. At the end of the day, it's you.

Simone's voice invokes this history. Her long neck bent toward the keys, her dutiful drummer providing the scaffold, Simone brings us with Sinnerman as he looks for help. He goes first to his familiar haunts—the rock, the river, and the sea—begging, "Please help me. Please hide me, Lord." But the Sinnerman finds no refuge. The river boils. The sea bleeds. The rock says, "I ain't gonna hide you." Even the Lord rejects him. "Where were you when you ought to have been praying?" asks the Lord before telling Sinnerman, "Go to the devil." The devil is, of course, waiting.

In this parable, constructed from the traditions of the southern black church, Sinnerman cries out for mercy but finds little in the world. "Power! Power to the Lord!" he says, confessing his sins and submitting himself for judgment. But the devil will never be satisfied. Sinnerman knows his debt won't be repaid no matter how much torture he endures. The song ends as Simone wails and saunters and plays and claps, ushering us from the haunts of the Jim Crow South to the racial violence of the northern ghetto. Channeling this same energy, she recorded "Mississippi Goddam" and "Four Women" and, in the wake of Dr. King's assassination, the lament "Why (the King of Love Is Dead)."

I sat at my desk over a half a century later trying to make sense of it all, "Sinnerman" and "See-Line Woman" playing in the background. Fela, Louis Armstrong, and Gil Scott-Heron joined her in urging me to think more clearly as I pored over my notes from hundreds of hours of interviews and observations. The careful social scientist in my tradition studies minutiae, analyzing facial expressions, body movements, and seemingly innocuous conversations to make sense of a given moment. Moments make history.

It was 2013. I had just taken a job at the University of Michigan, in part to launch my study of what life was like for formerly incarcerated people living in Detroit. I met with ninety people who were released from jails and prisons and returned to neighborhoods throughout the Motor City. The men and women I sat with shared their trouble finding work or places to live; they described the faces of property managers when they revealed their criminal records. I wrote down what they said and compared it with what I saw when I accompanied them on their daily routines. I wrote about the tone of these interactions in the margins of a notebook I kept in my back pocket; a note like *condescending* or *welcoming* or *scolding* or *surprised* would later help me make sense of the encounter. And I'd pay attention to their expressions—if they were fidgety or looked down or if their eyes danced to avoid a gaze or when they shook hands firmly or if they made eye contact when talking. The outcomes were almost always the same. Very few people landed jobs. Fewer still could rent apartments. They moved from couch to couch as their lovers and family members grew exhausted caring for able-bodied adults who could not find their way. I gathered these notes and tried to place them in order, reconstructing their experiences as best I could. And then I went back to the people I'd met with to make sure I got it right.

The people I followed were rejected, and they were rejected at every turn. I could hear myself saying that word—*rejection*—with Ms. Simone playing in my head. It all made sense. The rock, the river, the sea, and the good Lord all rejected the sinner. This is the nature of sin. It separates and marks you, like Cain, the cursed son of Adam who killed his older brother. God didn't kill him, but Cain walked the earth an outcast. Just as sin puts a barrier between people and their God, a criminal record separates people accused of a crime from the life-giving institutions of a free society. The rock, the river, and the sea give no refuge.

The psychologist Geraldine Downey studies the weight of rejection in people's lives. She studies how the anticipation of rejection affects psychological and physical health. She finds that rejection, whether it happens early or late, is prolonged or acute, breeds "rejection sensitivity." In kids, this sensitivity shows up as poor academic performance and behavioral problems at school. In adults, it leads to anxiety and depression and a sense of dissatisfaction with life and intimate partners.[3] No wonder so many relationships dissolve when a lover comes home from prison; no wonder so many people struggle to get their footing after hearing *No* dozens of times.

Locked out of the political and economic life of the city, formerly incarcerated people must depend on the mercy of others, although they rarely find it. They look for housing, but options are scarce or unaffordable. Social-service agencies refuse to help them or have long waiting lists. Employers rarely even review their applications. Family and friends turn them away or remove their support at the worst possible times. Almost everyone they know has faced a similar situation, because most of the people from their neighborhoods have spent some time in a cage. A whole people with no place to go, a whole society rejected.

I lived and taught in Ann Arbor, Michigan, a small, mostly white, affluent city forty-five minutes west of Detroit. The state was in a water crisis, or at least Detroit was. One hundred thousand people had had their water shut off. This was absurd. Nearly one in seven Detroit residents lost access to running water in a city between two lakes and a river. I learned that this level of disrespect was part of a long tradition.

George Clinton might call Detroit a chocolate city, like Newark or Gary or Atlanta.[4] Nearly all of the city's residents are black, but it wasn't always this way. Detroit bears the scars of transformation.[5] In the early twentieth century, the auto industry pulled successive waves of black migrants to the city. The war effort of the 1940s called still more migrants north. Despite its place in history as one of the last stops on the Underground Railroad, a place of refuge and opportunity, Detroit has consistently greeted black migrants with violence. Black people competed with poor white people for jobs on the factory floor and were hired for the worst jobs in the auto plants. They were redlined in their neighborhoods. The nearly all white police force cracked heads everywhere, even in the storied Black Bottom and Paradise Valley neighborhoods, where black celebrities like Joe Louis, the famous Brown Bomber, lived and where so many black businesses thrived. The message was clear: black labor was needed, but the black people who filled those jobs were unwanted.

Between 1950, when Detroit's population exceeded 1.8 million people, and 1967, the year of the most famous race riot in its history, many of the factories closed. Others moved to the suburbs, initiating the first great wave of white flight with nearly three hundred thousand white residents moving just outside of city limits. Black unemployment soared. In the name of slum clearance, an all-white city council razed Black Bottom to the ground. The Chrysler Freeway paved over its remains.[6] Another three hundred thousand white residents fled when Detroit elected Coleman Young, the city's confrontational, if beloved (by most Detroit residents), black mayor. More of the great auto plants closed as the industry struggled to keep pace with changing fuel-efficiency standards and foreign competition. Even more white residents left, blaming the mayor for driving them away. By the onset of the great recession of 2008,

Detroit had fundamentally transformed; in just under fifty years, 1.3 million white residents had left the city, taking their tax revenues with them. The once-thriving metropolis, full of energy and industry and with a population that was 84 percent white, was deindustrialized and abandoned. Today, there are just 717,000 residents, nearly 80 percent of whom are black. Detroit is the only major city to grow to well over one million residents only to see one million people leave. A whole society cast to the side; a whole black city rejected.

In July of 2013, Rick Snyder, the governor of Michigan, announced that Detroit would be placed under emergency management. That same week, Kwame Kilpatrick, the city's young and charismatic former mayor, was convicted on two dozen counts of federal corruption and bribery. The reins of the city were handed to Kevin Orr, an expert on bankruptcy and corporate restructuring from Washington, DC. The city council protested. Its members had a plan in place to address the city's fiscal crisis that the governor had already approved; 60 percent of the Detroit residents polled said they opposed declaring bankruptcy, but 71 percent of the city's suburban residents said they supported it. It was clear to anyone paying attention—a black government, elected in a mostly black city, was rejected by the people who had long since abandoned it. But it wasn't just black government. The giant auto industry had long since left the area. The Detroit Pistons were on a hiatus from the city that ended up lasting thirty-eight years; they did not return until 2017, three years after the election of Mike Duggan, the city's first white mayor in four decades. The crime rate, vacant buildings, and city blocks that had been abandoned for so long they were returning to nature were all the evidence one needed to understand that a whole people had been rejected. But more than that, any fairly conscientious observer could tell that black Detroit was being punished and left without protection.

Detroit residents complained that the police stole money, planted drugs, and beat them during routine traffic stops. And these were more than just allegations.[7] A consent decree from the Department of Justice issued in 2003 found that Detroit residents were being arrested without cause and held for days without charges being filed. The DPD arrested crime witnesses and the family members of suspects.[8] People were kept in temporary holding cells for days to months at a time while district attorneys built cases against them, a practice that's unconstitutional. Most cells had inadequate light, and some had no light at all. Officers had to use flashlights to check on the people they'd crammed in cages.[9] The food was unsanitary and served infrequently.[10] The toilets were often broken. In one district, just five out of twenty-one toilets flushed. This meant detainees had to be escorted to a working toilet by officers, who were seldom available, every time they needed to use the bathroom. And there was no formal complaint mechanism. All complaints were to be sent to a police district supervisor, but there were no forms to do so and no official appointed to handle them.

Each year, over one hundred thousand Detroit residents passed through these facilities.[11] It took years of requests from community activists and dozens of media reports before the federal government finally stepped in. At a cost of eighty-seven thousand dollars a month, the federal government monitored the Detroit Police Department to ensure they addressed the issues spelled out in the consent decree.

There were new signs of hope. Nearly one hundred million dollars was awarded to Detroit residents due to allegations of police abuse while the city and the DPD were under the consent decree. But when Detroit entered municipal bankruptcy, its residents who had been beaten or shot or whose family members were killed or who were arrested without cause and held in medieval conditions were last in a long line of creditors. They would not receive compensation. The river boiled. The sea bled. The rock refused to hide them.

In August 2013, just a month into Detroit's bankruptcy, after a decade of failure by the DPD to address the issues spelled out in the consent decree, the State of Michigan stepped in. The Michigan Department of Corrections (MDOC) took over the police station lockups, streamlining the process of detention. They rehabbed and reopened the Mound Correctional Facility, a prison that had been closed on Detroit's east side the year before. The compound was renamed and repurposed; the Detroit Reentry Center would take up half of it and the Detroit Detention Center would take up the other.

I learned about the two correctional facilities after a meeting with a senior administrator at the MDOC. I was hoping to do research in Detroit, and he had just the spot; a "hard-ass place," in his words. In a highly unusual move, anyone arrested within Detroit city limits could no longer be held by the DPD. They were instead sent to the Detroit Detention Center, where they would be booked until their arraignment and held by prison guards.[12] Likewise, everyone who was released from a Michigan jail or prison would go through the Detroit Reentry Center.

Anthony Stewart was the warden of the new facility. A Marine, a University of Michigan graduate, and a proud member of Omega Psi Phi, a celebrated black fraternity, Warden Stewart was "squared away." He wore a mustache but no beard; his bald head was always freshly shaven and his shoes were noticeably buffed. Every time I saw him he was wearing a well-tailored suit complete with a vest, a handkerchief, cuff links, and a tie clip. He was cerebral and creative, following our conversations wherever they went, from Detroit politics to the specifics of the consent decree to the needs of and requests from community leaders to the complaints of the people held in his facilities and their families.

Warden Stewart had begun as a prison guard nearly twenty-six years before and shot up through the ranks. His first task was to establish some semblance of trust among three police departments, the Michigan Department of Corrections, and community leaders who provided services or protested the treatment of the people he held in custody. Stewart walked the grounds several times a day to ensure the staff stayed on their toes, had hundreds of cameras set up around the facility, and ordered the installation of an ATM-like kiosk that issued debit cards, eliminating the need for guards to handle the cash of the people they detained. Accusations of theft decreased.

Stewart made sure that all the facilities worked and that the building stayed clean; he had flowers planted on the yard and arranged for a roving detail of incarcerated people from the Detroit Detention Center to sweep and mop the floors. He initiated video arraignments so people did not have to be transported to the courthouse. He instituted a new rule: anyone held for more than forty-eight hours without an arraignment would be released. Cases were processed much more quickly, and the average time detainees spent in cells was cut nearly in half. He installed a medical station and hired six registered nurses and an on-call physician to care for the people being held. By providing a newer, cleaner detention facility, medical care, and expanded access to the courts, the City of Detroit satisfied its consent decree. For the first time in over a decade, the city was free from a federal monitor.[13]

I started research in Detroit in January of 2014, splitting my time between the detention center and the reentry center. I visited twice a week. One guard at the desk would make a call and another would escort me into the facility. We'd go from bullpen to bullpen, and I'd get to pitch my wares to a dozen or so men who were standing around or lying on benches or, if it was early and crowded enough, lying on the floor.

"Listen up, guys!" the officer would shout to get the men's attention. "This is a professor from the University of Michigan. He's got something to say."

"Good morning. My name is Reuben Miller. I teach at the University of Michigan. I'm doing a study, trying to understand the lives of men and women who have been incarcerated. I'd like to learn about you," I'd announce, before going over the details of the study. Some men would ask questions. Most would just sign up. I was offering three-day bus cards and a promise to compensate them for their time. After that, I'd walk over to the women's side, meet a new guard, and repeat the process.

On the reentry center side of the campus, I'd wait with the family members who were there to pick up their loved ones. After a few minutes I'd be buzzed through a series of corridors. An officer would pat me down, check my shoes, and send me through a metal detector. Another would draw a line on the top of my right hand with an infrared marker to signal to other guards that I was a free man. Yet another officer would hand me a panic monitor. If there was trouble, I could pull a tab, and more officers would come running.

I'd head to the muster room. This was a cell where people

who were about to be released waited for the final buzzer and the final gray steel-and-Plexiglas door to slide open. They didn't know that their loved ones were on the other side of that door, eating overpriced concessions, waiting to pick them up. A different officer would escort me to the cell and introduce me to the people who sat there, some of whom had waited decades for their freedom. I'd pitch my wares the same way I had in the detention center.

I took down their names and the names of people who could reach them to set up a meeting later in the week. Most times I'd have the attention of the men who sat there waiting for their release. Other times I'd have to compete with whatever was happening on the yard, which they could see right outside the window, or the conversations they were having about their plans, or the papers they held with their conditions of release and instructions for their next steps. Then the steel door would buzz and slide open for their reunion.

A father would hug his boy close. A grandmother would reach up from her seat to embrace her long-since-grown child, her walker between them. Children weren't often there, but there was always some exchange between the people released from their cages and the people who picked them up, even when they were in a hurry to leave. There'd be some intimate conversation or just a few words between each pairing; maybe a nod or a glance or eyes that danced nervously from a lover to the floor, or maybe a parent would acknowledge how much a child had grown since the last transfer. All of it signaling their loved one was known and cared for, even if he'd made a mistake and even if she hadn't visited in some time. Some people made a beeline for the exit, their loved ones trailing close behind, but the relief on their faces when the last door buzzed was almost always there. They had been in prison, but now they were on their way home. Taking in the scene, I almost missed Jimmy Caldwell, who walked out of the detention center alone.

It took four tries for me to reach Jimmy. The call dropped twice, then his phone was out of service. After a few days, I got hold of his mother. She was warm and promised to pass along the message. Jimmy called back within a few hours and scheduled our interview. He showed up early and had a cup of coffee in the waiting area of the University of Michigan's Detroit Center in Midtown while I finished an interview with a woman whom I'd met at the Detroit Detention Center the week before.

The office in Midtown was chaotic in those early days. Ronald, whom I had just hired as a research associate, was down the hall interviewing the son of a man who had been locked up for fifteen years. Finn, my PhD student, at this point was my right hand, and he had just interviewed a woman in her fifties whose brother was sleeping on her couch. He had been cycling in and out of prison since they were teenagers. I hired Emily, a new graduate student, as my project manager. She was going over her interview notes with Kyle and Adriana, my undergraduate research assistants, wrapping up a two-hour interview with a man who had been locked up for nearly thirty years. And Yvette Singleton, who had started working with me earlier that month, was busy tracing sources. We were tracking down women who had been released the week before but whose phone numbers had already changed.[14]

Everyone who met Jimmy commented on how nice he was. Although he was a stocky man, he appeared somehow vulnerable, hanging on a speaker's every word like it mattered in some profound way. He was five foot ten but seemed short; he smiled easily and joked often but not so much that you didn't take him seriously. And while he looked at you directly when he talked, he never quite made eye contact.

I invited him from the table where he was drinking coffee with lots of cream and sugar to the room where we'd have our first interview, and Jimmy moved quickly. We covered the basics in short order. He had a tenth-grade education and had been arrested at least twenty times, starting when he was sixteen. High school was hard. He tried Job Corps, but it wasn't for him. He sold dope, used dope, and went to prison for property crimes. After a three-year sentence for grand larceny, he finished a six-month drug-treatment program at the Detroit Reentry Center, which was where we met. He was happy about completing treatment. He did a twelve-week program at the community mental-health clinic and a six-month treatment group at the Pontiac Correctional Center. Before he went to prison, he spent thirty days at a halfway house not two miles from my Midtown office. And he used lots of treatment language. He talked about "people, places, and things" and "co-dependence" and "enablers" and "my madness" and "my disease." I wondered about his life, but I wanted to get beyond the things he'd learned to say in treatment groups and beyond the stories you hear when you watch black gangster movies from the 1990s, like the hard and tragic life of violence and addiction that poor black kids are presumed to find themselves in every day. I needed to get past the stories of ducked bullets and crackhead mothers and teachers who hated kids who lived in the ghetto.

Black life in cities like Detroit has been so caricatured, and these caricatures have led to bad policy: Welfare reform. The War on Crime. A million mentorship programs that try to replace missing black fathers despite two decades of research that show black fathers are there.[15] Black fathers help with homework and go to games and share moments of affection like all fathers. In fact, black fathers spend more time with their children than fathers from any other racial group, even when they have multiple children and even when those children have different mothers—what social scientists call *family complexity*.[16] But the news about exceptional black men who teach low-income kids complicated handshakes and the YouTube clips of white principals doing the latest dances with little black girls and boys and the viral videos of police officers playing basketball with kids in dreadlocks and the memes where a hundred black men show up for the first day of school with a prominently displayed caption like *Real Fathers* or *Real Black Men* convince us that this is abnormal. And there's not just bad policy. Lessons from a thousand studies on missing black men and a thousand more on what sociologists call *social disorganization* show up in the first interview I do with almost everyone I sit down with. So do slogans that moralize black life along with phrases like "You know how we are" and some version of "What our people really need to do is..." And there are the things the preachers and pundits and presidents say at gatherings of black men. All of this typically comes up within the first hour of the interview. Social scientists might call this *social desirability bias,* meaning people tell you the stories they think you want to hear. There are interview techniques to get past all of this, but it takes a while to move beyond the noise in people's heads, and it takes more than a few hours and a few cups of coffee to really learn about someone's life.

I had a plan. I would ask Jimmy about his family and about what it was like for him to grow up on the east side of Detroit. I'd ask him about how the city had changed since the last time he was locked up, and I'd ask what it was like for him to come home.

"Um, I'm the only boy," he said quickly, confidently. He had four sisters. When I asked where he was in the pecking order, he sat up in his chair, laughing. "I'm the baby."

"You're the baby!" I said, thinking I knew what he meant. When I told him, "I'm the baby too," we laughed together, loudly, two middle-aged men sitting in an office in Midtown, decades removed from our childhoods, thinking about some pleasant thing from so long ago. But Jimmy stopped laughing abruptly. I was surprised by how quiet he got and how quickly the mood changed. He wiped his eyes, sighed, leaned his head on his hand.

"So..." He took a long pause. Tears started to stream down his cheeks. "I was kind of spoiled. I got pretty much everything I wanted." Thirty seconds of silence. Jimmy was full-on crying now, no longer bothering to wipe his face. His dim brown eyes red and full, his voice soft and broken, he went on. "So when crack came, it was a lot of disappointment, I being the only boy."

"Is that why you're so upset?" I asked. What a dumb question. I didn't really know what to say. There was a grown man crying in my office. I handed him the box of tissues we kept for times like this and sat with him in silence.

"It's not where I want to be right now," he whimpered after a while. "My sisters. They getting there. It's getting there, you know." I wanted to know more. He told me his sisters had helped raise him and that they were close growing up. He'd wanted to keep it that way, but that's not how things turned out.

"I'm forty-six," he said. "My sister is like maybe fifty. No, she like forty-eight. And I have another sister a couple of years older than that. And I've got two more sisters and their children."

He explained, "Everybody kind of looked up to me." He was back to wiping the sides of his face. "Like I said, it was a lot of disappointment. Time after time, they give me the benefit of the doubt, man. Basically, I shit on 'em."

"What about your parents?" I asked, trying to find my bearings.

"Well, my father, he was married, [but he] wasn't married to my mom. I got four sisters," Jimmy said, explaining they were his half sisters—that is, they were not all his father's biological children. His mother had children from a previous relationship, and his father had a family of his own. "He took care of two families," Jimmy said. "He treated all my sisters like [they were] his. He'd go home, but I seen my daddy every day."

"Were you close?" I asked.

"Yeah, we was close at the time," he said.

Jimmy's father died when Jimmy was young. "Cancer. It was '82 or '83," he said. Jimmy was just starting high school then. He was fourteen and at a new school with a mother raising five children on her own.

"Things started getting different. I don't know if it was because my mother didn't really know how to raise a boy. I was the baby. So, if I want it, I'ma tell my daddy and I get it," he said. "[But] after my father died, I stopped getting all the perks," Jimmy said.

Jimmy's father was an autoworker at a time when people still had pensions. His mother made Jimmy and his four sisters take their dead father's last name to ensure that they would be "taken care of financially," in Jimmy's words. But their share of their late father's Social Security income was all that they got, and that wasn't enough. There were no more perks other than the few hundred dollars that came in the mail each month from the Social Security office, and that went to Jimmy's mother. Jimmy's father, the man who Jimmy saw every day, the one who took care of his sisters as if they were his own, was gone.

"I wanted to wear all the good shit like I been wearing," Jimmy said. "But it wasn't that kind of a party. It felt like everyone was against me, so I started doing dumb shit."

Jimmy would wait for the mailman to come each month. "I figured, 'Well, that's my check. I should be able to do what I want to with the money.' And I wouldn't think about bills or none of that," he told me, reflecting on his route into trouble. This was the reasoning of a fourteen-year-old, one who didn't realize that the mailman *was* delivering his check or that the place where his father developed cancer might have some responsibility toward his family. And it wasn't just *his* family. Cancer rates among black autoworkers rivaled rates in the famed "cancer alley," that eighty-five-mile stretch along the Mississippi River of petroleum refineries and chemical plants that claimed the lives of a generation of black men.[17] Autoworkers were dying. Leukemia, colon and pancreatic cancers, lung cancer, cancer of the stomach, cancer of the liver, brain cancer, cancers of all kinds claimed the lives of so many black people in Detroit.[18]

"I started to steal," he said. "Like, me and other guys in the neighborhood, when the mailman come, we'd take the mail. Tried to cash the checks ourselves." A whole group of boys had lost their fathers to the auto plants—the same plants that convinced the government to use eminent domain to demolish fifteen hundred homes on the promise of good jobs in the 1980s. These same plants provided just a fraction of those jobs, then packed up and left.[19] The same auto plants did not cut checks to the boys' families.

Jimmy and his friends stole the meager Social Security checks the state sent to their mothers. But "that plan didn't work," Jimmy said. No one would cash the checks. So there the boys were, their names on checks their dead fathers had earned with no way to access the funds. "That's when I left high school," he said.

The rest of this story is predictable. Jimmy ran the streets, stole, and started selling dope. By sixteen, Jimmy was using. By seventeen, he had been to jail. By eighteen, he was in prison. He lied to his family and lost jobs. He stole things from people's homes. He used more drugs and did time over and over again: Six months for stealing car radios. Twelve months for drug distribution. Eighteen months for grand larceny. Dozens of arrests for trespassing, for using, for stealing scrap metal, for not reporting to his parole officer on time when he was high.

Jimmy stayed with his sisters in between bids. He loved his nieces and nephews. Having no children of his own, he spent as much time with them as he could. "Like last night, when you called," he said. "I had been with my nephew all night. I spent nine months with my sister at my niece house before [I went back to prison]."

The kids wrote to Jimmy while he was locked up, sending pictures and visiting as often as they could. But over time, he became more difficult to support. Jimmy told me that worse than the guilt for stealing and using and lying, worse than all the consequences that came with it, was "the separation" he felt from his family. "A lot of time [with] my addiction, I wouldn't come around. It's a lot of hurt. They was saying, 'Don't leave,'" he said. But after a while, they learned what to expect.

Jimmy would disappear for months at a time, then call collect when he ran out of money or knock on their door when he got out of jail. When he showed up again, the kids were older, and he was older too. He was middle-aged now, and the kids were grown. They had lives of their own. And despite the challenges and the separation he felt every time he was arrested, he was proud of them. "I got to say, all my nieces, my nephews, everybody doing good. They can be successful!" he said, looking to the side with a smile. I wanted to leave on a high note.

"What do they do?" I asked while he was still smiling. His nieces lived in Pontiac, Michigan, a suburb of Detroit. They worked and had families. So did his nephews. "My nephews, one of them, he was in the navy. [He] got married. He moved to Arizona. I talked to him last night." He told me about another nephew who lived in Rochester Hills. "He married too." Another nephew lived in Texas. "He finna [sign] to a record label."

"Wow!" I said, happy to hear the news. Jimmy beamed when he talked about the kids. I wanted to end our time together at that point. But things took another turn.

He put his head down and teared up again.

"What makes you sad about that?" I asked, surprised at the sudden shift.

"I don't know." He took a breath. "I guess…I guess I'm happy on that part." His voice breaking, Jimmy said, "But it's hard. I look at myself and all the potential that I had. How I let myself down. And I feel like, wow, I got left behind." I understood.

Jimmy had spent twenty years cycling in and out of different kinds of cages—workforce-preparation programs, mandated substance-abuse treatment, prisons all across the state. One was a five-hour drive from home. He was in halfway houses, jails, detention centers, and almost everything in between. All this time, the baby was separated from his family. Jimmy was all alone, and he had felt this way since he was fourteen.

I wondered how he dealt with it all. I wondered if he had seen anyone for help.

"With mental problems?" he asked me. "I have mental health," he said.

About a decade ago, a caseworker at a halfway house sent Jimmy to a psychiatrist. The doctor's diagnoses would have been obvious to anyone paying attention. He had bipolar disorder and a co-occurring crack addiction. He had no insurance, but the doctor at the halfway house kept a stash of sample meds. Jimmy got treatment as long as he lived there, but he had to stay "clean and sober." He started using, left the halfway house, and was arrested soon after for setting up a "home depot" in an abandoned building on Detroit's east side where he sold the appliances and copper he stole from construction sites in the area. When he reported to prison, a mental-health technician took him off his meds. In recovery herself, she said his problem was drugs, not mental illness. He spent the next three years without access to meds, much like he had most of his life. Of course, he cycled in and out of many different kinds of prisons. Of course, he used drugs and stole things and kept to himself.

We sat in the office quietly for another few minutes. He wasn't crying anymore, but his head was down, and he was looking off to the side of the room. He sighed, turned his head, and looked at me directly, this time making eye contact. "You not the only one doing time," he said. "They get tired too."

Later that week I met Jimmy for lunch at the Whole Foods around the corner from my office. He was happy to reconnect. He told me that the last session was "like therapy" and cracked jokes about how violent the South Side of Chicago was. He had just come from a meeting with his parole officer. When I asked how it went, he whipped out a photocopy listing his "conditions of release." He could not cross state lines without the court's permission. He could not possess a firearm. He could not return to or be near the vicinity of his last arrest. He could not "associate with known offenders." That is, he could not live or work with anyone who had a criminal record, and he could not spend time with anyone on probation or parole. He could not drink alcohol or use "any controlled substance."

The restrictions were straightforward, but the sheet also listed tasks he was required to accomplish. He had to report to his parole officer once a week to submit a urine sample for drug testing, which he was expected to pay for—ten dollars for every test. He had to complete a job-skills training program at the Michigan Works! Association, a workforce-development agency. He had to attend Narcotics Anonymous meetings twice a week. He had to attend all other "physical or mental health treatment" the courts or his parole officer deemed necessary. He had to search for employment. He was on an electronic monitor, his whereabouts tracked through an ankle bracelet and GPS satellite technology, so he had to do all of this between 8:00 a.m. and 3:00 p.m. each day. If he violated any of these conditions, he could be sent back to prison.

I wanted to know how he was going to feed himself. I knew that he was broke. "I really don't know," he said. "In the summertime I can wash some cars, things like that," and in a good month, he could make a thousand dollars. But "clean and sober, [and] being wintertime right now, I might make half that." He said he might go to relatives to get "a little handout here and there." He would find whatever resources he could.

"Like I said, the bus card you gave me [the last time we met], it really [helped]. Because I was able to take care of my business," he said. Jimmy activated his Bridge Card (Michigan's food-stamp debit card), and he went to the Social Security office to fill out forms for a new ID.

"Last night, I was thinking, *What are you going to do about this week coming?*" Jimmy said. He needed to "stay connected" if he wanted to get back on his feet. His girlfriend, Cynthia, had given him a prepaid cell phone, but the minutes ran out. Another friend gave him a different phone, one that could be used with a monthly plan, but the activation fee was fifty dollars. I gave him forty dollars as compensation for our interviews. "I might be short," he said, "but I might come back to borrow the ten dollars, because I know it's going to benefit me."

Jimmy was hopeful that his life would come together. He reminded me that in just a week he'd managed to get a phone. "I might can get on the internet," he said. "I need that internet. I need that e-mail. Once I get my résumé put up, [job leads] can go straight to my phone." Jimmy had a plan. He would go to the workforce-development agency and fill out job applications. Once he had a steady stream of income, he would be able to start a new life. "I just believe in more opportunities that work," he said, nodding his head with certainty. I decided to tag along.

I pulled up to the Rosa Parks Transit Center, the city's main bus terminal. It was sunny, but it was February and cold. I hated the idea of getting out of the car. You could see people's breath. A bus pulled up. The group that departed walked quickly inside the terminal, some hunching their shoulders, their arms crossed to close their jackets, others with their hands stuffed into their coat pockets. I sat at the parking meter for a few more minutes, soaking in the heat, then made my way inside.

I walked around, looking for Jimmy. There were no open benches. I didn't want to sit anyway. I wanted a hot cup of coffee, but I didn't want to hold anything, and I certainly didn't want the feeling of dripping coffee down my wrists while I walked in a freezing wind. Besides, I didn't see a coffee stand or a store of any kind. Jimmy got off the number 17 bus. We smiled, exchanged pleasantries, and started our trek. The agency was just under a mile from the terminal. There were no bus routes that would get us within more than a few blocks, so we walked.

Jimmy had on a black Detroit Tigers baseball jacket and a worn brown skullcap. He was chatty, making small talk as we walked. I'd never much liked small talk, and I liked trying to breathe, walk, and talk through the scarf covering my face even less. Jimmy seemed overly concerned with my comfort, asking, "You good?" more times than I cared for. He told me that he appreciated "spending time with a brother like [me]" and he was "glad to do something positive" at least three times. I felt awkward. I smiled and laughed with Jimmy, but I thought to myself, *What's he on?*

When we got to the address, a gray high-rise not far from Midtown, I understood in a deeper way why he was acting like this. No one was there, and no one would come. We weren't too early. The building itself was closed; there were no lights on. There was a loose-leaf printout taped to the door that had addresses of a few—hopefully open—workforce agencies. The closest one was a full nine miles away.

"That's by where I'm staying," Jimmy said. He was sleeping in a house that he was helping to rehab. Leon, his old dope dealer, owned that house. He was letting Jimmy crash there at night while he got back on his feet. Leon and Jimmy were friends. They'd met nearly twenty years ago. Jimmy detailed Leon's cars, and he was good at his job, so good that they'd stayed in touch. "He calls me on my bullshit," Jimmy told me. He'd opened up his home and allowed Jimmy to stay there despite having a wife and eight children of his own. "When I told him I had no clothes," Jimmy said, "he opened up his closet."

There were other people who helped Jimmy. Pastor Smith, from Full Gospel Tabernacle, the small church Jimmy's girl-friend attended, wrote letters to him while he was in prison. Pastor Smith ended each letter by saying, *I'm counting the days until your release.* But the parole officer sent Jimmy to an agency that was closed. That was not unusual; these kinds of places folded all the time. But it had taken Jimmy an hour to get to me on Detroit's notoriously unpredictable transit system, and we'd still ended up walking a mile. I wondered if there was somewhere else we could go, somewhere closer to Midtown. But that would just make it harder for Jimmy to get there when the bus pass I'd given him eventually expired. Besides, there was no phone number on the printout for the agencies we might go to, and in any case, Jimmy's phone had run out of minutes. There was no way to know which place would be open. We decided to go to the one closest to Leon's property and Jimmy's temporary home.

Jimmy asked me to advance him the bus card that I usually gave him at the end of our interviews. He was counting on the new card to get around for the week. If the workforce-development center had been open, he could have gotten a bus card for the month from a case manager. Without a bus card, Jimmy would have to walk nine miles to the other center. He would have to walk to his court-ordered AA meetings and he would have to walk to the parole office to give his weekly drop. He told me he could be sent back to prison for missing any of these appointments, and he was right.

We both knew men who had been "flopped" for similar reasons. Nearly a quarter of all prison admissions the previous year were for parole violations like these, and the price of violation was steep. Parolees who got flopped had to finish their sentences, and Jimmy had eighteen months left on his. Even if his PO didn't think Jimmy's violation was serious enough to warrant prison, he could be held for ninety days in the "eye-drop" unit at the detention center. Guards talked about the eye drop as a way to "lay offenders down." And Jimmy had been laid down many times. He did seventy-seven days at a work camp for stealing something from a garage with a partially open door. He did thirty days in the county jail for "pissing hot"—failing a drug test—and another thirty days at the eye drop for missing his very next appointment. He was smoking crack and was afraid to report to his PO; he knew he would send him back to prison. The stakes were high. A mistake—like picking up an outdated resource list or missing an appointment because he overslept or not going to a treatment group because he couldn't borrow bus fare—could cost this man his freedom.

Jimmy's careful work to ensure I was comfortable paid off. I gave him the bus card early, and after we walked back to the bus depot where my car was parked, I gave him a ride to the other workforce agency. This wasn't a part of my research protocol. I was trying to figure out how he got around on his own and hadn't planned to give him a ride.

I could say I gave Jimmy a ride to the agency because he

needed me to or because I liked him. He was easy enough to be around. And I was convinced he was a nice guy in a bad situation. Besides, it wasn't a big deal. But if I were being honest, I would admit I gave him a ride because I was cold. I was going to accompany him to the second agency, and I couldn't imagine walking a mile back to the transit center and then jumping on a bus to take an hour-long ride to the east side of Detroit, after which I would have had to take the bus back to the depot to pick up my car and then drive an hour to get back home, all of this on one of the coldest days of the year. Jimmy made it to his next appointment and avoided a potential arrest because I *felt like* giving him a ride—or, more precisely, because I didn't feel like taking the bus.

The agency was busy when Jimmy and I arrived. A receptionist sat at the front desk answering calls and helping clients with their paperwork. There were a dozen people in the waiting room and activity in the back. People walked quickly between the gray dividers separating the front lobby from the area where the training classes were held. We walked to the counter together to sign Jimmy up for a session. The receptionist told us that all the classes were full. She instructed Jimmy to put his name on the waiting list and to come back the next week because a parolee might fail to show. They did not give out bus cards to people who were not yet in the program, and they could not guarantee him a spot.

We grabbed brochures and headed to Coney Island, a Detroit diner chain near his worksite and temporary home, to debrief. Jimmy thanked me for the seven-dollar lunch I bought him and the forty-dollar gift card I always handed him at the end of each interview. It had been a hard day. He thanked me twice in the course of our conversation for "being there" for him. Being there? What had I done?

In that moment, I understood why Jimmy worked so hard to make sure that I was comfortable. He lived in an economy of favors.[20] With so many rules to follow and so much risk involved—one mistake could cost him his freedom—he needed favors from people he barely knew to meet his basic needs. Life for Jimmy was so chaotic in part because he was so often rejected. He moved from one catastrophe to the next. There was no way for him to anticipate that he would need a ride from me, but he had to stay in my good graces just in case he needed me. But I wasn't "there for" Jimmy because I liked him; I'd helped him because I was cold. I did Jimmy the favor of giving him a ride based entirely on my mood. In the end, my help didn't matter. The agency had no room for Jimmy, and it would make no room for him, even though he'd spent a good part of the day trying to get there. The river boils. The sea bleeds. The rock just won't hide you.

*   *   *

Detroit is a beautiful and strange place that's rife with contradictions. In 2019, it was rated the poorest big city in the nation. In addition to the water crisis[21] and a policing crisis and a crisis of confidence in the local government, this city full of abandoned homes is somehow in a housing crisis. One hundred thousand properties were lost to tax foreclosure, the most since the Great Depression.[22]

Since the city went bankrupt, parts of Detroit have dramatically changed, but the headlines about the "New Detroit" and the city's "comeback" are truer in some places than others. For all the blight on the east side, downtown crackles with possibility. Two years after the city declared bankruptcy, property values in Midtown had increased 250 percent. Much of the redevelopment has been spurred by Dan Gilbert, the billionaire CEO of Quicken Loans, one of the nation's largest subprime lenders. Microsoft opened an office downtown, anchoring a hub of tech incubators with open-concept workspaces and coffee shops that lined the avenues. Several new "made in Detroit" retailers have moved in, hocking two-thousand-dollar bicycles and thirty-five-dollar T-shirts boasting of Detroit's grit. *National Geographic* named Detroit an "unexpected food location." You can buy coffee beans roasted in the city and find hundreds of local beers made at dozens of microbreweries. And the farm-to-table movement is alive and well. The young, middle-class white urbanites who flocked back to the city have launched urban gardens, a trend that had a long history in Detroit's historically black neighborhoods. But the pastry shops and gastropubs in the Corktown, Midtown, Downtown, and Riverwalk neighborhoods don't often patronize black farms.

Black farmers and black entrepreneurs complained they didn't have access to land or capital and said they were all but shut out of Detroit's comeback. This is part of a national problem. An analysis of start-up funding across the United States found that black business owners received just 1 percent of venture capital investments despite making up 11 percent of the nation's start-ups.[23] And a report from the Federal Reserve found small, black-owned businesses were less likely to get small-business loans than white-owned businesses with similar, and often worse, credit profiles.[24]

Flush with cash from investors, government grants, and community-development incentives, parts of the new Detroit, with their tech incubators and bistros and more people out walking dogs than out with their children, are unrecognizable to long-term Detroit residents. Detroit's city government is a machine, like Chicago's, but one that seems to have made room for newcomers. And the new networks of scholars, creatives, and entrepreneurs doing work in the city feel welcoming to them. These people aren't from the old Detroit; most residents from the old city can't afford the higher rent and property taxes of the new.

After going to a church service led by another Chicago transplant, Janice, Jonathan, and I met friends at the kind of brunch spot where you need a reservation. We were reconnecting with Bernadette, a Chicagoan and law professor who was studying residential displacement amid Detroit's tax-foreclosure crisis. She brought her friend Rodrick, then the CEO of Detroit's Economic Development Corporation. Our table was the only one in the restaurant with black diners. Almost no one passed by the picture window, though the restaurant was on a main thoroughfare. Where was everyone?

As we left and walked toward our car, Jonathan called out, "Dada, look!" A man with a handlebar mustache wearing a fedora, a blue tank top, and matching spandex shorts waved at my boy. He was riding an antique unicycle down the empty four-lane street.

– II –
WAGE

CHAPTER 4

MILLIONS OF DETAILS

Hello. This is a collect call from"—some voice that sounded like my brother's—"a prisoner at the Michigan Department of Corrections Newberry Correctional Facility. If you feel you are being victimized or extorted by this prisoner, please call customer service at—" Some number that was rattled off too quickly for me to catch. The digital woman gave instructions: "To accept this call, press zero. To refuse this call, press one. To prevent calls from this facility, press six."

I was home in my nightclothes, sitting at my desk, trying to write the proposal for this book. I'd added money to his phone account, or at least that's what I thought. Did I forget? "Shit!" I hissed out loud, but not quite loud enough for Jonathan to notice. He played and did his homework or drew and read his books close by my desk. He has done this for as long as he's been alive. There's a picture of Jonathan at six years old sitting on my shoulders while I sat huddled over my desk writing my dissertation.

I fumbled through papers, moving books, a coffee mug, and a glass of water, trying to find my wallet. I pushed the lamp to the side to search the corners of the desk. Why was Jeremiah calling collect?

In the state of Michigan, and maybe in other states too, the Department of Corrections doesn't issue phone cards. Loved ones have to set up accounts associated with their phone numbers and fill them with enough money for the person behind bars to be able to call, if there is an available phone in the housing unit.

There should have been money left. I added twenty-five dollars to my number's account each payday, more when there was something bothering my brother. I put twenty dollars on his wife's line, which was something I hated to do. The last time the two of them had visited, Jeremiah's wife tried to start an argument with Janice in front of our kids. And they'd crashed for longer than we'd agreed they could stay and broke the wooden frame of our living-room futon. Jeremiah said she was broke or sick and couldn't put money on his books. In any case, I always added the twenty dollars. And I'd added twenty dollars to Joseph's line too. They didn't talk much, although they should have. Jeremiah needed his big brother. And I put fifteen dollars on Bradley's line. He was like family. Bradley had promised to rent Jeremiah his basement apartment at a discount so Jeremiah would have some place to go when he got out. This was on my promise to cover the rent, another bill to brace myself for.

I spent eighty dollars a month for phone calls alone, and that was just for the people I knew. I had no idea who else he might talk to, but they needed to put money on their own phone numbers or accept his collect calls, which added up. There was a $2.95 processing fee each time you accepted the charge, plus 24 cents for each minute you talked. You could have conversations in fifteen-minute blocks, after which the service hung up the line, so each call cost $6.55. I paid in advance to avoid some of these charges, but there was still a $2.95 processing fee each time I used my debit card.

Why was he calling collect? Did we use up the money already? There was a week left until payday, and my bank account was low. Did he forget whatever complicated combination of numbers he needed to enter to make the call? Had I paid the wrong company?

The MDOC posted a notice on its website under "Inmate Information." They were switching phone accounts from JPay to ConnectNetwork, a competing telecommunications service. ConnectNetwork would handle phone calls and "inmate trust-fund" accounts, the money you put on the books for your loved one to buy ramen noodles and soap.

I would still need to use JPay to send letters to Jeremiah. Starting at twenty cents a message, you can write your loved one an e-mail. You can upload a picture for an additional twenty cents, though the file can't be too big or contain explicit images. All correspondence is monitored. Add twenty cents for each additional picture; you can send up to five. Add an electronic stamp for twenty-five cents, and an e-mail with pictures or the electronic greeting cards JPay advertises when you log in on a holiday weekend can cost a dollar or more. Buying their stamps in bulk saves money: it's five dollars for twenty stamps, ten dollars for fifty, and twenty cents for the "return stamp" that ensures your loved one can write you back.

We'd correspond frequently, sending letters back and forth. I'd log in to retrieve his JPay note, and each letter, while different, would open the same way. He'd give an update: he was exercising; he'd read a book; he'd gotten his GED (a test he'd avoided for years but passed on the second go-round); he'd completed a certificate in food preparation and a certificate in anger management; he'd finished a class on how to be a more responsible person, and now he was taking a different class—some variation on the same theme.

Jeremiah's JPays would always include lists of things for me to do. He'd ask me to look up college grants or job-training programs or take screenshots of his Facebook page. Sometimes he'd ask for books. *The Forty-Eight Laws of Power.* Machiavelli's *The Prince. The Art of War. The Autobiography of Malcolm X. Nobody,* by Marc Lamont Hill. And *Dreams of My Father* by President Barack Obama, because he wanted to "fuck with these republicans." I sent him Ralph Ellison's *Invisible Man,* because that book changed my life, and *The Sellout,* by Paul Beatty, because I thought it was funny. I bought him subscriptions to half a dozen magazines—*Esquire* and *Popular Science, Popular Mechanics, GQ,* the *Atlantic,* and *The New Yorker.* He asked for a few motorcycle and foreign-car magazines, and I tried a subscription to the *New York Times,* but none of these delivered to people in prison. On top of the phone calls and e-mail, I spent between ten and fifty dollars each month for books and another thirty dollars for his subscriptions. Car magazines, at about five dollars each, had to be bought and shipped separately, adding another ten dollars a month.

Sometimes he'd ask me to scan clippings from car magazines or look up the cost of a used truck. He used to work in "transportation services." His first job was as a bike messenger, delivering packages in downtown Chicago. He did this for a decade. He moved up to car delivery. He got his CDL a few years before he got into trouble. His license was suspended during his last DUI, which was the first time he'd been paid to drive a truck. He hoped to drive trucks again, knowing this skill could lift him out of poverty.

He'd always ask me for money. Sixty-five dollars for gym shoes from the commissary that cost thirty dollars at Marshalls. Ninety dollars for boots you could pick up for forty-five dollars at DSW. One hundred and fifty dollars for an antique television set. One hundred and twenty dollars for an MP3 player, with each song costing one dollar to download. Forty dollars for a radio. An AM/FM radio? Who listened to the fucking radio? But he was in prison. What else would he do?

Most letters would end the same way: He wanted to know how my daughter, Adé, was doing. He called her "Little Foot." He'd tell me to say what's up to Jonathan, whom he called "Little Scoober"—the same nickname he had for me when we were kids. He'd write that he was praying for me and that he prayed for Janice and my children and that he was sorry for throwing a crack party in my house. Then he'd say he wished he would've listened and that he was grateful for my help.

I'd stare at something from my to-do list and send what I could, though sending trust-fund deposits through Connect-Network meant another private company had my financial and contact information and that another private company would charge a fee. I'd go to a website, mainly Amazon, to order the things he asked for. Books and magazines had to be bought new and shipped directly to the prison. I would then log into ConnectNetwork to add money to his books and money to the phone numbers of the people he called most. But no matter how much money I sent through these services, the MDOC decided how much money my brother would actually receive.

One month, I sent him two hundred and fifty dollars so he could buy boots and the TV he'd asked for. We were both surprised to learn that half of everything he received over fifty dollars in a thirty-day period would be applied to pay down his legal debt. He owed thousands of dollars. He was charged six hundred and fifty dollars for the privilege of being represented by the checked-out public defender he'd met just once, on the day of his hearing, and sixteen hundred and eleven dollars for "court costs." Judges, stenographers, bailiffs, and clerks had to be paid, I suppose. There was a four-hundred-dollar extradition fee and a sixty-eight-dollar fee for the "state minimum costs" to record his felony conviction. They applied one hundred dollars to his debt from the two hundred and fifty I sent and put the hundred and fifty that remained on his books. This was just enough to buy boots or a TV but not both and not enough to stave off his hunger. I sent two hundred dollars the next time I got paid, thinking the MDOC had made a mistake. They gave him a hundred and twenty-five dollars from those funds and applied the rest to his debt.

The digital woman on the other end of the line was repeating herself, asking, for the third time, if I would accept the charges. I found my wallet. It had fallen under the desk. I pressed 0 to accept the call and followed the phone tree to enter my debit card number. I'd have to pay the collect-call processing fee plus 24 cents a minute. Another $6.55. Why was he calling collect? I wondered again.

On the last day of each month, I sent Jeremiah fifty dollars—the amount we were sure the MDOC would not confiscate. Each time we talked, he told me that most of the people he did time with didn't receive anything from anyone and that he needed that fifty dollars. "I can't explain it, Scoober," he said. "You can eat all that shit"—meaning the food they serve. "It's hard to get your head around why you're still hungry." Then he rattled off the list of things he wanted me to buy.

The MDOC suspends its commissary rules once a quarter. You can buy your loved ones an "access pack" from a company called Michigan Packages. You're allowed to spend up to eighty-five dollars on food or toiletries but never on the big-ticket items like radios or TVs or boots or coats or shoes. Prisoners had to use their trust-fund accounts to purchase those things. Jeremiah would need to save whatever was left over from the money that the MDOC did not confiscate to purchase big-ticket items; that, or I would need to send him twice the cost of the things he needed. We thought buying a stash from Michigan Packages would help save money. His list looked something like this:

30 packages of chili-flavor ramen noodles
3 packages of precooked long-grain rice
5 packages of hot summer sausages made with beef and
    chicken
2 spicy jalapeno-cheese-snack-spread tubs
1 peanut butter package
1 package each of lemon cream and chocolate cream
    cookies
29 cinnamon raisin bagels
5 strawberry cheese Danishes
1 package each of sugar flakes and cinnamon square cereal
1 tube of cocoa and shea butter body lotion
1 tube of fresh mint fluoride toothpaste
4 packages of instant coffee
A calendar

I put in these orders after registering with a third online service that stored my personal details and coming up with a third password I'd have to remember. Jeremiah went through each new food stash in about two months, which left him hungry for the rest of the quarter.

Every month, I spent hundreds of dollars on e-mails, phone calls, trust-fund deposits, and food for my brother, more when he needed to make a special purchase, like shoes that didn't give him blisters, and more still on holidays and when I visited him, something he never asked me to do. He knew how busy I was, and he didn't want to impose. But this was my brother, and he was alone. I had to go and see him.

The first time I visited, I flew in from New Jersey. I was on a fellowship in Princeton at the Institute for Advanced Study, the place where Einstein worked until his death in 1955. My wife and I had packed a moving truck and, with our silver Honda Accord in tow, drove ten hours from a storage facility in Chicago to New Jersey. On the night we arrived, Jonathan stood in front of a bronze bust of the wild-haired physicist and posed for a photo, his hand stroking his eleven-year-old chin.

Our place there was not a half a mile from a forest preserve. The scene was pastoral: meadows; small herds of deer grazing outside our kitchen window. There was a chef who made meals for the faculty and their families; a library for me to work in with floor-to-ceiling windows that looked out onto a pond. My colleagues joked that this was summer camp for academics. We lived and worked at IAS, playing soccer with our kids while debating theory and world events during teatime and happy hour. Janice and Jonathan loved it there. And our daughter,

Adé, was in college on the East Coast, so we saw her more that year than we had in the previous two. Life was good.

We binged *Atlanta* and *Dear White People* and *The Hand-maid's Tale* with our new friends and drank wine late into the night. We made pancakes and shared dishes and spent time together as often as we could. I learned about stinky cheese and that wine didn't have to be expensive to taste good. We sang and danced with friends from places I had never heard of, and I read scholarship I might never have encountered otherwise. This was one of the best years of my life. But every time I got that phone call, I'd be snapped back into our reality. Was my brother sick? Had he gotten into a fight?

I was breathing hard now, my chest tightening. I couldn't remember if you pressed # right after putting in the sixteen digits of the debit card or if you were supposed to wait and then put in the expiration date and the security code. *Shit,* I thought. I'd put in the wrong number. The electronic lady was making me start all over again. What must it have been like for Jeremiah standing at the phone on his unit? Was there silence? Did he hear the digits as I entered them? What if this wasn't him? I'd answered so fast, I couldn't be sure. Could a skillful conman make out the digits and steal the few dollars I had left in my account? After I had spent much too long in my head, the charge was processed. The call was finally connected.

"What's up, Ruby Scoober? What you doing?" Jeremiah asked.

I said, "Nothing, really" or "Writing" or whatever it was that I would say when he called.

We caught up like we always did—quickly. He told me some funny story about the men he lived with. We laughed about old times and talked shit about Joseph and some mutual friends. He asked about whatever was going on in my life and gave me advice about my family and work and driving and told me not to worry about my kids. He was always so supportive. But we mostly talked about him and his needs.

"Let me ask you this," he said, which was what he always said before he asked me to look something up or send him money or give me an update on someone he cared for. I was always relieved to hear his voice, but I was also always in the middle of something. That time I was working on this book, something I hadn't done before. The previous time, I was in a faculty meeting. The time before that, I was on a date with my wife, and before that, I was asleep. Sometimes I'd be sitting, trying to clear my mind. Sometimes I'd be in an airport. Sometimes I'd be with my kids. But no matter what I was doing, when the call came, I had to answer. And each time I answered, there was some new request.

Any boxer will tell you that it's the punch you don't see coming that puts you down: The collect call you didn't expect. The court date you didn't have the gas money to attend. The conversations you dreaded having with your children about why their uncle was in prison and when, exactly, you expected him to come home. (The honest answer was that you weren't sure.) The $2.95 processing fee that brings your bills above your budget. The $292 that you've overdrawn your account.[1] The six $34 overdraft fees because you didn't budget the last collect call. The overpriced boots. The unexpected embarrassment as you sit at your desk entering your loved one's order for thirty packages of ramen noodles. What it feels like when Michigan Packages runs out of the flavor of ramen noodles he wanted. The fact that you know, or at least you think you know, that no one else is in your shoes. It's these little things, the daily disruptions, that manage to put you down. Shame does it too.

How could he know how it felt to run into him on campus in Ann Arbor? Like in those early days of his case, before he copped a plea, when he was sleeping on the streets on and off. He hadn't been to my place to shower or shave in weeks, and you could tell. I took a meeting with a colleague at an overpriced coffee shop and complained about my pay—the lowest in my department at the time. My colleague said, in that smug and awkward way some senior scholars talk to juniors, "Someone has to be on the bottom."

"I'm not going to be on the fucking bottom!" I said loudly, and I packed my things to signal the end of our meeting. Had that been a joke? He might not even have known that I was upset or why.

That was when I saw Jeremiah walking with someone across the quad. I introduced my brother to my tone-deaf colleague, and Jeremiah introduced me to his friend, a formerly homeless veteran he ran with from time to time. My brother was always so gregarious. This was part of the problem. People loved him—sometimes the wrong people. We stood there laughing, cracking jokes about the day and the students he drank too much with at the bars. He was disheveled and obviously high, but I was happy to see him, as always. My embarrassment faded as quickly as it had come—that is, until he leaned in, smiling, and asked me, "You got some change, little bro?"

"You have one minute remaining," the digital woman said. Our phone call was coming to a close.

"All right, bro, I love you," he said.

"Love you, man," I responded and waited for him to hang

up. It was November of 2016. I had been in Princeton for just a few months. It was already time to go back to Michigan.

Most of Michigan is flat—grass, cows, more grass, a few rivers and streams. The drive from Chicago or Detroit or the airport to just about any correctional facility is sleepy, uninteresting, and long enough to be dangerous. I was always on my way somewhere else when I visited my brother. I had fieldwork in Detroit or a meeting in Ann Arbor or a layover I could extend at DTW. This was the only way I could afford to see Jeremiah with any regularity, squeezing visits into an already tight schedule to make the trips less costly, although it also made them less pleasant. And I was always tired.

This time I needed to be at a conference. I was giving a lecture about what citizenship means in a country where one in three black American men lives with a felony record and where almost nothing they can do will save their children from meeting the same end.[2]

Back then, I didn't share my personal experiences in the context of my work. I was embarrassed. My family was "complex," the kind my colleagues studied, the kind in which the children have different last names. I always felt like something of an outsider in the academy; I couldn't shake the trappings of poverty. While I wasn't exactly an insider in the neighborhoods that I studied, familiarity bred insights that my colleagues either rejected or just didn't write about. Jeremiah was in prison, like our father and like Stephen, our father's other son. And I was studying prisoners. I knew what it meant to visit a loved one in jail, to spend more money than you can afford to buy microwave cheeseburgers from an overpriced vending machine. I knew the relief of seeing a family member after he's been in a cage for a few months and how your heart quickens and drops, just a little, when you glimpse the single-file shuffle of men making their way into the visiting room, their wrists and ankles chained.[3]

The conference started early Wednesday morning. My hosts would cover the hotel fee if I flew in the day before. This was a lucky break. Visiting hours were on Tuesday. I caught a red-eye, leaving Newark at six a.m. and arriving at DTW by eight. I convinced the conference organizers to pay for a rental car, since it was cheaper than a cab. I drove four and a half sleepy hours to the prison. Jeremiah called me three times during the trip to make sure that I was still coming. I stopped once for breakfast, once to stretch, and one more time for coffee; I caught up with our brother Joseph, chatted with my wife, and listened to an audiobook.

I pulled into the parking lot of the prison and walked to the visitors' center. The officer behind the desk was pleasant. There were two families sitting in the waiting room, watching whatever was on the television. *Shit*, I thought. I needed a quarter to store my car keys in a locker, but I'd forgotten to break the twenty-dollar bill I pulled from the ATM and I had no singles, so I couldn't use the change machine. I'd passed a gas station about ten minutes before, but I wasn't quite sure where the town was and I didn't remember passing any stores. *Shit*, I thought again, and I headed back to the car. The pleasant officer stopped me, reached in his pocket, and handed me a quarter. That was nice of him. He looked up my name while I went to store my things. I felt relieved he'd given me the quarter and embarrassed that I'd needed one. I studied prisons and visited them frequently enough to know you couldn't bring your car keys inside. What if he hadn't had a quarter? What if he hadn't wanted to give me one? What if I hadn't had a car to drive to find a place to get change? It turned out that none of that mattered. I wasn't on the visitors' list.

Jeremiah had put me down as a visitor weeks before, but there was a visitor's form that I needed to fill out, and I hadn't. Why didn't I know this? How was I supposed to know this? The form was on the MDOC's website and could be faxed to the main office in Lansing, but it took up to two weeks to process. *Fuck,* I thought. I walked back to the parking lot feeling a strange mix of anger, sadness, and exhaustion. I hadn't visited Jeremiah, but I had to prep my talk for the conference the next day. I hopped back in the rental car and started the five-hour drive to my hotel.

I was tired of the audiobook by the halfway point of the trip. For some reason, it was hard to follow, and I had listened to as many of my playlists as I could stand. I had been in the car for seven hours, and that was after a forty-five-minute cab ride and a two-hour flight on a day that had started at four in the morning.

The phone buzzed—a 517 area code. I was nervous. I didn't want to tell Jeremiah what had happened. He had been in there for months. How long had he waited for me to show up? I pressed 0 and accepted the call.

"Shit," Jeremiah said after I explained the incident. Then he consoled me. "That's okay, little Scoober. I appreciate what you do." Jeremiah's cellie told him to tell me to tell the officer that I'd driven from Chicago. He *had* to let me visit, the cellie said. But I was two hours into the return trip, and I doubted the officer would care. Why would he bend the rules for me?[4]

A million families live this way: Sending money they can't afford. Making court dates they don't have time for. Driving five hours only to be turned away because there's been a lock-down at the facility or their names weren't on some registry or they showed up on the wrong day or someone's dress wasn't quite long enough. It's the way the guard talks to you when you get there and herds visitors, single file, through dingy corridors to pay too much for microwave concessions.[5] It's watching the guard march your loved one away when the visit comes to an end. Everyone you know has experienced this. You still some-how feel alone. It's like this for millions of grandparents and for the one in two black women with a loved one in a cage and the one in nine black children frustrated, in much the same way, each time they visit their parents.[6] Over half of all Americans, including nearly two-thirds of all black people in this country, have a family member who has been to prison. But it's not just the family members who are frustrated. It's especially hard for prisoners.

The combination of bad cell phone reception and a busy life means some days your loved ones can't reach you. It's the four different phone calls at four different times of the day that make them wonder if your distance is intentional. It's missing out on the small things that make life happen for most people—birthdays and graduations, a nephew's performance, a niece's track meet. It's your tone when you finally accept the charge from frustrations they couldn't have caused. It's going weeks without mail and months without a visit and hearing *No* for the thousandth time from people whom they've supported all their lives. It's hearing another lecture about what they should be doing and having to stand there at that pay phone listening to you complain about things they can't fully under-stand because they need you, and they know what they've put you through. The law stands in between you.

But it's not just like this when they're locked away. Trouble follows your loved ones because the prison is like a ghost, preceding them into the unemployment line and into the welfare office and into their lovers' arms. It meets them at the table when they share meals with their families, exerting an influence on almost every encounter they'll have. It will do this for a lifetime.

The jail, the prison, the courtroom, and the places where they did dirt, the same places where they were arrested and the places that sent them away—these places all stay with them. Even when their convictions were from lifetimes ago and from when they were the kinds of people they've worked nearly a lifetime to forget.[7]

I couldn't help but notice Yvette Singleton when she walked into the coffee shop in Ann Arbor. Her blond, curly, shoulder-length hair, her manicured nails, her wide smile and smoky voice that she never deployed to flatter. She was always ready with some well-timed joke or an observation that was less cutting than astute. Yvette was a force of nature. Anyone who knew her would say the same. She packed the lobby of the Detroit Institute of Arts during Black History Month in 2012, singing Paul Simon's "Bridge Over Troubled Water" under a 1933 Diego Rivera fresco painted in tribute to the laboring class. She led a marching band through the streets of Ann Arbor, wearing all black save for a gold-sequined fedora, singing a blues-and-gospel-inspired version of the University of Michigan Fight Song. The school went on to win the Sugar Bowl that year. She's a playwright, a social worker, and a well-known figure in the nonprofit sector, sitting on the boards of some of the best-funded organizations in the state and founding or leading, as president or vice president, four criminal justice–reform organizations.

Yvette sent me an e-mail the week before asking about my research. After a half an hour sitting across the table, she said, "I'm going to work on this project in some kind of way. I don't know if that's as a volunteer or if you'll find funding to hire me, but I'm working on this project." I hired her right away. She had that kind of effect on people. We once gave a talk at an East Coast law school about the dangers of risk assessments in the criminal courts. I got a call from her a week later. The dean and board of directors in attendance had been so impressed that they offered her a full scholarship. "What do I look like, going to law school?" She laughed, flattered by the offer. She was in her sixties, and they knew she had a record.

It had been over thirty years since Yvette walked out of the gate of the Women's Huron Valley Correctional Facility. She had been caught in the kind of sting operation that young black women from poor black neighborhoods find themselves in every day. A handsome man she met at a bar convinced her to pick up a package. She didn't know he was an undercover officer. She did half a year for a delivery charge, was released, relapsed, and was rearrested. She did another few months at Huron Valley and was released on two years' parole.

"I'm so excited. I'm finally getting out," she said, reflecting on that time. "The problem was, when I went in, I was addicted. And I detoxed in prison. So I hadn't really made the complete transition from the first life. I mean, from my past life."

Yvette paroled to a recovery home in Ann Arbor just a few miles west from where she'd grown up and a few blocks west of the bar where she'd caught a case. Her parole officer picked her up, so there were no loved ones at the gate with welcome-home signs like you see in so many documentaries. There was just Yvette sitting in the back seat of the government-owned vehicle on her way to some troubled block in Ann Arbor, a place considered one of the nation's "most livable cities."[8]

"At the halfway house," Yvette told me, "my roommate was using and selling drugs and boosting." Her roommate was supporting a heroin habit by stealing clothes from local department stores and selling them on the street. "Of course she gave me some," Yvette said, "which started me back up, you know." Yvette was using again just a few days after her release, a parole violation for sure. She knew she would give a dirty drop. She knew she was headed back to prison. "I went on escape," she told me.

"Where did you go?" I asked, surprised, thinking she must have left the state. But she'd gone to Ypsilanti, the same small city where the prison was located, just a few miles east of her Ann Arbor home.

"[I went] to friends' houses. And I don't want to say [this]," she continued, embarrassed to tell this part of her story, "but [we stayed in], like, flophouses, you know, [where] you could end up staying overnight."

Yvette and a few girlfriends stuck together in those early days, sleeping on couches and alternating nights at some "guy's house" that one of them was "talking to." Nights on the street. Nights in dope houses. Nights in the beds of people they didn't know very well. Yvette lived like this for a year. A whole life just a few miles west of the prison, the same place she went on the run to avoid, and a few miles from the little house where she'd grown up with a family that loved her and would be there for her, even now. This wasn't the life she'd imagined.

Yvette's grandmother was the elder of the Light of the King Full Gospel Tabernacle, the church she'd founded in the living room of their Ann Arbor home with her two daughters, their husbands, and her three grandchildren. The congregants were mostly family, but there were some folks from the community. They came each week from Ann Arbor and Ypsilanti, and cousins and friends from Detroit visited the ministry. Wednesday nights, there was Bible study. Saturday mornings were for prayer group. Each Sunday, they'd hold a full service, the kids singing and playing instruments. Her grandmother "gave the word," she said.

"We went to church so much," Yvette said, "and I grew up around all of this music." Blues. Soul. R&B. Church hymns. She took piano lessons. She was always singing—in the choir, on the playground with her friends, around the house with her sisters. She fell in love with gospel music, but more than anything she loved Motown. Those were the songs on the radio and on the records her cousins brought when they visited. She performed every chance she got.

"I've been singing for as long as I can remember," she once told me. "I sang things I couldn't say." I don't know why I was surprised to hear this.

What was happening to Yvette? She said her mother was her best friend. Her grandmother was loving and well respected. They owned their home and a car, and her family ran a church. But so much was happening in that little house in "Tree Town."

"Basically, I wasn't happy at home," she said. "There's a picture of me. I must have been three or four years old. I don't know what other three- or four-year-olds are thinking, but I was serious," she said. "There was something wrong with me!"

In the picture, a young Yvette sits on the lawn in front of her family home. She looks directly into the camera. She's not smiling or posing like she would years later in her denim prison blues. She just sits there, looking squarely at whoever is looking at her. I wouldn't have noticed how serious she was if she hadn't told me to pay attention.

"Don't forget," she said as if we'd had this conversation before and I should have known what she was about to say, "between four and six, one of my half sister's husbands had sexually molested me. Oh yeah," she continued, "then at thirteen, I was raped. So I had this inside me."

Our first conversation about these matters was in 2016. I'd worked with Yvette for nearly three years and talked with her dozens of times. I knew she had a record. I knew she had been to prison. I knew she'd struggled with addiction and experienced hard times, but I didn't know this. I only knew how she worked every room we were in together and how sharp her wit could be and how well people responded to her whenever she came around. I saw only her strength, her hats, her hair, and the call-and-response from the crowds that gathered to hear her sing. In all that time we worked together, I never asked her about her troubles. And I wasn't the only one.

"Nobody talked about anything back then," she said. "Matter of fact, the thirteen thing... I don't think I told my folks about that. So I had no outlet. I definitely [thought] something was wrong with me. With all of *that* happening?" she said. "So I acted out."

Her story will seem familiar to anyone paying attention to the lives of poor black women in this country, especially those who have been incarcerated. Just about every woman I talked with had been sexually assaulted. An uncle. A boyfriend. A parent. A half sister's husband. One in six women nationally and a staggering 86 percent of all incarcerated women are survivors of sexual assault. Three-quarters of these women were abused at home, and over half were abused as children.[9]

Yvette started getting into trouble at a public high school in Ann Arbor. The white kids from the rich houses were using. "To this day, they say Ridgemont is the worst place to send your kids...well, if you don't want them to be exposed to drugs...and better drugs too," she said. "You're around the more affluent kids who have access to it, and they have money, and they get things out of their parents' medicine cabinet," she explained.

But the rich kids didn't get arrested; people like Yvette did. This was the early 1970s. With just three hundred thousand people in cages and a population that exceeded two hundred million, the U.S. incarceration rate was relatively low. Mass incarceration at the scale and concentration that we know it today was in its nascent stages. But black people, both men and women, have always been arrested at wildly disparate rates. Yvette was getting started in the drug scene as the incarceration rate began to climb. The rich kids offered her drugs, and she took them. And while those kids never saw a day in court, Yvette was a poor black girl in a mostly white town, even if that town was progressive, and her first arrest was at the age of fourteen. She was charged with vandalism. By fifteen, she had possession and delivery charges pending in juvenile courts. By sixteen she was addicted, and she found herself in trouble of a different kind.

Yvette met a man in his late twenties at a hangout spot in Ypsilanti. He was doing political education for a black nationalist group, an offshoot of the Black Panther Party.

"I thought he was handsome," she said. "And he was talking *strong* rhetoric. I hadn't really met anyone who basically acted like that." She was a child, a young, dark, and beautiful girl, and this was the 1970s, a time for new ideas about blackness, about struggle, about who you were and what your place in the world was. "I almost joined the party!" she said.

"Was that you?" I asked, wondering about the black nationalist streak that might have been hiding underneath her curly blond hair and long eyelashes.

"No!" She laughed. "I thought we were in love."

They hopped on a Greyhound to Santa Fe. When Yvette and the black nationalist got there, they moved to a small town not far from the border. He made trips to Mexico to rob weed dealers. He would be gone for days. Before he left for the first trip, he introduced her to a man who ran a topless bar. She quickly realized that her job was to strip to pay the couple's bills.

She had experimented with drugs in high school. "It was marijuana and pills in those days." But she got addicted to heroin while working the clubs in that small border town. "Of course the drugs were better," she said, her tone more serious than before. "All my troubles started following somebody else."

They moved again, but under duress, this time to a border town in Nevada. He made her work the strip clubs and took her money when she got paid. His trips got longer and more frequent.

"I did all these things to support him," she said, now sullen, "the so-called provider." This was human trafficking, even if it felt consensual and even if no one would recognize her as the sixteen-year-old victim that she was.

Things changed when the handsome man started seeing someone else. He came home less often and only to pick up cash. But Yvette was quick on her feet. She told him her mother had taken ill and she needed to get home to visit. She boarded the next Greyhound to Detroit and then took another to Ann Arbor. She never went back.

Yvette and her mother were close. She welcomed her daughter just like she would years later when Yvette returned from prison. But Yvette was still a teenager, and it was time for her to get used to being back home.

"I wasn't a member of nobody's church," she said. She joined a community choir where Pastor Meadows, a local minister, was the director. She hadn't yet shaken off her old life. "When I joined this community choir, oh my God," Yvette said, laughing. "You should see some of the looks I got from some of the saints. I had on a miniskirt, some Peter Pan boots! I had an Afro, [and I had] a missing tooth in the front," she said, laughing even harder. "But I could outsing the whole soprano section. Of course I could," she said, looking at me with a smirk. "I don't know how he could direct the choir with a straight face," she said.

"Why?" I asked, wondering if it was the boots or the missing tooth.

"I never realized I stood out like a sore thumb. Woo!" she said. "And if they would have said anything at all, I would have cursed them out from 'Amazing Grace' to a floating opportunity," she said. "I would have cursed them out!" she repeated. "Ooo-wee! I was a piece of work."

Yvette toured and sang with the choir despite the looks from the saints. She was home, after being gone for nearly a year. Yvette was home, and she was happy.

It wasn't long before Yvette met the next handsome man to put her in danger—the undercover officer. He was a user like every other man who had gotten her in trouble—her half sister's husband who raped her, the rich white boys who gave her pills, the wannabe Black Panther who made her work the strip. Maybe the officer was trying to catch a bigger fish, some dope dealer up the food chain. Maybe he was filling a quota. Either way, a police officer gave a package of heroin to a young woman with an addiction. He was a user like all of the others.

After a year in prison for what some might call entrapment and a year on the street on the run, Yvette was tired. She turned herself in to the police. She was convicted, again, for narcotics delivery and was handed another conviction for absconding while on parole. Sentenced to another twelve months in prison, Yvette returned to Huron Valley. It was 1981.

Mass incarceration had begun in earnest, though these were still its early years. The tough-on-crime era had not yet reached a fever pitch. President Reagan had not yet declared his version of the drug war, a campaign he inherited from Richard Nixon. In Reagan's version, which sounds like a conspiracy theory, the U.S. government agreed to sponsor arms deals with "anticommunist forces" whom officials knew to be drug lords, and they relaxed security measures along the once well-defended Western border. The nation's "inner cities" were flooded with cocaine, launching a crack epidemic whose effects would linger for a generation, all while "Just Say No" ads blanketed the nation's airwaves.[10]

Yvette was twenty-one and by then, she was used to prison routines. She knew how to ration food and make the most of her time on the yard or at medical or at chapel or wherever it was that she could steal away to sit and think. She posed for photos in her best prison blues, stealing moments of freedom when she could. She avoided the guards who stared too long for her to misunderstand their intentions. And she learned to avoid the guards who might not have been particularly interested but who were having a bad day. Commissary. Visitation. Waiting to make a phone call. The politics of the TV room. All of this felt familiar, but for Yvette, this bid was different. She told me she got "serious about religion," in part because Pastor Meadows started a prison ministry and a choir in Huron Valley and in part because of her friendships.

"I bonded with a woman who had natural life," she said. "She was the sweetest person you ever want to meet." After years of beatings and being left for dead when things on the stroll got dangerous and being sold to groups of men, Yvette's friend killed her pimp. "It's not like it was no pretty storybook thing," Yvette said. "They did horrendous things to her, and one day she just couldn't take any more." She grew close to another lifer, a woman in jail on three murder counts. "Three life sentences," Yvette said, "and that was before they had laws about proximity. She dropped her husband off. He ended up killing a bunch of people. She wasn't even there when it happened."

The women had met at the law library, but they got close worshipping together. Yvette said that there was "something about those services that made you feel like you were a part of something bigger." The women would sing and study and spend time together. And they shared their lives and their commissary and their many, many gifts. While they would meet in the law library and in the dining hall, in the chapel and on the yard, their friendships would extend far beyond the prison.

"I remember when I was incarcerated, singing on the couch," she said during a lecture at a university. "And I remember that music made a real big difference. Things I couldn't say, I could sing. I could act out. It calmed me," she said.

"This whole time I've been looking to work with myself," she told me, sitting in my living room three decades removed from her last bid. "A lot of the word was important," she said, "but there was a freedom to be found in those church services. In worshipping...And you knew, the best thing you could do was use that time to plan on how you were not going to come back." She had seen so many people who were released come back to prison in just a few months. A new prostitution charge. A parole violation—pissing hot or missing appointments or getting into a fight with a boyfriend.

"I knew I would be going home soon," she said. "And I remember being in one service, and a woman came from the outside. And there's a little poem called 'Footprints,' but she had turned this poem into a song...she sang, and it just broke me down." Yvette remembered reading the poem. There would be a painting or maybe a photo of a beach, the sun rising in the distance, and one set of footprints next to the words to the poem; there was a print of that hanging in every other church office and every other kitchen in black homes throughout the 1980s. "You're walking along. God comes and picks you up. You go from two [sets of] footprints to one," she explained, "'cause he's carrying you."

Yvette was weary of the routines—being cuffed to a bench in some police station. Waking up next to some man she barely knew. "I was tired of the whole struggle that leads you to the point where you're sitting there contemplating life choices," she said, "where you're trying to figure out how you're going to do things different. I'll never forget that song."

Twelve months later and now twelve months sober, Yvette

Singleton walked out of the Women's Huron Valley Correctional Facility for the very last time. It was 1982. She joined Pastor Meadows's church and started to write letters to the women she had done time with, a practice that would last for decades. By 1983, she was accompanying Pastor Meadows in his prison ministry. She would sit and pray and sing with the women, listening to their stories as often as she could.

A decade passed, and Yvette was still visiting the prison; she was cleaning houses and doing temp work at offices in Ann Arbor to support herself. She met her husband. They were going to have a child, and she needed a job with benefits, one that paid enough to buy a home and raise a family and establish herself in the city where she'd grown up.

"I could type," she said. This was an understatement. She typed ninety words per minute. "So I applied for a job at the Health Department." The Office of Public Health and Welfare had an opening for an administrative assistant. There was a box on the application that the candidate was supposed to check if she had been convicted of a crime. This was the 1990s, before the era of "big data" and before credit-reporting agencies sent alerts when a so-called felon moved into the neighborhood. Background checks weren't used as often as they are today. Yvette had a husband and would soon have a child. She didn't check the box.

Yvette had experience, strong recommendations, and a magnetic personality. She was called in for an interview, and she was hired on the spot. Two months went by without a hitch. She was a hard worker and brilliant and easy to be around. It was clear to anyone paying attention that she was good at her new job—a job with benefits and room for her to grow.

In the third month, right before her probationary period

ended, Yvette broke her ankle playing volleyball at a church picnic. Her boss said that he would miss her while she recovered. Yvette needed help to make ends meet. Her boss suggested she sign up for unemployment and get public aid until she could return to work. Yvette went down to the social-service center to sign up for benefits, something she hated to do. "I'm not a dependent," she said. "I'm not waiting on anybody to do anything for me."

The woman in the aid office knew her from church functions, from working temp agencies downtown, from the neighborhood where they grew up. She didn't know about Yvette's troubles. There was no reason for her to. Yvette had put her old life behind her. She hadn't been arrested in over a decade. She was sober. She had a family.

The woman behind the counter at the public aid office went through her checklist: contact information and prior addresses, marital status, employment history, and the reasons she needed support. She asked Yvette if she had ever been arrested. Wanting to be honest, Yvette said yes.

The woman went through the rest of the form and said her office would be in touch. Yvette's boss called a week later. The woman at the social-service center had told a friend at the Health Department that Yvette was an ex-con. That word got back to her boss.

Yvette explained that she was a different person, that the old her was dead and buried. She told him she made a mistake but had been clean for over a decade. She was active in church and needed the job to care for her family. Besides, she was good at her job. She came in early and left late. She always finished her work on time. She had missed days only when she'd broken her ankle.

Her boss understood but said there was little he could do. An employer could be sued for having a felon on the payroll.

A decade free and a decade sober. A volunteer. A hard worker. A good daughter and wife, and soon to be a mother. In the end, none of that mattered. She went to the office to gather her things.

It was 1991. Mass incarceration had reached its midpoint, with 1.2 million people held in American jails and prisons. And while the infrastructure for the supervised society had not yet matured, the machinery was in place.

Changes in liability law, beginning in the 1980s, started in housing. Tenants sued negligent landlords when they were robbed or mugged in their buildings. The courts sided with the renters, finding that crime prevention was part of every landlord's responsibility. More lawsuits followed. Landlords were fined under nuisance ordinances for letting their buildings fall into disrepair, for harboring drug users and gang activity, and for leasing apartments to felons.[11]

Almost overnight, property owners became part of the crime-fighting machine. They responded to this new responsibility by evicting tenants with even decades-old criminal records, and denying leases to people facing criminal allegations.[12] This move was emblematic of the new way of managing crime. It didn't require that anyone help the people who had been labeled criminals.

Americans hated the idea of welfare, and so-called criminals were viewed as the least deserving of care.[13] The verdict was in on prisoner rehabilitation—much of the public and most policy makers believed it simply did not work. Crime could not be treated, the public thought, because criminals were born, not made. A suite of new laws provided a way to avoid the risks posed by "criminals" without having to deter crime.[14] Employers could simply refuse to hire "ex-cons" or fire them once they learned of their convictions.[15] Whether prisoners were locked away hundreds of miles from home for months or years at a time or kept out of the workplace by having their job applications rejected, this was a policy of social exclusion.

When the gossipy woman at the public aid office told a friend who told a friend who told Yvette's boss that Yvette had a record, the world had already changed. Employment discrimination was illegal. Were Yvette fired because she was black or because she was a woman, she could have filed a lawsuit against her employer. But she was fired because of her record, and there was nothing that she could do. She didn't have the same rights as other people. She lived in an alternate legal reality, because the laws and policies that we've enacted have created an alternate form of citizenship.

The very first sentence of the Fourteenth Amendment offers the famous "citizenship clause." It reads, "All persons born or naturalized in the United States, and subject to the jurisdiction thereof, are citizens of the United States and the state wherein they reside." Citizenship has benefits, including "equal protection of the laws" and the right to live free from any infringement on "life, liberty, or property." But people with criminal records don't have these rights. The Fourteenth Amendment guarantees "the privileges or immunities of citizens" unless those citizens have been convicted of a crime. And the Thirteenth Amendment abolishes slavery and involuntary servitude, but that does not apply to those with criminal records. The amendment's sole exception: "as a punishment for crime."

Yvette had changed quite a bit in the decade since she'd walked out of prison. She was a wife, a minister, a mother-to-be, and a professional with experience. But her track record didn't matter. She had a criminal record, and once you are labeled criminal in this country, your life will never be the same.[16] The record whispers of the potential for danger in the ears of all who will listen, and it changes the nature of one's relationships with almost everyone one encounters, because the record is all some people can see.

The same way an interpreter communicates the meaning of a phrase, the criminal record communicates the nature of the people labeled criminals. And just as a language can be translated in many different places—at the UN, at a restaurant, in school, or at home—one's criminality can be read across time and space through one's record. Judges and prosecutors declare it in court when they say "Repeat offender," and employers and landlords read it in every job application and lease. Criminal records serve one purpose: they announce shame and danger and one's propensity for violence and grift. They communicate a history of drug use and promiscuity. That is, they declare risk. And much like a phrase that's been poorly translated, one where the deeper meaning gets lost in translation, the distinguishing features of so-called criminals are flattened or discarded, their lives forever defined by crimes they might once have committed.

CHAPTER 5

IN VICTORY AND SPECTACULAR DEFEAT

The children, having seen the spectacular defeat of their fathers—having seen what happens to any bad nigger and, still more, what happens to the good ones—cannot listen to their fathers and certainly will not listen to the society which is responsible for their orphaned condition.

—James Baldwin, "A Report from Occupied Territory"[1]

There are so many ways to lose a child—an accident, an illness. So many things, far outside of your control, can take your child away. A stray bullet, an aimed bullet, some stranger with a badge. The dangers from without and within. The dangers from people sworn to protect your child from danger or from the people we least expect to cause harm—police and store clerks and homeowners with itchy trigger fingers. Anyone

161

who is not black and happens to own a gun. They can take your child away.

The murder would be justified. The murderer would go free. The courts, which are dangerous too, would proclaim the murderer's innocence. Of course they would, and of course they do. You know this as you sit in the gallery of that courtroom, watching some judge make life-or-death decisions about your child—a child he does not know and did not spend a single day raising. These are the same courts that took your siblings and your cousins and the children who lived on your block. They put them on some bus and sent them too far away for their mothers to visit. They took the children of almost everyone you know.

You sit in that gallery with many parents in your situation, but somehow, you feel alone. You remember working extra shifts and borrowing money you couldn't pay back and selling things you needed, but there was never enough cash. You spent all of the money you were able to find on bail and an overpriced attorney whose discounted rate you can't afford. Your child will still be shipped away, no matter the lengths you've gone to to raise the money and no matter how hard you tried to raise him right. That judge, who can't know what it costs, will send your child away. And everyone you know has gone through this, but you don't know anyone in that gallery.

It was this way for my grandmother, who watched her family separated by some judge in some courtroom and saw two of her grandchildren shipped away. And it was the same for every grandmother I knew growing up. And it was the same for every grandmother I met over the years I spent doing the research for this book. Some court sent away their children—to group homes or job corps, to juvenile detention or jail, to prison or some alternative school. And sometimes those same courts sent away the children of their children. It didn't matter how many times a grandmother took her grandbaby to church or how many afterschool programs a mother took her children to after working a double shift. They knew that it didn't matter how hard they hoped and tried to keep them safe. When they gathered the money or found the time or got the ride from their family or the people they barely knew, when they called in the many favors that it took to mount a legal defense, they knew it wouldn't matter, that their loved ones would still be shipped away, and somehow it felt like it was their fault.

Every black mother in every American city knows this fear all too well. Every black father that I've encountered has recounted the same bad dream—that their children would pay for their sins. That their child would get shipped away. In some ways, it is like the crisis at the border, where parents are separated from their children and the children sleep each night in a cage, but it's been like this for black children for so long that it's easy to overlook.

On any given day, there are forty-eight thousand incarcerated children living in the United States.[2] Seventeen thousand are in juvenile detention; eleven thousand are in "long-term secure facilities," those training schools and reformatories that use work and school and moral teachings to turn bad boys and girls into good ones. Ten thousand are in residential treatment for drugs or alcohol or a sex offense or for mental-health or behavioral problems. Thirty-four hundred are in group homes, and forty-five hundred children do time in an adult jail or prison despite what we know happens to children when we lock them away with adults.

So many children living in cages need us to pay attention. So many parents are afraid for their children, who can be snatched away in the blink of an eye. But there is a different fear every black grandmother knows, one that's all too familiar to every black parent. They know it from their flesh. The courts that take your children away from you can take *you* away from your children.

Half of the nation's prisoners have minor children.[3] That's a million parents locked up on any given day. That's 2.7 million children who have a parent, at this very moment, sitting in a cage.[4] Five million American children have lived this way, their parents experiencing their children's first steps or their first words or their first real disappointments from a cell.[5] A million fathers watch their kids "grow up through family pictures." A hundred thousand mothers raise their children fifteen minutes at a time through the collect calls their loved ones struggle to pay for or the visits they manage to arrange. But these are the lucky ones. Most parents who go to prison hardly see their children at all, and many will never see their children again.

In the past decade and a half, thirty-two thousand prisoners lost the right to raise their children although they were not charged with child abuse or neglect.[6] And while nearly all of them were poor, and many were addicted, some five thousand had their parental rights revoked simply because they were incarcerated—as if their incarceration weren't punishment enough.[7] Mothers are almost always the primary caregivers for their children, and incarcerated mothers were five times more likely to lose their rights than incarcerated fathers. And while the reports didn't show additional racial disparities in the number of prisoners whose parental rights were revoked, they didn't need to. The U.S. criminal justice system had long since done that work.[8] The legal scholar Dorothy Roberts tells us that the same kind of racial disparities found in American jails and prisons "exists at every point of decision making within the child welfare system."[9]

So many black parents have had so many of their children snatched away—a fact that would be alarming to people if they were paying attention. These parents can thank, in part, Public Law 105-89, the Adoption and Safe Families Act, passed during the Clinton administration. The hope was to increase the annual number of adoptions in response to an expanding child welfare system.

Between the late 1980s and the mid-1990s, foster-care placements more than doubled. But the children who were sent to foster homes were hard for agencies to place. They were older. They were poor. They were black and brown and queer in a world that was hostile to them. Many were disabled. Many more were "troubled" and had parents cycling in and out of jail. They were born "crack addicted." At least, that's what the newspapers said. Researchers have since established that much of what people thought was wrong with so-called crack babies was due to poverty rather than the effects of crack on fetal development.[10]

The child welfare system was in crisis. There were horror stories. Foster children were abused (there was a 50 percent increase in reported cases between 1985 and 1993) and neglected (there was a similar increase in reported cases of neglect during the same period). Because these children were hard to place, many never found a permanent home. Instead, they "aged out" of foster care as they became adults. And we know from studies of foster-care outcomes that these children had a terrible time. More than half dropped out of high school. Nearly half were arrested. Over half were unemployed. Nearly 40 percent became homeless.[11] Some had children of their own much earlier than they'd expected. And many of their children ended up in foster care.

Policy makers presented the Adoption and Safe Families Act as a way to right the ship, saying it offered modest financial incentives for states that increased the number of adoptions and it set federal guidelines to "streamline" the process for would-be adoptive families. In the words of then President Bill Clinton, "We have put in place here the building blocks of giving all of our children what should be their fundamental right—a chance at a decent, safe home; an honorable, orderly, positive upbringing; a chance to live out their dreams and fulfill their God-given capacities."

After twenty years and nearly one million adoptions, the act is vaunted as a success. But the act's passage had deleterious consequences for the nation's poorest families. As part of the streamlining process, the federal government set guidelines to terminate the rights of parents whose children had been in foster care for fifteen of the previous twenty-two months.[12] The average prison sentence in the United States is 2.6 years,[13] over a year beyond the fifteen-month guideline.

Proceedings began, terminating the rights of thousands of incarcerated parents, most of whom were never charged with child abuse, child endangerment, or neglect. And since child welfare and criminal justice agencies operate within separate spheres, some people lost their parental rights without even knowing it. They received letters in their cells telling them their rights had been taken away. Their children were adopted. The adoptions were closed. They could never contact their children again.[14] Others received notice that proceedings to terminate their parental rights would begin, but the Department of Corrections had no legal obligation to take the parent to family court.

There were other grounds, too, to take parental rights away from incarcerated parents. In some states, being convicted of three felony charges within a five-year period is grounds to establish "depravity," and being "depraved" is sufficient reason to take away someone's parental rights.[15] People can lose their rights if they've been convicted of a violent crime or if a judge has determined their prison sentences are too long. None of this is directly related to one's ability to raise one's child, yet thousands of prisoners have lost those rights simply because of their incarceration.

Amanda Alexander, founder of the Detroit Justice Center, has worked with parents facing the threat of losing their children. She started out as a lawyer in Detroit representing incarcerated mothers as they tried to keep their families together. We met as new faculty members at the University of Michigan and while writing together, we learned that both of our fathers had been incarcerated.

"Almost all the guys locked up are fathers," she said of the men she represented. "The majority of women in prison are the primary caretakers of their children. [This was] one of the main findings from our bail-fund work, [that] most people locked up are parents."

That most people in prison are parents and that their incarceration means a child's life will be fundamentally changed might cause others to pay attention to how often they call the police. A judge might consider these children when handing down a sentence. A prosecutor might think about these children when he or she proceeds with a case.

"Most people don't ask," Amanda said. Judges set bail, or don't, without thinking twice about the children. They aren't trained to consider it, and there are few resources available to judges who do think about the kids. But children are somewhere waiting for their mothers, and their mothers are in cells. "In a lot of the cases," Amanda told me, "[family separation] happens early on, beginning almost at the moment of arrest. 'I was supposed to pick up my kids,' the mom might say. 'I got pulled over for a taillight, and when I didn't show up, the school called [Child Protective Services].' In other communities, the first call would never be to CPS," Amanda explained. "The first call would be to an emergency contact. But in black poor communities, we're calling CPS to deal with this."

The "this" to which Amanda refers is the color of child welfare, and the research on the matter is clear. In the United States, black families are more likely than white ones to be reported to child welfare agencies. They are less likely to receive the services they need to keep their children out of foster care. Their children are more likely to be removed from their homes, and once removed, they receive services inferior to those offered to white families. This is despite the fact that black families are no more likely to abuse or neglect their children than white ones. Half of all foster children in New York State are black, and they are admitted into foster care at ten times the rate of white children.[16] In Chicago, the overrepresentation is just as bad, and it's like this in every major city.[17] Detroit is no exception.

"The parent is picked up," Amanda said. "Jail. Bail. She can't pay. It's tricky because no one is really tracking this. A bail fund may ask if the women have kids," she said, "but they won't know whether CPS was called."

Whether or not CPS is involved makes all the difference in the world. A well-meaning teacher or a neighbor who notices the child's mother is gone or, really, anyone with access to the CPS hotline can make the call and initiate an investigation.

"Just when the mom starts to figure out her case, it's like, 'Oh, shit, my kids!' It's hard to legally appoint someone to care for your kids—most criminal defense lawyers don't help with that," Amanda said. "[A mom might say,] 'I've got kids, and I think my sister has them.' Maybe CPS was called. We have to find out," she said.

"There's things they can't account for," she continued. A kid could be sent home from school, and CPS gets called because the teacher wondered, "Where's the kid's parents?" or "What connection does the person who came to the office have to this child?" "Danger!" Amanda said. "There's [now] an open CPS case. And this is a case against a woman with a looming criminal conviction. Suddenly," Amanda said, "the procedure is ticking along. It's hard for a mom sitting in jail to make the case that 'I'm the best possible caregiver for my baby.' And there's a line of people who want a beautiful newborn."[18]

Amanda's job was to make sure her clients could mount a vigorous legal defense and, in the meantime, find a way for the mothers to keep their kids. While there's been considerable attention paid to pregnant prisoners who give birth behind bars—the practice of shackling a woman in labor to a gurney being common in most states until a few years ago—there's another, equally insidious problem that seems more logistical than anything.

"The truth is," Amanda said, "no one is arrested at an opportune moment."

All the people I met doing research for this book were on their way somewhere when they were arrested: To work. To the grocery store. To visit a relative. To the hospital. One woman was arrested the day before her graduation from an alternative high school in Detroit. She got into a fight with a cheating boyfriend while getting her hair done at a beauty salon. The police were called. She had a Taser and a criminal history. She spent the next few months in jail.

Amanda said, "Incarcerated parents face enormous stigma. Judges and prosecutors see them as stereotypes. I remember a prosecutor who didn't bother to look into the details of my client's case and basically just said, 'She's a felon! She's a felon, Your Honor!'" That is, the prosecutor was saying the woman was depraved. She'd burned too many bridges. She was a criminal and a bad mother. She should not have the right to parent her child. But in most cases, much of the pressure comes from the clock.

While "fifteen months is the federal guideline," Amanda said, "some states start proceedings in six." That is, if the child is in foster care for just six months, some courts have jurisdiction to terminate the rights of the parent. But whether it's six months or six years, there's never really enough time. Between figuring out how to deal with her case or finding a place to stay after the last encounter with an abusive boyfriend or adjusting to life in a cage, an incarcerated mother has to prove to a judge that she *wants* to raise her children, and she has to provide evidence that she's fit to do so.

"This is when things kick into high gear," Amanda said. Filing court appearances. Correcting old motions. Requesting appeals, which will be denied. Asking for continuances to gather evidence. More continuance requests will come from the prosecutors, trying to lengthen the process. The inevitable wrestling match to get the officers' statements that were used to put these women in prison. These are all the things we expect from good lawyers, but dotted in between those actions, Amanda and other family defense attorneys do the things we don't associate with the law at all.

They write grants to raise funds to represent clients who can't otherwise afford their services. They track down the women's children, and they track down family members willing to keep them while their mothers sit in cages. They arrange visits and prepare their clients' loved ones for the long road that's surely ahead. But just as important as the case itself, Amanda and her team have to help their clients demonstrate they have a connection with their children.

"[We might] get mom in a knitting program to knit booties to show ties," she said, or they might enroll a mother in a program that records her reading books to her babies. The women might very well have done these things on their own, but Amanda has the burden of proving to a judge that the mothers they represent love their children. And all of this effort is needed, no matter what the mother has been charged with.

"Right before Christmas, the Bail Project Detroit bailed out a woman who was nine months pregnant," Amanda said. They fought to set bail and to raise the funds to get the woman released. "She had an emergency C-section shortly after she got out." If she hadn't been released, she would have had the baby while she was incarcerated. When that happens, Amanda said, "it's twenty-four hours with the baby and back to the cell." The baby would be handed off to a guardian, but if one wasn't identified, the baby would go straight to CPS.

Half of the women in prison are there for a property crime,

like shoplifting, or a drug offense, sometimes with intent to sell. Forty percent are there for a crime of violence. Sixty percent will leave an American jail without ever being convicted of a crime, but almost all of these women will be separated from their children.

I caught up with Jimmy Caldwell on the east side of Detroit. We met at the construction site where he slept. As was our custom, we hopped in my car and drove to the Coney Island diner just west of Gratiot Avenue. He ordered his usual: Eggs sunny-side up. Grits. Bacon. Toast. So did I: a veggie omelet with hash browns, this time, I hoped, without the curly black hair I'd found in my breakfast the last time we met. We drank coffee and orange juice, sitting across the table from each other like two old friends catching up. Jimmy was happy, and I was happy to see him.

"What's up with homegirl?" I asked, thinking about his girlfriend. She'd seen him through his last two bids, sending letters and putting money on his books for three years without fail. She'd visited him every two weeks when he was transferred to the Detroit Reentry Center, and she was still standing by him, offering a hot meal and a place to sleep when he managed to stay out of jail.

"Cynthia?" he asked with a wry smile. "Don't get me wrong. She was there for me," he said before blurting out, "I want me a hot girl." He was laughing, but he meant what he said. Cynthia was sixty-two. After spending most of his adult life in one correctional institution or another, Jimmy wanted to be free. That is, he wanted to feel free. He wanted to date someone he chose, not someone who chose him. The world was open to him now. At least, that's what he said. He wanted to be with someone he was excited to sleep with. And besides, Jimmy said, "Yolanda all in my business."

Yolanda was Cynthia's sister, and the two were close. Yolanda said Jimmy was a user. While he was in prison, he'd used most of Cynthia's disposable income on his requests for ramen noodles, toiletries, and phone calls, and he used her for a place to sleep, but only when it was convenient—mostly between jail stays and drug treatment. He claimed he had been sober for three and a half years. He'd detoxed in prison and was in drug treatment at the reentry center. But Yolanda saw no evidence that things had changed. To Yolanda, Jimmy was an addict, and Cynthia could do better. Yolanda had advised Cynthia to leave him on more than one occasion, and sometimes while Jimmy was within earshot.

"Even the way she talks to me," Jimmy said, made him feel disrespected. But that feeling, while unwanted, wasn't unfamiliar. "She just like Tabitha," Jimmy told me, referring to his middle sister. Tabitha called Jimmy a crackhead and cursed him out in front of company. He said that she once kept her children's toys locked in a car at a birthday party and told the guests that Jimmy would be the culprit if her kids' toys went missing.

"They know I'm out here," Jimmy said, meaning his sister knew he needed help. Everyone in Jimmy's circle knew that he had been to prison. But this was an old problem the two had had since they were children. His mother, Ruth, would usually step in to settle their disputes, but things were different now. Jimmy had gotten into too much trouble, and he'd burned too many bridges. They weren't children anymore, and Jimmy's actions had consequences.

Even so, Ruth was used to the cycle. He would turn to her for a place to stay each time he was released. And she would always help him, letting him sleep on her couch or giving him a hot meal or cash when she could afford it. But her landlord started asking questions. He told her he saw Jimmy come and go at night. He didn't want trouble in his building. And he knew, like everyone else, that Jimmy had been to prison. He told Ruth that he liked her, but if Jimmy moved back in, he would be *forced* to put her out.

Thousands of families have been evicted, and thousands more live under the threat, for housing relatives with criminal records. Many can't afford the risk, so they must turn their relatives away. This, too, is a kind of family separation. But it's separation through housing policy, so it's easy to overlook.

In his January 23, 1996, State of the Union address, President Bill Clinton named "the challenge to take our streets back from crime, and gangs, and drugs" as the fourth of the "six great challenges...faced by all Americans." The president hoped to "take on gangs the way we once took on the Mob" and directed the FBI to target those who "involve juveniles in violent crime" and to "prosecute as adults teenagers who maim and kill like adults." But it was his next pronouncement that changed family life in most American cities. "And I challenge local housing authorities and tenant associations," Clinton said. "Criminal gang members and drug dealers are destroying the lives of decent tenants... The rule for residents who commit crime and peddle drugs should be 'one strike and you're out.'"

People with criminal records had long been denied access to public housing, and the one-strike rule didn't introduce any new laws. But Clinton's address coupled with the fervor of the tough-on-crime movement led to new and more restrictive ways to implement housing policy. In a celebratory report, the Department of Housing and Urban Development, led at the time by a rising political superstar, Andrew Cuomo, described the initiative as "strict" and "straightforward" and said it would ensure that residents who committed crimes would "face swift and certain eviction." But the initiative went further. Within two months, Congress passed the Housing Opportunity Extension Act of 1996. The act required public-housing agencies to evict tenants for "any criminal activity" that threatened the "health, safety or right to peaceful enjoyment" of any other resident. This included any crimes committed "on or off such premises" as well as crimes committed by "any member of the tenants' household... any guest, or other person under the tenants' control." Put differently, tenants could be evicted for allowing someone with a criminal record to simply visit their home.[19]

Housing-application denials for people with criminal records doubled in the first six months after Clinton's address. By 1998, almost every public-housing authority in the nation had taken up some version of the initiative, barring people with criminal records from the premises and evicting entire families who let formerly incarcerated loved ones sleep on their couches. Exclusion became official housing policy.

While the government made the call to evict people with criminal records, families were responsible for putting them out. Most families wanted to help their loved ones. They knew everyone needed a home. But the stakes were too high. They had other children or partners or their livelihoods to consider. With an announcement and the stroke of a pen, housing policy changed the family dynamics for millions of Americans.

"When was the last time you saw your mother?" I asked Jimmy as I sat across the table from him at Coney Island.

"I don't really come around like that," he replied. Jimmy certainly needed his mother. He was homeless. He was in drug treatment, doing his best to stay clean and sober. And Jimmy was Ruth's baby, the youngest of her five children. She would have taken him in. But he and Ruth both knew that she would be evicted if she did. He'd decided to avoid her *because* she wanted to help.

"I understand," I said. I asked about Cynthia again.

"Too much drama," he told me.

We finished the meal as he talked about his job hunt and his relationship with his parole officer and how his treatment was going and how it felt to be "free." I paid the bill and handed Jimmy the bus card and the forty dollars I gave him at the completion of each interview. I dropped Jimmy off at the construction site and made my way home.

The next time we connected, Jimmy had changed his tune about Cynthia. He was sleeping at her house more often, away from the drafty, sometimes damp, almost always too hot or too cold buildings he gutted. And he told me that her sister had stopped insulting him. They got along better. I wondered why. It turned out Cynthia had had a stroke, her fifth, and was in what Jimmy called a convalescent home. This made him sad. He was no more attracted to her than he had been a few months before, but now they were making plans to get married, and Yolanda said it was a good idea. Marriage, he said, was the only way he could secure an apartment. He also said he wanted to help Cynthia make decisions about her medical care. But Jimmy wasn't happy. He described the upcoming marriage as a debt. "She stuck with me in prison. I'll stick with her now."

In a moment of reflection about his life and his relationships, Jimmy said, "I feel needy." I asked if he thought his relationships would have been the same had he not gone to prison. Jimmy sipped the last of his weak diner coffee and finished chewing his toast. "No," he said, signaling the end of our conversation.

In a lecture I gave at a legal aid convention, I talked about citizenship in the supervised society, where thousands of laws dictated where and with whom a previously incarcerated person could work or live and what it meant for the law to come between a person who has been incarcerated and the people he cared for most. I discussed how law and policy granted many kinds of people immense power over the lives of people with criminal records. I told Jimmy's story about Cynthia, whom he slept with but didn't love, the woman he was going to marry out of a sense of obligation, or need, or desperation—the one to whom he owed a debt. And I talked about the way his sister treated him and how he had to rely on people he barely knew just to meet his basic needs. I talked about what an economy of favors looked like and, more important, what it felt like. How it showed up in Jimmy's life. How it changed his perception of himself. How the power that others had over him changed the nature of his relationships.[20]

An attorney, flanked by two colleagues who were also public defenders, came up to speak with me at the end of my talk. Sheila, who did most of the talking, had worked for years in housing law, representing clients in central Illinois, almost all of whom were facing eviction. Many had criminal records. Many more had children who had done time. "In the private sector," she said, "if a landlord has decent housing to provide, they probably won't even rent to someone with a criminal record... But there are plenty of landlords who do, [and they] rent to people with extensive records or people [they know who are involved in] criminal activities . . . But often times," she said, "those places aren't fit for people to really live in."

I had heard as much from dozens of previously incarcerated people, that it was nearly impossible for them to find a place to live regardless of their credit or income. And they told me the conditions in the apartments they found were unbearable. Vermin. Rusty water. Broken appliances. Lights and electric sockets that didn't work. Some places were dangerous in other ways. They were next to crack houses, or they were in neighborhoods where the police rode through to make arrests but didn't have a real presence otherwise. The schools were the worst in their districts. Nothing ever worked. The landlords abused their rights, and the tenants had little or no recourse.

Sheila said, "I had this client a few years back. This was my first day in a new office. We have things known as emergency cases. You drop everything," she explained. She represented a tenant who had withheld his rent, citing the conditions of the unit.

"The landlord turned off water, utilities, all that madness," she said. "To me and everyone else [who works in tenants' rights,] that's what we call a lockout emergency. [You] run to the courthouse, get a restraining order," she said. "It's illegal for a landlord to shut off the utilities, even for nonpayment." It was called a breach of the warranty of habitability, she told me.

Landlords have a legal obligation to ensure a unit is habitable. No one could reasonably be expected to live in a place with no running water.

"The only defense," Sheila said, "was that my client had an extensive record. Professor Miller!" she said, raising her voice. "I mean the record was *ex-ten-sive*." She assured me his convictions were "awful" without saying what they were. "But he's still a person," she said. "He still has rights."

The case went on for over a year. Eventually, there was a ruling. Tenants have rights, and Illinois, according to many landlords I've spoken with, is a tenant-friendly state. The landlord was in the wrong and the client had a history of paying his rent on time. But her client had a record.

"You can always use those records to impute credibility," Sheila told me. "The judge found he wasn't credible," she said, meaning that after a year in court and a clear violation of her tenant's rights, the client didn't have the grounds to bring a lawsuit *because* he had a record. The conditions of the apartment and the actions of the landlord didn't matter in this case. In fact, Sheila said, "he wants *me* sanctioned for representing someone not worthy of legal aid assistance!"

We spoke again a few months later, this time over the phone. "I had this epiphany," she said. "I care about my clients. I want them to have housing and be content. But sometimes we'll prepare an agreement that says, 'So-and-so'—meaning a loved one with a record—'is not allowed to live here. So-and-so is barred from the premises.' But quite frankly, where is So-and-so supposed to go?"

Sheila asked if she was part of the problem. With so much at risk, sometimes telling a mother to evict her child was the best legal advice she could give.

Connie was separated from her children but not because of her criminal record. And she lost them to the prison, though she never did any time. We sat at a diner outside Ann Arbor in the spring of 2017.

"I went to college originally to become a social worker," she said, "and then I ended up quitting college and getting married." Her marriage was hard, perhaps loveless. She went into nursing. It scratched an itch to help others, an urge she would later joke was pathological.

In nursing school, she made a friend, Mary Pat. They studied together, graduated together, and found jobs at the same hospital on the same unit. They were close. Connie shared her marital problems with Mary Pat, and Mary Pat shared hers with Connie. And they would go out together on weekends.

"I would take my youngest daughter over to her house," Connie said. Jake, Mary Pat's husband, "would take care of their two [children] and mine. When I saw it in the paper," Connie said, looking at me directly, her voice elevated, "it was like I couldn't believe it."

Jake had been arrested. He'd stalked and sexually assaulted five young women on a dirt road in a town just a few miles over.

Connie was worried about Mary Pat. "I called her after a couple of days, and I said, 'Mary Pat, you don't have to tell me anything. I'm calling to tell you that I'm in support of *you.*'" If she needed a babysitter or someone to go to the grocery store or someone who would just listen, Connie said, Mary Pat could depend on her.

"Jake is not denying the allegations," Mary Pat said.

Connie told me she felt sorry for Jake. He had been "seduced" by a sixteen-year-old camp counselor when he was ten years old. "He deep-sixed it," Connie said, calling it a "classic case of repression" as she walked me through what she believed to be his psychology. "All of a sudden when he was like thirty, all of this stuff started coming out."

Jake admitted he raped those women, but Connie understood something that she felt was important about his life. His behavior could be explained. Besides, she wanted to support her friend. She went to enlist other people's help. "I talked to my pastor about everything," Connie said. She told her pastor that Jake was guilty, but she said he'd had a hard life and that her friend Mary Pat deserved support. "If he did these things, there is definitely something emotionally wrong with him," she said. In her mind, everyone needed support, even people who committed heinous acts.

Her minister began visiting Jake in prison and counseling Mary Pat. Meanwhile, Connie was following the case. "I started going to trials and pretrials and all this. And we had a meeting of everybody that started going to our church," Connie said. "We wanted to do a 'mission,'" she said, making air quotes. "And so we had this all-day-long affair." After hours of discussion, they found a cause.

"All the people that we wanted to work with—the poor, minorities, people in prison," she said, "we could actually deal with if we started a prison ministry." They connected with a local advocacy group and began visiting local prisons. The pastor counseled incarcerated men at the prisons in Macomb County and Jackson and women at Huron Valley. The parishioners started a knitting class, making slippers with a group of lifers. (Lifers are people who have been convicted of felony offenses and have been sentenced to spend the rest of their lives in prison. In the state of Michigan, more than eight hundred people are currently serving life sentences.)

The worlds of the courts and forensic science, investigations, evidence, and trials—these worlds were so different from the ones she navigated as a nurse. But it was more than a fascination with the process; she began to care, in a much deeper way, about the men she visited each week. Connie had found her calling.

Daniel was a lifer in Connie's knitting class. He was twenty-five years old but had been in prison for a decade, starting his journey at the "gladiator school"—Michigan's infamous juvenile reformatory. His route from the notoriously abusive prison for children, where guards were rumored to "fight preteens like pit bulls," to the Jackson Penitentiary, which was then the largest prison compound in the world, was just as infamous.

Daniel and his friend Adam were just fifteen years old when, high on cheap beer and barbiturates, they broke into the home of a middle-school teacher while she was out. They knew the teacher. Everyone did. Daniel was her neighbor. The plan was to sneak in, sneak out, and sell the goods they stole before anyone was the wiser. But the teacher came home unexpectedly. Walking in the front door, she immediately recognized the boys; she called Daniel and Adam by name. Panicked, Daniel hit the woman in the head five times with the blunt end of a hunting knife, knocking her unconscious, and continued with the robbery. While Daniel filled bags with whatever valuables he could find, his partner, Adam, raped the woman, beating her in the head with a glass bottle and, eventually, a baseball bat. Daniel returned to the room where the woman lay dying. He slit her wrists, Connie would later tell me, "to take her out of her misery." The boys grabbed as much as they could carry and drove away in the teacher's car. They crashed into a pole and were arrested a short time later.

The town was small enough and the murder grisly enough for a white judge and an all-white jury to sentence a scared white teenage boy to life in prison without the possibility of parole. Adam, his accomplice, turned state's evidence, meaning he testified against Daniel in court. He was given a lighter sentence, paroling after just five years. Daniel couldn't afford an attorney, so it didn't matter that he was from the same small town as his jurors, and it didn't matter that he looked like the kind of American child for whom the public seems to marshal empathy. There were editorials in the local newspapers calling for capital punishment, though there hadn't been an execution in the state for nearly one hundred years. The war on crime had not yet begun, but it was 1972; there was a national violent crime wave. The boys had long hair, and the world was afraid of the cultural and sexual revolution that followed in the wake of the civil rights movement. And besides, who could blame the jurors? The evidence was clear. They were dangerous drug addicts in the eyes of the court.

Connie wouldn't meet Daniel for another ten years. He had become a model prisoner, meaning he avoided trouble in the facility, progressing quickly from maximum to medium security. He worked in the law library and became a successful jailhouse lawyer, advocating quietly for the expansion of prisoners' rights and working on his colleagues' cases.

"The lifers realized how intelligent he was," Connie said, "and what a good leader he was. And, you know, *we* certainly noticed."

The church group wrote to Daniel regularly, but Connie didn't sign up. "I'm not a very good pen pal," she said, laughing, but that changed over time. "I wanted to get involved in the reforming of the system," she said. "I wanted to know more about the psyche of the prisoner and the psyche of prisoners' families." Daniel told Connie he understood and that he would try to answer her questions. "But I must tell you that when a person comes to prison for as long as all the lifers are, they have a tendency to push all their emotions down the long dark tunnel," Connie said.

They wrote each other for a year, and their writing became more and more personal. "What was fortuitous for our relationship," Connie said, "is [that] he actually got into therapy." The therapist helped Daniel "bring up all of these memories [that] he had totally put out of his mind," Connie said. And there was a lot to tell.

She told me about Daniel's childhood. He idolized his father, who didn't return his love, and so the boy had attachment issues. She told me that he had been raped, "seduced," by a teenager when he was just a little boy and again by his sister-in-law when he was a teenager living with his brother.

"Daniel was ashamed," she said. "He never felt accepted." Connie told me that it was this series of psychic insults that sent Daniel looking for someone like Adam, his accomplice. And it was Adam who raped the teacher. Daniel said he hadn't stopped him, and he would have to live with this fact for the rest of his life. "He took responsibility for his crimes; he would be the first to call them heinous. He was always honest," Connie said.

"Daniel was fifteen years younger than I was," Connie said, but she admitted being struck by his maturity. "My marriage was a mess, and I knew it. Eventually, I just fell in love with this kid. So we fell in love with each other, and I did get a divorce, and we've just been together ever since then."

It had been three long decades. During that time, Daniel helped file and win a class-action lawsuit against the Michigan Department of Corrections. He was stabbed in what he said was a retaliatory attack. He'd had a heart attack, and he was transferred, without notice, twice. And there was loneliness.

They were not married, so there were no conjugal visits, and Connie had divorced years ago. She dated two other people while she and Daniel were together. One man, she dated for a year; another one, she dated for just a few months. But she was in love with Daniel. Those relationships didn't work. Connie missed physical intimacy, but as she got older, she said, "that was less of a problem."

It was important for Connie to maintain a sense of independence from Daniel and the prison. She had heard too many horror stories. "Those women gained two and three hundred pounds eating all that commissary food. They ruined their finances," she said. She put limits on their phone calls—they spoke just once a week for personal matters and twice a week for prison litigation. And she put limits on her trips, visiting just twice a year toward what turned out to be the end of Daniel's incarceration. But despite the challenges and the limitations, their relationship endured. After a change in state sentencing law and no fewer than four parole board denials, Daniel was released on probation, and Connie welcomed him into her home.

He was a "neat freak, and I was a slouch," Connie said. She worked hard to prepare her home, clearing out a room for his paperwork. She knew he would need a job and an ID and thought he might want to get a library card. The church sent an e-mail blast to the congregation and put a flyer in the church bulletin about his upcoming release. But not everyone was welcoming.

Connie had been friends with one couple since the 1970s. They stopped returning her phone calls when they got word of Daniel's pending release. Her son was worried for her safety but said he wanted her to be happy. He still called her about once a month, and he visited as often as he could. Her daughter's response was much different.

"When I told my daughter he was coming home, she told me that she wouldn't have anything to do with me," Connie said, her voice trembling. "She won't let me visit [her]. She won't visit me." Connie was now crying. "She won't let me see my grandson," she said.

I was twenty-eight when I met my father. I'd heard his voice maybe once before, but we hadn't had a conversation. I learned who he was only through an acquaintance's chance encounter with someone else. I got a phone call from a woman who went to my church and who was about my age. The woman, who was a hairdresser, said she'd met a man who looked just like me. He was working at a barbershop not far from her home. She'd gotten his number. He must have thought she was flirting. I called the number. The man turned out to be my brother Stephen, the eldest of my father's five sons.

I didn't know how I felt when I heard Stephen's voice on the other end of the line. He asked about my side of the family and gave me my father's phone number. I'm not quite sure why I called. I wasn't particularly curious about my father. It didn't matter much to me what he looked like. I never thought about the life he might have made for himself or why he wasn't around. This is also what separation does. My grandmother raised me. I hadn't experienced my father's absence as a loss. But I mustered up enough curiosity to make the call. By the next week, I was in a car riding shotgun with Janice on our way to his home.

The drive felt long. I didn't understand the west side of my own city. I'd lived with my brother for a few months in the very same neighborhood, but that was years before. Nothing felt familiar. I don't remember much of what I was thinking, but I do remember I was nervous and felt somehow guilty for feeling that way. Perhaps I had some distant sense of obligation. I had a family of my own, and there was something that told me I should meet this man whose voice I couldn't remember.

We pulled up to a large, white frame house not far from the Austin neighborhood where, years later, I would do some of the research for this book. Two of his boys, my brothers whom I had not met, sat out front. Inside, I met my sister, whom I vaguely remembered. And my stepmother had a kind face. She was warm.

Janice and I had been together for three years. I was so glad she'd come with me. We took a seat on the couch, making small talk with my stepmother as I waited for a man I had never seen. I wasn't sure what to expect.

He wore overalls, or maybe jeans. (This memory seems so long ago.) And he seemed big, but not fat and not particularly tall—maybe five eleven. He was bald and was about my complexion. I don't remember whether or not he had facial hair. I was lanky then, six two, maybe a hundred and ninety pounds, and still growing into a man's body. But it was clear to me, as it was to Janice, that this man was my father.

We did not shake hands at first or hug. I can't remember what pleasantries were exchanged. I mostly watched him watch me for what felt like quite a while. Then, as I do with my youngest son now, who at fourteen is already six one, he moved toward me quickly, put his hands on my shoulders, and spun me around. He seemed to smile, watching me twirl in front of him. Was this pride? I had been to college but had not yet finished. I had a job, was about to be married, and had children of my own. He directed me outside, where we walked and talked in what I remember to be an open field. And I remember it was sunny, maybe spring. And while I still can't remember what his voice sounded like, I remember what he said.

"Man, I'm sorry for all that shit," he told me, referring to the group homes and the poverty and the experiences he might never understand. Some things are best left unspoken. I didn't say much at all. I don't typically talk much around people I don't know. But I learned a lot that day. He had just gotten out of prison, again. By then he had done twenty years off and on, earning the title "Big Soul," a retired member of the Black Souls street gang. He said that he'd had no idea that we were in foster care or that my grandmother died and that I had been on my own for over a decade. He did know that two of my brothers had done time because he thought at one point he'd done time with Jeremiah. He apologized for mistreating him, saying he was ashamed. Something about Jeremiah acting soft and my father pretending not to know him. "I didn't stick up for him," he said.

I was angry now, which I wasn't before. Janice says I looked like I was standing over him, my chest out. I wanted to ask him, *What did my brother need sticking up for? Did they beat him? Did they rape him?* or say something like, *The one time you could have done something!* But I couldn't form words. A moment passed. I looked down and moved on, mumbling something like, "It's cool," and after my father made some promises I didn't expect him to keep, Janice and I left.

We lost touch shortly thereafter. I wasn't emotionally invested enough to pursue him. I'm not sure he wanted to be pursued. But I did call my brother back. His phone was disconnected. I tried to call the barbershop where he worked. A man answered;

the owner, I suppose. When I asked for him, he said he no longer worked there. "Your brother is in jail," he said.

Sixteen years passed before I heard from Stephen again. It was April 5, 2020. My state, like many others, was under a shelter-in-place order due to the COVID-19 pandemic. My stepmother, the one with the kind face, had sent a request to Jeremiah through his Facebook account. My father had died in August, and she was hoping to reach his sons.

I did not know my father, but his incarceration had a profound effect on my life. I don't believe that we would have been close had he never gone to prison, but I know my brothers followed him there. I don't know what his presence might have meant for his boys, but I know that my grandmother raised us alone. This is the afterlife of mass incarceration. It is the separation from the people you care for or have been told you should. And this is family separation, even if others can't or refuse to see it. Even if you've moved on with your life, and even if you didn't experience it as a loss, and even if, or perhaps especially if, it takes many years to notice the effects.

The people I met lost children, and they lost them for so many reasons: A missed appointment. A social worker came by the house, and the landlord hadn't exterminated in months. Someone had an addiction. Someone had a gun. Someone had one too many convictions. Someone was in jail too long. Some of this was justified; some of it was harder to explain. In the end, their children were taken, and there was nothing they could do.

The grandmothers lost children, too, in some of the same ways they lost their lovers. Some were buried, and some were buried but still alive, incarcerated for so many years. The fathers and mothers lost friends, even friends they'd known forever, because their loved ones did something wrong or because they were sent away. The children lost their parents. Some of the parents were made to leave. Some were taken away. In the end their families were separated, and their lives would never be the same.

In a supervised society, the prison and the jail and the law frays our closest ties. It pulls our families apart. It did this to Connie and Jimmy, and it did it to me, and it does this to millions of families. And while this happens in so many different ways and to so many different kinds of people, once the law gets between families, they are never quite the same.

It was December of 2015. We were wrapping up the first year of data collection on the Detroit Reentry Study. It was time for a party. We met at my house in Ann Arbor. It wasn't a terribly big house, but we had a fireplace and a dining room, and it was walking distance to Jonathan's school and the university.

My team had grown quite a bit by then. Ronald and Yvette were still with me, and I'd hired Daniel on Ronald's recommendation. While living in different penitentiaries, they had worked together on a successful class-action lawsuit against the MDOC, and Ronald's endorsement went a long way with me.

After a conversation with Daniel's parole officer, I understood what he was allowed to do. He could not conduct interviews for the project, because he could not, under any circumstances, "affiliate with known offenders." He could not do face-to-face interviews with their family members, whether they had criminal records or not, because he could not travel outside of the city without his parole officer's approval and most of the people in my study lived in and around Detroit. With very little left that Daniel could do, I put him on transcription duty. His job was to transcribe interviews, typing them out so that I could analyze the data.

Janice and Jonathan and I cohosted the party. Ronald came. T'Kara, my new research assistant, brought her mother, who told us stories about local politics and the world of local politicians. Adriana and Kyle were still on the team. They came to the party with their friend Alekos, who volunteered occasionally. My students Nicole and Emily were there. So was Finn, my PhD student and right hand. Connie had dropped off Daniel, but for some reason she didn't come in. I learned later that she'd waited for him outside, thinking the party was just for team members. She, of course, would have been welcome, and I regretted not telling her that directly.

The house was full. Everyone brought a dish, and just about everyone brought a friend. I made guacamole. Finn made some fantastic vegan dessert. Nicole brought chips. Emily brought cookies. Ronald brought fried chicken in a beautiful gift box that still sits in my living room. Daniel brought a dish he called "Daniel's famous cheesy potatoes." Yvette brought her voice. After a few jokes and the trademark flutter of her eyelashes, Yvette sang a full-throated version of "Bridge Over Troubled Water."

We laughed and played board games and ate and drank. While Yvette sang, Daniel sat in the corner grinning, watching us all watch her as she sauntered across the dining-room floor. When it was over, Daniel was smiling about something, shaking his head and wiping away a tear. He made eye contact with me, looked at Yvette, and said quietly, almost to himself, "Yvette crazy as a beetle bug."

I don't know if Daniel had been to a party since he'd gotten out of prison or what it had been like to spend so long in a cage. I don't know how long it had been since he'd had a panic attack in a grocery store. Connie told me he got anxious whenever they were in large spaces. And I don't know what it had been like to be separated, in the way he was, from the people he loved the most. I do know, in that moment, Daniel was happy.

CHAPTER 6

CHAINS AND CORPSES

Connie's mother died when she was thirty. She grieved privately. Quietly. But she didn't grieve alone. "I did have friends," she said. "People I could actually talk to." It took about a year, but she made peace with the loss. It felt somehow natural.

Connie's father died when he was ninety. She was middle-aged by then. He was "very sick" and much harder to get along with, she said. "I got to the point where I didn't like my dad." He was gone, but this, too, felt natural.

"What happened when Daniel died?" I asked, treading lightly. Connie had told me more than once that she'd felt relieved after our conversations. Connie liked to talk about Daniel. She liked to think about their happiest times—some funny thing he said or did or how they found a way to make it through the impossible circumstances of his life sentence. She liked to say his name, to remember his accomplishments. But our last conversation was hard.

They were together thirty-one years but unable to touch each other. After fighting for and losing dozens of appeals and being denied parole at so many hearings, Daniel was released. Not long after, Daniel, a man who had spent three-quarters of his life incarcerated, was dead. He had been free just eighteen months.

Connie and I sat across from each other at the same Greek diner where we met when he was alive. "All of a sudden, he was gone," she said. "For twenty-eight years I talked to him on the phone." She dabbed the corners of her eyes with a napkin. They'd talked three times a week for nearly three decades and every day since he was released. They'd talk each night before he went to sleep, and they'd talk more when he woke each morning. He would wake her at 5:00 a.m., his body still on the prison's schedule. She would accompany him to the parole office or to church or to doctors' appointments. She missed his words, and she missed his voice.

"I got cards. I got cards from him," she repeated, her voice trailing off but still matter-of-fact. "Now there's no communication at all."

When Daniel was finally paroled, he made lists of things to do around the house—his way of making a home in Connie's house. She wanted him to do that, to feel useful. But soon there were no more to-do lists. A very good oncologist at one of the nation's best hospitals told them that Daniel had pancreatic cancer. It had already spread. There was no time even for a second opinion. Daniel was dead within two weeks.

Connie and I met many times in the year after Daniel passed. She told me so many stories. She'd met hundreds of men with life sentences. But Daniel stood out even when he was young—just twenty-seven when they met.

Connie watched as he grew into his body and new disposition. He was tall. She found him handsome then, and he was still handsome to her so many years later, with his thick if mostly gray beard and almost full head of hair. His hairline had receded just a few inches since his arrest as a high fifteen-year-old. The "clear blue eyes" a social worker at Catholic Charities described in a newsletter in a piece about his short and eventful life seemed placid, calmer than they were in his mug shot that graced the front page of the town's paper of record. He was lanky in the picture, wearing oversize prison blues, and had the kind of dark, shoulder-length hair that somehow looked wet. Three decades later he was beefy, looking all of his fifty-seven years.

Daniel was gentle, or at least he carried himself that way, but not weak. His pastor said he was a "beloved soul" at his parole hearing and called him a "blessed member of the beloved community" in the church bulletin preparing the congregation to welcome him home. He would echo these sentiments at Daniel's memorial service just two years later.

At Daniel's final parole hearing, the director of a prisoners' rights organization testified on his behalf, something she said she had not done for anyone else in her eleven years working with lifers. "He is a model prisoner, and he mentors people," she said. And even though Daniel had done "great harm, I believe in redemption. And I also believe in deep human transformation."

Four decades is a long time. So many things had changed. The public had once called for his execution. He was a "notorious murderer" and a "depraved individual" in their eyes. He took responsibility for his crimes, and now a different community vouched for his character. In prison, he sought counseling. He volunteered on the hospice ward, caring for men who would certainly die in cages. And he mentored younger prisoners. One of his mentees, a former juvenile lifer who had been released a decade before, called him a role model. "You don't hear that a lot coming out of the big house," he said.

An attorney and legal scholar testified on his behalf. Daniel's humor "came through in his letters," the professor said. He was "one of the few people I've worked with who I wanted to get to know." A half a dozen people wrote letters of support that were read at Daniel's parole hearing. This was because, according to those who knew him, Daniel had changed his life.

And the laws had changed too. The Supreme Court of the United States ruled that it was unconstitutional to sentence a minor to life without the possibility of parole.[1] Thousands of men were resentenced, and thousands more became eligible for parole.

Daniel was special to Connie and precious to the community who knew him best. He made friends and had passions and hobbies, and he loved and was loved by others. But if statistics are to be believed, his death was unremarkable.

The hard truth is that prisons kill people like Daniel every day. The people the government has incarcerated, cut off from their family and friends, are twice as likely to die from any cause than anyone else in this country. They are three times as likely to die from heart disease and four times as likely to die from cancer. They are most likely to die within the first few years of their release.[2] If you consider death by drug overdose, incarcerated people are 129 times more likely to die within just two weeks of their release than members of the general population.[3]

In prison, Daniel had had a heart attack, and he was stabbed.

He had a history of drug addiction, though he hadn't been high in decades. He lived with men who contracted tuberculosis and hepatitis and HIV and all of the various illnesses that circulate in places like prisons.[4] The scholarship is clear: prisons make people sick, exacerbating preexisting health conditions.[5]

Studying the mortality of people released from prisons in New York State, the sociologist Evelyn Patterson found that for every year someone spends in prison, he loses two full years of life expectancy.[6] There's nothing special about prisons in New York. They look the same and smell the same and have people there for the same reasons as prisons in Michigan or anywhere else in the country. And the health care in prison is poor—when health care is provided at all. This means the people who live in Attica are exposed to the same diseases as people doing time in Jackson, Michigan. Incarcerated people are more likely than anyone else to contract most illnesses and communicable diseases.[7] Daniel had preexisting conditions, and he had been in prison for forty years. If the scholarship is right, no matter how special he was to Connie, he didn't stand much of a chance.

Daniel didn't have the problems most of the men I followed had when he was released. Connie provided a place to live and sleep. He had a job waiting at an advocacy group not far from where he lived. He enrolled in classes at the community college and did well. His parole officer was on his side, even approving a trip to attend a conference on criminal justice reform in Florida. But even with all that support, Daniel died just the same.

Like everyone else who's been released from prison, he didn't always have it easy. Daniel had trouble completing tasks. He didn't turn in his time cards and eventually stopped coming to work with my team altogether. (This felt strange, since he'd seemed to like hanging around the lab and had *Research Assistant at the University of Michigan* listed on his Facebook page.) And he couldn't go into a Costco without having a panic attack. The warehouse was just too big. With his conditions of release, there were many other places he could not go.

He was painting a house for extra cash when he fell off a ladder. This wasn't all that surprising. He knew from his heart attack and two long hospital stays in prison that he had poor circulation, and he assumed that was the problem. He went to the hospital that afternoon. The doctors ran tests and referred him to an oncologist, who ran more. He was diagnosed with metastatic pancreatic cancer. He had just weeks to live.

Daniel spent his last days with the friends who'd welcomed him home. And there were pleasant surprises. After cutting off Connie and refusing to see her for a full year and a half, Connie's daughter visited her mother in Daniel's hospital room. She snuck in and out but reassured Connie that she would see her grandchild again. Daniel's friends from church visited in shifts, bringing food, though he could no longer eat, and flowers and balloons, which he might not have noticed.

Daniel was heavily medicated for his pain. He had trouble breathing but panicked when the nurse tried to put an oxygen mask over his face. He refused life support. When he had just a few hours left to live, his pastor offered a prayer. A friend massaged his feet. And the group of people who loved him, the same people who'd welcomed him home, held hands around his hospital bed, singing hymns as he slipped away.

Ronald had introduced me to Daniel. They had done time, briefly, in the same prison, but it was their work that brought them together. Daniel was the president of the prison's library association and Ronald was one of the best jailhouse lawyers in the state. They worked on class-action lawsuits against the Michigan Department of Corrections and on a few smaller cases that helped set several men free. But Ronald wouldn't have been free, and I would never have met him, if it weren't for a bizarre twist of fate.

In 2013, when I arrived at the University of Michigan, Ronald was one of the two hundred thousand men in the United States serving a life sentence. Nearly forty thousand of them were on what advocates and policy makers called "virtual life"—a sentence of fifty years or more.[8] While he was one of few jailhouse lawyers who exonerated himself, it was an act of violence as much as any legal maneuver that set Ronald free.

"I always worked on [my case]," he said, explaining how he became a jailhouse lawyer. It was 1986, just a year since his wrongful conviction. He'd paid thirty thousand dollars to the city's top attorneys but was still serving fifty years in prison. "I told Mom, 'Don't spend not one more dime on this case,'" he said, and he took matters into his own hands "as a simple problem of economics." He filed his first appeal as a pro se attorney later that same year.

The reasons for the appeal were straightforward. Ronald was not at the scene of the crime. The officer who was shot had said so, but the police department denied the defense access to the officer's sworn statement that would have exonerated Ronald at trial. The judge had a contentious relationship with Ronald's attorney and his father, all reasons he should have recused himself. Even if Ronald's trial had been fair, the sentence was excessive. Fifty years for assault was far beyond the state's guidelines. In legal parlance, he was requesting an appeal based on prosecutorial and sentencing misconduct. The court denied his motion in less than a year. Ronald took his appeal to the state supreme court.

"I had like six issues," he said. "They agreed on everything but sentencing." The court found that while parts, perhaps even most, of his appeal had merit, they would "view [the case] in a light most favorable to the prosecution. I'm like, *The fuck you mean?*" Ronald said. "If I'm right, how are you going to view this in the light most favorable to the prosecution?" Ronald was left to serve the balance of a fifty-year sentence. It didn't matter that his case had merit. If the courts had their way, he wouldn't leave prison alive. The blow was "crushing."

Now it was 1989. He had been in prison for nearly four years, but Ronald was an optimist. "I said, 'Wait a minute. They really looked at the appeal. They agreed with my issues, but they just not giving me no relief.'" The very first case he had ever filed made its way to the state's supreme court. He knew he was onto something.

Ronald began spending more time in the law library, learning the jargon and the form and what it meant to mount a legal defense. He eventually enrolled in a paralegal studies program through the local community college and began working on other people's cases. After three years, he applied for and secured a position with Prison Legal Services, a national prisoners' rights–advocacy organization with a branch in the Jackson penitentiary.[9]

Ronald began filing motions for incarcerated people throughout the state. He helped people at Jackson represent themselves in cases where corrections officers issued them "bogus tickets." These weren't easy cases to win, because few people took the claims of incarcerated people seriously. Worse, the legal channels they had access to meant that judges and wardens were being asked to rule against their colleagues. Ronald won enough cases to establish a reputation as a skilled jailhouse lawyer. His reputation grew when he joined one of the largest class-action lawsuits against the Michigan Department of Corrections.

There was an incident in Jackson over the Christmas holiday the year before he was hired at Prison Legal Services. "Jackson was the largest prison in the world back then. It was the mothership," he said. The director of the Department of Corrections was touring administration segregation, and the people held in solitary confinement "dressed him out."

Ronald explained. "*Dressing out* means they put piss and shit together and slung it at him. They called it 'gunning him down,'" he said. "They gunned him down, all right! They put shit and piss in a cup and throw it on you. That was their recreation, really." He laughed. "They dressed his ass out!" he said.

Ronald said the director retaliated. He ordered the guards to empty all the cells in administrative segregation, throw the men's belongings on the floor of the wing, and then throw all of it in the garbage.

"This is now a standard practice, but back then," Ronald said, "we could have our clothing and property in the hole with us. You know, your TV, everything. They took all their property," he said. "They didn't even pack it up and just threw it—TV, everything—on the deck." Ronald told me that there was a three-foot-high, hundred-yard-long pile of property.

"A porter was ordered to shovel it to the sides. Nothing was spared, not even their court documents," Ronald said. "But because the prison, by law, had to provide access to those documents, they put them all in a central location in another unit." Prisoners now had to ask permission to access their paperwork.

This meant a guard had to take them to the new location each time they wanted to review their cases.

Paperwork would come up missing. "You know how it is. Once your shit is out of sight, it's gone," Ronald said.

This new arrangement made it nearly impossible for prisoners to access court documents, which meant it limited their access to the courts. "Our response was 'Hell no.' We put together a motion to file an injunction against an implementation of that policy. And it ended up becoming the largest class-action suit in Michigan history—a case called *CANE vs. MDOC*," he told me.

The case started off as a lawsuit based on a violation of property rights, but the scope of the case expanded. More plaintiffs joined. "It ballooned over the years into everything. Access to court. Medical access. It dealt with the telephone system," Ronald said.

Ronald got to be a named plaintiff. The case went on for eighteen years, but they won—six jailhouse lawyers with an under-resourced library and manual typewriters against the Michigan Department of Corrections, which had the full resources of the state.

Ronald, his reputation solidified, continued to work on his appeal. Despite these victories and the work that helped set many of his colleagues free, his own appeals kept getting denied.

Now it was 1997. Ronald was in the hole "for one reason or another." He said his angry years were behind him, and he hadn't been in a fight, but "retaliation wasn't beyond the MDOC." He had been to the hole more often than he could remember, so this time wouldn't have been remarkable had he not gotten a letter from Laila Stewart, a friend he hadn't seen in over a decade. She was the woman he'd spent time with when he was a tool-and-die maker at GM.

"I got her out of an abusive relationship [back then]," he said.

"Wait, what? How?" I asked. I knew Ronald to be a remarkable man. We had grown close over the years, sharing meals and drinks and the details of our lives. He had a million and one stories. I certainly hadn't heard them all, but this was a genuine surprise. "You can't just drop that and move on," I said. "How did this come up? She just told you? At work? Were you on a date?" I asked.

"She was cute, but not my type," Ronald said. "I'd run into her at lunchtime. We ended up sitting at one of the little bars around the factory where we cashed checks, you know, talking, eating." He told me he treated her like a sister. "You can tell when a woman is being abused. You can see that shit," he said.

Ronald was on the street then. He was, to use his own word, *wild*, but Ronald was consistent. "I hated bullies," he told me on more than one occasion.

After about a year of Laila coming to work with bruises and about a year of lunchtime discussions, Ronald followed her as she drove home one day, telling her he just wanted to make sure she got back safely. He walked in the front door and beat her husband repeatedly with the butt of his handgun. Laila moved out that night. Her husband never put his hands on her again.

It had been twelve years since Laila and Ronald had spoken. "Out of the blue!" Ronald said, smiling. At first, he didn't recognize her name. But she hadn't forgotten him. "I'm like, *Oh, damn. It's her*," he said.

Laila wrote that she was grateful for all that he had done,

that the judge who'd sentenced him had finally retired, and that she knew the new judge appointed to his case. She told him to be sure to let her know if she could help in any way. Ronald wrote back and asked Laila to see if she could get her hands on the officer's sworn statement, and he started working on his appeal again.

"During this time, I had been trying to get [this] evidence. They were saying it no longer existed. It had been destroyed in a flood in the basement. They were lying," Ronald said. "I had been fighting for this document for at least six years," he said. "She sent it within thirty days." After great effort and a decades-long legal battle, a federal judge ruled in his favor. Ronald's sentence was reversed, and he would soon be on his way home.

It's easy to focus on the victories. Some might say Ronald found purpose in his misery. Others might say he became an advocate and was vindicated because his sentence was overturned. But histories told in this way, ones that move from one event to another, hide what happens in between. Ronald, and all of his incarcerated colleagues, experienced a kind of death, one that, while different, is no less final and no less violent than the physical death Daniel endured. To be cut off from family for years—to be too far away for regular visits. To watch so many of your closest relationships fray and then dissolve. To see your children grow up through family pictures. To be hungry for days at a time because the food you eat is never enough, and there is nothing that you can do about it. To be isolated. To be in a place with thousands of men but to somehow feel alone. This is what it means to be socially dead.[10] To be subjected to violence and humiliation. To be shackled, one to another, during daily routines, your ability to work and provide for yourself taken away. To move in a coffle down long hallways like animals for "feeding time" or "meds." To be marched away from your lover and your children every time visitation ends. To be cut off from the human community or to have no community at all—at least, no community that might be valued by members of a free society. To have few benefits and fewer protections. To become a figure who walks the yard or haunts the neighborhood so many years after your release, unable to find work or secure a home, unable to participate in the politics of the city in the ways most people find meaningful. To have no say over where or how often you connect with people you love. To be made a "nonperson," in the words of sociologist Orlando Patterson, who gave us the term *social death*.[11] To be at once a part of the wider world, through labor or punishment or as a social problem of national concern, yet to be kept just outside of it.

"The first five years I was angry," Ronald said. "You didn't want to be around me, 'cause, like I said, I was in there for something I didn't do, and I was aggressive anyway." He got into fights. He went to the hole, often. He and his wife divorced; it wasn't just because of his incarceration, but who could have blamed her if it was? She was in a relationship with a man she could not touch and who would likely die in a cage. She knew his story, but after a while, it must have been hard to believe. And Ronald was a proud man. A tradesman from Flint, Michigan, when it was booming. A DJ and a dope dealer in his wild days, he was a person with flaws, like all of us, but he had not shot that cop.

In a speech he gave in a packed auditorium three years after his release, Ronald reflected on his time in prison. "I don't know what to say about it. It's something you wouldn't wish on your worst enemy," he said. "I wasn't no Boy Scout," he joked, before explaining in a much more serious tone, "It's karma. I got what my hand called for."

The stories I heard from formerly incarcerated men and women were almost always variations on that same theme: "I didn't do what they said I did, but I did many bad things and didn't get caught." But even if they internalized their guilt, claiming they in some ways had earned their place in prison, this was the kind of death they wouldn't wish on anyone, not even their worst enemy, as Ronald had put it.

"It's not the physical danger," he said. "It's the mental drain, the spiritual drain, and psychological drain that it puts on a person. The prison was designed to debilitate. To dehumanize you. You're no longer an individual," he told me. "You're a number, and you are a part of a bunch of other numbers," he said. "I spent twenty-seven years just battling the effects of trying to be made nominal. I hate being marginalized. I want to be important."

But this is how social death works: You become a nonentity, a nonperson, someone whose existence is superfluous. You're invisible, hidden in some cage just outside the city or within it or perhaps hundreds of miles from home. The effects are all the same. You are a number among a bunch of numbers. You might have a family. You might do great things in your community. You might help others, regularly. You might be a person of great faith. But you are dead to the world that matters to you most. The prison robs you of your importance.

*   *   *

Ronald credits his faith and his legal work with saving his life. It slowed him down, he said, giving him a new sense of purpose. He became active in the Moorish Science Temple of America, eventually becoming a minister, and he got serious about legal advocacy, taking on other people's cases. He admits this took time.

"You do incarceration in stages," he said. "The first [years] were my angry years." Years where he said he "fought and fought." But in his fifth year he had an epiphany.

"Back in 1990," he said to the crowd that had gathered to hear him, "I was reading a book called *They Came Before Columbus*. And in it there's a quote: 'I am a vital force among forces, and I refuse to be a victim of a prearranged destiny.' As I sat in prison, I said to myself, 'I refuse to be a victim of *this* prearranged destiny.'" Another book moved Ronald: *Visions for Black Men*, by Na'im Akbar, which he credits with teaching him to take responsibility for himself and the betterment of others. "I became an advocate," he said. "When I stopped being angry, I looked up."

Prison, to Ronald, was "depraved, unfair, a place where so many good people that made bad choices weren't going to be given a second chance. Who doesn't want a second chance?" he asked. "Who doesn't deserve it?"

Ronald was innocent. He found a way to make peace with himself through his work, but life certainly wasn't easy. Even after counseling dozens of men, helping them to cope with the social death of the prison, he still couldn't touch his lover or see his children when he wanted to or send money home with enough regularity to provide for his family in ways that he saw fit. After fighting and winning one of the largest class-action lawsuits in the history of his state and after working to free half a dozen men, he still sat there in a cage. And he would need every bit of his newfound faith. It would be tested.

It was Father's Day of 2001. Ronald had been incarcerated for sixteen years. His son, Ronald III, was coming to visit.

"He said, 'Dad, I'ma go and get the girls, and we'll come by later,'" Ronald told me. This was his only son and the child who bore his name. He also carried the name of Ronald's father, the man Ronald had buried so many years before.

"I wait and I wait. I wait," he said, his voice starting to trail off. "Afternoon draws on, four or five o'clock. It's kind of strange they hadn't shown up yet. I started calling around."

He called his family and his son's family. "Couldn't catch anybody," Ronald said. He said he called his ex-mother-in-law "on a whim a few hours later." She asked if he'd heard what had happened. Ronald said no, he hadn't been able to reach anyone.

"Little Ronald was shot and killed," she said.

Ronald has told this story many times. I've heard him recount it in packed halls and full classrooms and as he sat in my home on my couch and as we broke bread and shared a fifth of Hennessy Black or Rémy VSOP or whatever we'd picked up to catch up on old times and celebrate our recent accomplishments. Each time his voice breaks. He has to at least pause. Sometimes he takes a breath. Sometimes he looks up. Sometimes he wipes away a tear. Sometimes he waits to regain his composure. Sometimes he soldiers on, but "it hits me different each time," he said. It's a memory, but it's also a feeling, a kind of knowledge from his body. "My only son," Ronald said. "He was shot and killed by a fourteen-year-old juvenile. On Father's Day 2001."

He tries to explain how this feels when he does his advocacy work, but how can he relay what it's like to lose a son and to lose him in that way? "You cannot begin to understand the magnitude of the hurt, the anger, the anxiety," he says. "The whole range of emotions. The rage that you feel." He appeals to the parents in the room. "Any of you can imagine losing a child," he'll say, "but imagine losing a child under the conditions of incarceration. You blame yourself for not being able to get there. Not being able to be there," he says. "Feeling like it's part of your responsibility. Your problem. Your fault," he says, now raising his voice, "that it happened because you weren't there."

Ronald lost his only son after spending sixteen years sitting in a cage on a wrongful conviction. He would sit there eleven more years before his eventual release. And his son was killed by a child—some fourteen-year-old with a gun who'd ruined his own life and the life of his entire family.

"I'm still in a rut," Connie said. "For twenty-eight years I thought of our life together. After I retired and he got home, my life was with him. And I was just so angry."

When Connie's mother died, she said she "felt her" from time to time. "My mother came to me," she said, her voice no sturdier than before we'd begun our conversation. "I had hoped that I would feel Daniel when he visited. He didn't," she said. It was all so final.

"I had had this one therapy session. I was so disappointed he hadn't visited me." The very next day, Connie said, "I was walking out of a Speedway gas station. [There was] a shiny brand-new penny." She was laughing now, hard, almost cackling, in the restaurant where we usually met in the year after her lover died. Daniel had called Connie his "Moneypenny," after the secretary from the James Bond flicks, the one that Bond would flirt with after he got out of one spy jam or another. "I never go in gas stations," she said. "I just pay at the pump. Everything was different about this. And there was this penny." Connie said she felt Daniel for the first time in nearly a year, and it was just what she needed.

On April 10, 2012, Ronald Simpson-Bey walked out of prison a free man. The brothers he'd spent so much time with cheered as a guard escorted him off the wing with his property. His mother met him at the gate with two of his sisters.

One night, five years after my dear friend Ronald was released, after we ate a good meal and drank too much and laughed together way too late into the night, he put his drink down and stopped laughing.

"The things I have now, I used to pray for when I was in prison," he said. "I wouldn't change how things ended up. But, man, shit." Ronald picked up his glass of Rémy and took a sip. "I sure as hell would change what I had to do to get here."

– III –

SALVATION

CHAPTER 7

TREATMENT

Zo had been free for just thirty-two days—that is, he was almost free. After serving nine years across four maximum-security prisons, he was released on five years' probation. Zo left the prison with bus fare, twenty-five dollars in gate money, and a voucher from the Illinois Department of Corrections good for thirty days' rent. He was given the address of a halfway house in Auburn Gresham, a neighborhood on Chicago's South Side, and told to report to the parole office on Eightieth and Cottage Grove Avenue. He wasn't sure he should go.

Zo was from K-Town. He hadn't been there in years, but the South Side was a different country. It was 2001. The Twin Towers had not yet fallen in New York City. There were no gang registries to speak of; at least, there were none that the public knew about. The murder rate had dropped by a third during the nine years Zo was downstate, but there was no evidence that he could see that things were any safer in the neighborhoods where he would travel.[1] He felt on edge and, to him, so did the neighborhood. Besides, the crime decline didn't keep police from stopping young black men, and it didn't mean that it was any better on the blocks where most murders happened.[2] The halfway house was in a foreign land. Zo was nervous, but he had to go. It was a condition of his release.

Zo knocked on the door wearing khakis, his prison-issued oversize button-down white short-sleeved shirt, and black plastic boots, the kind that gave most men blisters. The man who opened the door took Zo's paperwork to another office, showed him his rack, and went over the rules: You can smoke outside. No drugs. No drinking. No guests. No pets. You must sign up for food stamps right away and turn over your Link Card (a debit card for food stamps issued by the State of Illinois) to the house manager; he would use it to buy groceries for Zo and the fifteen other men who lived in the house.[3] No food in the rooms. Get your own toiletries. Check in with your parole officer once a week. Stay sober. You have to leave each morning and piss in a cup when you return at night. Curfew is eight p.m. You have to get a job. The IDOC covered the first thirty days' rent, but it was four hundred dollars a month after that. Rent must be paid on time. This was a halfway house (the kind of place my grandmother would have called a flophouse). There were no five-day eviction notices. You could be put out any day of the week for any reason.

The thirty days went by fast. Zo had lost most of his family connections. His mother was dead. His younger brothers were in no position to help. He had never been in a romantic relationship, at least nothing long term, so there was no warm bed to sleep in at night. He hadn't been called for a job interview. Even if he found a job, he wouldn't get a paycheck for at least two weeks, and it probably still wouldn't cover the rent. Where would he get the four hundred dollars?

Zo faced eviction. He had been to many different kinds of prisons—to juvie, to jail, to penitentiaries downstate—but he had never been homeless. Worse still, homelessness was a violation of parole.

When Zo was in prison, outreach workers had held an information session about Emmaus Road, a prisoner-reentry program in North Lawndale, not far from where he grew up. They offered six months of free housing, and they helped men get jobs. You could earn a high-school diploma there instead of the GED you could get in the prison. And men learned culinary arts and got training for something called "green jobs." He put in an application to parole to Emmaus, but they had a long waiting list. The halfway house in Auburn Gresham was the only place that had room.

Zo started walking around the neighborhood to clear his mind. He knew he needed to check in with his parole officer, but what would Zo say? That he would soon be homeless? He got to the bus stop on Seventy-Ninth and Cottage Grove, just a block from the parole office, when he saw two dope boys "talking shit, flashing they little money." The experience was surreal.

"I didn't know what to do," Zo said, but he did. He had a routine; the muscle memory was still there. "I thought I could choke one out. It was crazy. Literally, man, it was crazy," he said. Zo didn't have a weapon, and if things went wrong, he would be sent right back to prison. "I cried," he said. "I cried, man. Right there." Right in front of the two boys he had been planning to rob at that bus stop on that busy intersection.

"That was it," he told me. "I came down to Emmaus that day to beg them to let me stay."

The trip to Emmaus was a long one. Zo had to take the bus at Cottage Grove Avenue to the Seventy-Ninth Street El, the train station on the Dan Ryan Expressway. The Red Line extends from the northernmost edge of the city to Ninety-Fifth Street on the South Side, leaving about a third of the city's mostly black South Side residents without a railway. City limits stretch to 138th Street.

High-school teachers and college instructors have students ride the train to demonstrate residential segregation in Chicago. Students board at the Red Line's northernmost stop, Howard Street, and ride to Ninety-Fifth Street, the last stop on the South Side. As they head into the city, students notice that, with few exceptions, the train passengers are white. The train runs on time. The tracks are well maintained, and so are the neighborhoods surrounding the stations, with bistros, pubs, universities, and, at one point, a city zoo. It takes forty-five minutes for an appreciable number of black Chicagoans to board. This typically starts downtown. By Twelfth Street, about a mile into the South Side, the passengers, with few exceptions, are now black. Chinatown is off Twenty-Second and State Streets, walking distance from the El. After Thirty-Fifth Street, the stop for the famous Comiskey Park, now Guaranteed Rate Field, where the Chicago White Sox play, the train runs much more slowly. It's less well maintained. The neighborhoods look different, with fewer businesses and almost no grocery stores. There certainly isn't a city zoo. This continues for the remaining six miles along the Dan Ryan, the east/west dividing line for Chicago's South Side.

Zo had the opposite experience. He got on the train with mostly black passengers at the Seventy-Ninth Street station and made his way north. By the time he got to the Madison

Avenue and State Street stop, which was the first time he had ever been downtown, he was confronted with a much more diverse but mostly white city. He waited twenty minutes for the Madison Street bus that took passengers to the West Side. His stop was in North Lawndale, a neighborhood that was rapidly gentrifying.

To Zo, North Lawndale was unrecognizable. There was still a quarter-mile stretch of vacant lots just outside the new condo developments where Harpo Studios used to be an anchor, signaling to speculators that the former meatpacking district was ripe for cafés and gastropubs. Those speculators had gone farther west. The United Center used to be the outer limits of the trendy district, tourists in taxis shuttling past the blight to get to Chicago Bulls games. Now, half-complete developments pushed beyond Western Avenue, where you could see vacant rehabbed brick-and-frame homes configured to mimic the new urbanist design. But Madison Avenue, the city's north/south dividing line, still bisected the neighborhood, laying bare the contradictions of the new economy. Zo knew that he was almost home.

There was a currency exchange, a pawnshop, a diner, and a few liquor stores just off the intersection of Madison and Western, where high-school kids bought chews, potato chips, and Black and Milds to roll their blunts. In the mornings, the younger kids stopped by gas stations to pick up Little Debbie Snack Cakes, bottles of blue juice, and Doritos with jalapeño peppers soaked in nacho cheese sauce. The even busier fast-food restaurants still sold pizza puffs to the regulars from the high school and the staff from one of the five correctional institutions within a half-mile walk.[4] There were still more half-way houses and detention centers here than anywhere else in the city. It was striking that so many different kinds of prisons sat in this neighborhood. North Lawndale used to be the place for black politics.

Dr. King led a housing campaign in North Lawndale in 1966—the vacant lots provide evidence of the night the city burned, right after his assassination. There's a picture of Madison and Western taken a few days after they murdered King. The streets were in ruins, most of which remain. But just a few years later, this neighborhood was the site of the free health clinics and food programs where organizers from the Chicago chapter of the Black Panther Party planned demonstrations. It's the same neighborhood where Fred Hampton, the deputy chairman of the Illinois chapter, was assassinated. The police raided his home and shot the man in the back of the head while he lay sleeping in the arms of his pregnant lover.

The residents of this neighborhood might hate the police under different circumstances. They might see the many different cages that were built here as a part of the problem. But if it weren't for the vigil held each year by Fred Hampton's son Fred Hampton Jr., chairman of the Prisoners of Conscience Committee, we might not talk about this history at all. I've sat in a local diner talking with people about their neighborhood not three blocks from the apartment building where the police murdered Fred Hampton. His assassination doesn't come up. The Panthers don't often come up, and their food programs and health clinics never come up without me asking. Dr. King comes up around his birthday, most often when the "I Have a Dream" speech is playing on the TV in the corner of the diner, but crime and violence come up all the time. The crime rate doesn't help. For years it was one of the highest in the city. The murder clearance rate, a paltry 17 percent, certainly doesn't help, and it was no better when Zo got out of prison. Unemployment, crime, and poverty rates were triple the national average, and economic development, before the condos started pushing people out of North Lawndale, meant erecting a new Dollar General or repaving the parking lot of the McDonald's across the street from the juvenile-detention center.

Journalists from Chicago to Fairbanks, Alaska, have spent years diagnosing the problems with the neighborhood. Bestselling books have been written about its decline. Documentaries catalog the violence and the children's dashed dreams and what it means to live under these conditions. After just a three-day visit, one journalist wrote an article asking, "What's it like to live in hell?" It made sense when I asked people what they thought of their neighborhood or why their children were arrested so often that they'd tell me "crack" or "black-on-black crime" or "single-parent homes" or "deadbeat daddies." "We need programs for these kids," they'd say, "something for them to do," or some version of "the police can't do nothing. The gangsters won't snitch." In the face of disinvestment, police brutality, and clear accounts of racism—systemic and otherwise—the people I talked with would say what the politicians said and what the pundits on their favorite talk-radio stations said. Black people were responsible for their own problems. They had bad families. They had bad culture. They needed to change their ways.

Zo certainly needed a change. He got off the bus just east of Western Avenue and made his way to the halfway house. What he didn't know was that Emmaus Road was the gold standard in care.

About forty men lived there. They slept on racks, up to six men per room, just like they did at the flophouse, but the rooms were mostly clean. The buildings were old, some built in 1885, but the staff did what they could to keep things tidy. And there was always something to do. There was a rec room with exercise equipment. A TV room with mostly clean couches. A cafeteria where the men had house meetings. A den where they played chess and took foreign-language classes or knitting classes or classes in public speaking, taught by student volunteers from local universities. Addiction-treatment groups. Anger-management groups. Groups on what they called "life skills." Job-preparation groups, where men learned how to write résumés and practiced their interview skills. And there was weekly one-on-one psychotherapy. You couldn't spend a decade in a cage and not need to talk to somebody about something.

Emmaus staff gave the men food and clothing and a warm place to sleep, and they helped them find jobs once they were done with their classes. The place had rules of its own. No guests. No pets. You must stay sober. Remember, you have to piss in a cup at least once a week and each time you return to campus. You may smoke only in designated areas. But Emmaus had a mission: To "help ex-offenders reassess value systems, reorder priorities and develop socially and legally acceptable patterns of behavior." The organization was good at what it did, having been at it since 1954, when an Episcopal priest let men who had just gotten out of Cook County Jail sleep on the floor of his home. He started Emmaus to serve the men's needs, naming the halfway house after a divine encounter that occurred on the road to the village of Emmaus between the disciples and their Messiah (Luke 24:13–35). He walked with them on the road to their village, so says the scripture, explaining the deeper meanings of life and their relationships with their God, but they did not know who it was until their "eyes were opened."

Zo was convinced that his eyes were closed. He was tired of prison and violence, and he was tired of being poor. He needed every bit of what Emmaus offered. But the halfway house had no room. With everything he owned stuffed in a black garbage bag, Zo begged the staff to let him stay. Andrew, the program manager, handed him blankets and a pillow. He slept on the rec-room couch. A bed opened up a week later. Zo hasn't looked back since.

It took just four months for Zo to complete programming. He attended anger-management classes, substance-abuse treatment, and parenting groups, although he didn't have children and had never had a drug problem.

"I was addicted to money," he told me.

I asked Andrew why men who didn't have children needed to take a parenting class. Andrew had been through the program himself and he wasn't a father either. "I tell people all the time, even if you don't have kids, you know somebody who does," Andrew said. "You might be a parent to somebody else's kids...sometimes you got to learn to parent yourself."

Emmaus gave Zo his first legitimate job, working as a groundskeeper, right after he completed the program. He cleaned bathrooms, swept hallways, and picked up litter. He was a good worker and a clear leader. He was referred to a long-term housing program at St. Michael's Way, an affiliated social-service agency just a block east. They had rules. You must stay sober. You may smoke only in designated areas. No one else may live with you in the unit. But he had a key to his own apartment. This was Zo's first time signing a lease. He was thirty-two years old.

After six months of working the grounds and doing general maintenance, Zo was promoted to house staff. A year later he became house supervisor, a management position. He oversaw the resident dormitory and took urine samples when the men returned from work or a family visit. A year later he was promoted to case manager. He helped men get into programs for their addictions or their anger or to be able to see their children. After a few short years he was promoted again, this time to intake coordinator, which meant he selected the new residents. And he made the presentations at the prisons that brought men like himself to Emmaus's front door. It was more important than the job or the place to live or finding a way to stay out of prison; Zo told me, "My eyes were opened," just what programs like Emmaus were for.

I met Zo in 2008. The country was facing the great recession. We had reached the height of mass incarceration, the targeted arrest and imprisonment of poor black men like Zo on a scale that had never been seen before. On April 9, President George Walker Bush signed the Second Chance Act into law. He said the country needed the "healing touch" of organizations, what he called "armies of compassion." He was evoking the words of his father, who, as the forty-first president of the United States, had called on the nation's volunteer and civic organizations, its "thousand points of light," to guide the country out of its troubles, including the high unemployment rate he presided over that likely sank his chances for reelection.[5]

The one-hundred-and-sixty-five-million-dollar legislation was the largest federal appropriation for community-based services for formerly incarcerated people in history, shifting away from the tough-on-crime policies celebrated by the Nixon,

Reagan, and Clinton administrations. The purpose for it was simple. There were 2.4 million people held in American jails and prisons, and almost all of them were coming home. Policy makers knew that mass incarceration was unsustainable. Members of the Congressional Black Caucus had been calling for this level of investment for years, and activists had been warning about mass incarceration's fallout since the mid-1980s.

The passage of the act rekindled the debate about whether someone could find redemption after prison.[6] The United States, according to the younger Bush, was the land of second chances. He said the act would ensure that "where the prisoner's spirit is willing, the community's resources [would be] available."[7] Programs like Emmaus provided people who were willing to change with the means to do so.

By the time I met Zo, he had been home for six years. I started following men at Emmaus, going to group meetings, spending time in treatment, and sitting with them during smoke breaks. We ate meals together and talked about their families and the life they hoped for after prison. But I was curious about Zo's work. I wanted to know why he'd stayed at Emmaus and what had kept him there all those years.

"Emmaus saved my life," Zo said without hesitation. "It gave me a second chance." I could see that. He had a job and an apartment. He was getting married in a couple of months. He drove an SUV and was preparing to close on a home. It's true that, minus the wife and the real estate, he'd had most of those things as a teenager, but he lived under threat of arrest. Now, years later, he was the one who selected men to join the program. He was offering a second chance. This wasn't easy. Emmaus got hundreds of applications each year, but it had only forty beds. Every one of the men needed help. I wondered how he decided whom to admit.

"If I get a person who applies with a one-year sentence," Zo said, "[he's] served sixty days. He's been convicted fifteen other times over the last ten years. The odds is, he's looking for a residence, that he's looking for room and board. He's not looking for a program," he said. It wasn't enough for a man to need a place to stay. Every one of the applicants did. His job was to figure out "whether or not he's sincere," Zo told me.

"If I get a person that did some job-skills courses," he said, "there's no confusion, no conflict about why he's in the institution"—meaning the man admitted he was wrong and took full responsibility for his actions. "And his letter, his words, depict what he wants out of life. I'll be more than likely to give him an opportunity, [because] this man wants an opportunity," Zo said, then paused before continuing. "He has to want change." That is to say, this man was looking for his redemption. I understood the sentiment.

I once spoke to Steny, a man who worked up through the ranks like Zo but who had done it three decades before. He was a serial bank robber in the 1970s and did a decade and a half in prison before he made his way to Emmaus Road. He was a reentry specialist now, working with men who finished the program to make sure they stayed out of prison. The men loved Steny. He was short, maybe five four, but commanding; he wore a Marine Corps utility cover that, at least to me, looked authentic. He was a masterly public speaker, clean-shaven with a clear but deep voice with enough character that you could tell him apart from the other group facilitators. Sometimes he ran the class on relapse prevention. Sometimes he gave guest lectures at local universities. He'd been going to AA meetings for thirty years and was a frequent guest speaker on their circuit.

I asked what he hoped to accomplish with the men and what he thought were their major obstacles. "The main thing we try to get done with individuals is to get individuals to change the way they talk to themselves," he said, making sure to enunciate *individuals*. "Whether we're talking about how you see things or whatever, because it's not what you think it is. It's only what *you* tell *you* that creates all the disturbances." This time, emphasizing *you*, he said, "How *you* talk to yourself causes *you* to act out. Handle a gun. Pick up drugs. Whatever." According to Steny, "That's the most difficult, because I'm up against deep-rooted beliefs."

The year that I met Steny and Zo, the same year President George Walker Bush signed the Second Chance Act into law, policy makers knew that people with criminal records had a terrible time in the job market and had housing doors shut to them and were arrested over and over again, most times for parole violations.[8] In the face of these structural barriers, the president called for a program of personal transformation on a mass scale. Emmaus Road and the collective work of the armies of compassion would solve unemployment and housing discrimination by helping men change their lives. Personal transformation was the way out of drug addiction. A commitment to change was the way to address homelessness. Tenacity and grit were the answer to racism. You just had to change the way you "talked to yourself" about the situation that you were in.

This wasn't the case at Emmaus alone. A look at the most popular treatment programs offered in American jails and prisons tells you all you need to know. With programs titled "Moral Resonance Therapy" and "Thinking for a Change," it's clear that redemption is the currency in the American criminal justice system. But it's the felony record that excludes you from a job or a place to live, not the extent to which you've committed to a life of personal transformation and change. The irony isn't lost on Emmaus residents.

I joined a group of men at a workforce-development program discussing Chicago's labor market and what it meant to have a felony record while looking for a job. A professor from a local university was leading the discussion. The twenty-one attendees sat at a square table, some listening, some taking notes, others peering out the window of the Mann Workforce Center. Two of them began to argue.

Ricky, who was in his fifties, was agitated. "All you get is fucking day labor," he said. "Day labor ain't shit. Show up six days, you might get work, what, two, three? What, they pay you forty dollars?" he said. He was tired of talking about work possibilities that he said he had never seen.

Lionel, a man about the same age, jumped in. "I came up on day labor." He looked around the room, taking note of the group's now rapt attention. "I always get work," he said. "You show up, be consistent, they see you."

"They give them Latinos work," Ricky replied, his voice raised. Lionel, now looking like he'd had enough, scanned the room. He sighed loudly, looked at the facilitator, looked at me, then looked at Victor, the only Latino in the group, and said, maybe for his benefit, "Ain't nobody gonna *give* you shit! They pick Latinos because they work."

The facilitator stepped in and tried to redirect the conversation by asking Lionel where he worked now. "The Beach

Bistro," he answered. "That was a come-up. I show up on time every day. People talk that race shit, but it's on you!" The remaining minutes were quiet but tense.

Lionel stuck around afterward, laughing and joking with the other residents. Ricky was still angry. He had been that way since the presentation started, annoyed that they were talking about jobs when they all had an X on their backs. And he knew he was right. Nearly all day-labor agencies in the city were in Latino neighborhoods with high concentrations of immigrants, and many of Chicago's restaurants, meatpacking floors, and waste-disposal and construction sites were staffed with undocumented workers.[9] For Ricky, you can't talk about employment without acknowledging the X, and you can't talk about day labor in Chicago without acknowledging that day-labor agencies seem to prefer to hire Latinos.

But for Lionel, employment prospects hinged on your work ethic, despite evidence from Ricky that a black man traveling miles to a day-labor site has less than a 50 percent chance of earning a day's wage. Lionel's analysis was supported by his success. He got a job at the Beach Bistro. But the Beach Bistro was an outdoor lakefront restaurant in a city notorious for unpredictable weather. Lionel complained, often, that bistro employees were sent home during rainstorms, paid only for the short hours they worked that day, and put "on call" during inclement weather. With unpredictable hours and a rotating shift, it was nearly impossible for Lionel to find a second job or budget for his monthly expenses. And the bistro opened in early spring and closed in late summer, leaving Lionel unemployed three-quarters of the year. Despite this, he counted the bistro job as a success, which was understandable given his record and Chicago's already hostile labor market. Lionel told me during a smoke break, "People *like Ricky* talk that race shit to hide their lack [of] character."

Reentry programs don't seek to remove the barriers formerly incarcerated people face. They can't. Criminal records are stored in electronic databases. Anyone with thirty dollars and a debit card can pull them up. Some are even free to the public. In Chicago, there are over seven hundred policies that keep people with criminal records unemployed. More than fifty bar them from housing. There's just very little social-service agencies can do. Instead, these organizations try their best to improve the "soft skills" of formerly incarcerated people, making them the kinds of workers that employers want to hire. They try to use moral lessons to help improve their character and remind them to make informed, rational choices when they're faced with a problem. People with records are taught to reassess their situations and endure hardships with grit and tenacity. Put in criminal justice parlance, the reentry program tries to make "criminals" into "productive citizens." They can't change the reality these people face, so they try to change how the people who face those realities see, understand, and respond to them.

The focus on employability comes out of efforts by policy makers to enhance what economists call "human capital"—the skills, competencies, and qualities associated with a healthy workforce. Human capital has two sides. One has to do with the education and training an employee uses to complete a task. The other has to do with "noncognitive skills," attributes like mental toughness, trustworthiness, and grit.[10] To reduce the poverty and address the cycles of unemployment that formerly incarcerated people face, policy makers seek to enhance their personal qualities, making them more desirable job candidates.

The nature of this endeavor wasn't lost on Bryant Stanley, the director of the city's reentry and workforce-development programs. Running late and overbooked, Bryant met with me in an open conference room in the basement of a West Side branch of the city's social-service center. Bryant described himself as motivated. He was passionate about being the fiscal agent for a consortium of reentry programs, providing financial support for many of the city's work-related services for formerly incarcerated people. Rattling off well-rehearsed recidivism and unemployment statistics and the crime and poverty rates of the poorest communities, he explained the relationship between employment and dignity. "The prison system does a person an injustice," he said. "Ex-offenders go in with no education. They come out with no education. And you know about what kinds of neighborhoods they come from. What does that do to a man?"

Bryant laid out the structural dilemmas formerly incarcerated people faced, from the decay of public education to employment discrimination to racism on the job. He told me about programs the city ran to ease men into transitional employment. The goal was to teach them how to work and get them a résumé bullet, making them more employable in the long run.

"What about job placement?" I asked. "How do you make sure formerly incarcerated people have jobs in the long run?"

Bryant's tone changed. "We're not into entitlements," he said. "You can give a man a job, but with no education, what does it mean? Our goal is to make them self-sufficient and more marketable." He went on. "Some will say, 'When I did the program, when I went out to find a job, I couldn't find a job.' I tell them, 'All we can do is get you dressed, teach you to tie a tie, write a résumé, do an interview. At the end of the day, you've got to go out there. At the end of the day, it's on you.'"

The goals of the Second Chance Act couldn't have been stated any more clearly. One hundred and sixty-five million dollars to teach men how to shake hands and tie ties, but nothing to help secure their long-term employment. There was funding for case managers who might find a man or a woman just released from a cage a place to live, but there was no money allotted for affordable housing.

As our interview progressed, so did Bryant's irritation with the questions I raised. I asked him how his organization measured success, since they didn't track employment outcomes beyond the number of temporary jobs they provided as a way to train men for the worlds of work.

"We ensure [that reentry programs] are living up to [their] contractual obligations. That they pay transitional-job wages, that they give [former prisoners] a stipend."

"But what happens when the stipend runs out?" I asked.

Bryant took a deep breath. "We look for participation. That they complete the program. We look for certificates of completion."

"Certificates of completion?" I asked, surprised that this would matter. I thought these were just documents that service providers passed out. They were all over the place at Emmaus, at St. Michael's, at every halfway house I visited. People were always having graduation ceremonies and handing out certificates of completion, sometimes just colored documents I could print using Microsoft Office at home. But Bryant explained that funding decisions were based on the number of people who completed a program. The certificate provided the evidence. The number of certificates an organization handed out let the city know how many people received services and, by extension, whether the organization was living up to its contract and fulfilling the conditions necessary to be funded the next year. Organizations would invite funders to the graduations where men wore caps and gowns and marched down an aisle and even made graduation speeches, but the funders had no way of knowing what happened after those ceremonies, and the men I talked to doubted whether those certificates mattered.

"Who you know would take that shit?" one of the brothers said when I asked about the certificates he earned. "Which [certificate]? [I'm supposed to say,] 'Yeah, I'm in a drug home' or whatever? I don't show that shit," he said. "You might could use it, though, when you go to another program. But that's it."

This was in 2008, during the first few months of the great recession. The men that Bryant served didn't need graduation ceremonies or transitional jobs to teach them soft skills. They needed jobs to cover their rent and bills and landlords that would rent them apartments.

I was sitting with a small group of men in an anger-management session. Manny was a new resident at the time. He said he had a problem. Emmaus welcomed visitors for tours, so many people passed through Emmaus and asked him questions about his personal life. He got tired of sharing his story. Fielding his complaint, Jennifer, the intern from the Psychoanalytic Institute who facilitated the group, said, "That's completely understandable. I suppose it can feel like you're in a zoo." She asked if anyone else felt that way.

It was the summer of 2010. Cortez, drenched in sweat, a towel draped over his large balding head, walked in late but right before the five-minute cutoff period when facilitators would lock the door. He looked around and whispered a few words to Gary, who was sitting next to him. Sighing through a long deep breath, Cortez sat forward in his chair, looked directly at Manny, and said, his East Coast accent uncharacteristically muted, "I feel like you've got to deal with that wherever you go. On your job. At work or whatever. Shit, on these streets. People is constantly watching." Cortez looked around and smirked as he watched the men watch him as he talked. "That's what you signed up for," he said. "We did what we did. So I say, 'Fuck it. Take a look.'"

Manny was snickering like he was in on a joke, but he took the challenge. "What am I supposed to say? I'm saying it's fucked up here." He looked around, grinned, and raised his voice just enough for the room to get the point. "We got bed bugs and shit!" he said. "I can't do shit I want to do."

Cortez's accent was more pronounced, his voice raised, when he spoke again. "You got to do you, pimp. I'm saying. Do you. But that's what you signed up for."

Gary interrupted. "For what they do for us"—meaning Emmaus—"we don't pay for shit. If they need me to talk to some kids about my shit, I'll do that. My life is an open book. This place helped me," he continued. "That's what I'm here for. Take a good look. Shit, I don't have to be here."

For some reason this upset Manny. Maybe it was that so many people were piling on. Maybe it was that he was trying to make a point. Either way, he was frustrated. He looked directly at Gary, something he didn't usually do. "I'm saying, bro, I don't need people looking at me like I'm all fucked up," he said. Manny looked around, making eye contact with me and a few other men in the group who were watching him closely. "I do need this place, though, bro," he said, almost pleading. "I mean, I ain't got no place. But why people always like, 'You don't have to be here'?" he said, mimicking Gary. "I mean, I need help, but I not fucked up, bro."

"We all fucked up!" Gary said, cutting him off. "We all fucked up," he repeated.

When Manny responded, his voice was more pleading than angry. He didn't want an argument; he was just trying to make a point. "Naw, bro. I wasn't gone no long time. Only one year. No offense, but you been gone a long time. I mean, bro, I respect that," he said, lowering his voice. "I ain't been gone no twenty years." He shook his head, his eyes wide, acknowledging the time Gary put in. "I ain't have no long bid, bro," he said. "I not fucked up, bro. I don't has that problem. I not fucked up."

At this point, Leonard, who normally sat quietly through anger-management sessions, chimed in. "I understand everything you saying, man. But the thing is, bro, we all fucked up." He then asked, "How many times you go down?"

"Three times, bro. Just three times," Manny replied quickly.

"Three times is a long time," Leonard said. "Who am I to say that this man"—he was looking at Gary—"don't know what the fuck he talking 'bout. Shit, man, we all need these groups." At that point, Leonard pulled off his sunglasses, revealing the exposed white of his partially blinded left eye. "We all fucked up," he said. "But some of us need to pull our head out our ass to see when the shit come down. We need all this shit, man. All these groups," he continued. The room was quiet. "I'll be honest with you. I didn't think I needed that shit. But I do. And if I can't share, I don't need to be here."

This conversation went on for twenty minutes of the fifty-minute session, men taking turns discussing the importance of sharing their experiences, how they were all "fucked up," how they all needed Emmaus, and how they needed to change their lives. And while Manny was trying to express his frustration, in the end, the idea that his life should be an open book and that the problem was him was too seductive for the group to move on.

In this version of the story, all of us are fucked up and all of us need change. Manny's job was to embrace that. And his colleagues had a job too. They were to hold him accountable for changing his life. But while Manny had many problems—he told the group he "went down for some bullshit," which he later shared meant beating his wife—the problem of reentry is not simply a problem of behavior. There are rules that formerly incarcerated people must follow that other people just don't have to. There are laws that regulate their lives that do not apply to anyone else. Manny was in a zoo whether he deserved to be or not.

There is no question about the need for reentry programs. They relieve real human suffering in real time. But the problem of mass incarceration is ultimately a problem of citizenship. As long as formerly incarcerated people are legally excluded from the labor and housing markets, investing in their human capital won't do much to improve their lives. Reentry organizations can't erase their records or change their social situations. And while it's true that programs like Emmaus help prepare them for the worlds of work, if no one restores their rights as citizens, the worlds of work won't make a place for them. They make people more competitive applicants in an undesirable candidate pool. They teach only how to cope with their position on the bottom of the social order.

On one of my last days conducting research in Chicago, I met with Jarrett, an administrator at a human services agency. I asked him about the work he did and the job prospects for the men. "They do everything they're supposed to do," he said. "[They] jump through hoops. Stay clean. More hoops. What for? They want a job. What can I say to that?"

"What about all those graduates from the program?" I asked. "What happens to them?"

"We're not keeping up our end of the bargain," he said. "My guys got fourteen certificates and no job."

CHAPTER 8

POWER

I was riding shotgun in a 1996 Chevy Caprice Wagon. Yusef Shakur was driving, his phone ringing every few minutes. This was our first time riding together. We were picking up one of the brothers on the first stop, an elder from an East Coast branch of the Black Panther Party. Yusef flew him in for an event later that night, the Restoring the Neighbor Back to the Hood banquet, an awards ceremony that spotlights the work of black revolutionaries' organizing in Detroit. He was walking me through his influences.

"As a young person growing up who had a nigga mentality," he said, "I looked at other niggas to imitate. You know, gangbangers. Dope dealers." Those were his heroes then. "So, following that same suit, now I become a brother. And recognizing what that means, I look for other brothers," he said. "George Jackson, Bunchy Carter, Huey Newton, Malcolm X, Frederick Douglass." These were the men he looked to, men who had changed their lives and changed the world. "I didn't have the knowledge of the black struggle or what it meant to be black in America," he said. "I just had the knowledge of suffering and things of that nature."

We pulled up to the hotel. I hopped in the back seat while Yusef got out of the car to hold the door open.

"Boy, you looking super-cool!" he said to a young brother wearing a newly pressed dashiki who couldn't help but smile. This young man's job was to escort an elder, make sure he got around the city safely. Yusef ran a tight ship.

"What you got a taste for?" Yusef asked as he greeted the elder.

"Nothing with pork," the elder said, smiling. He got in the car, and we pulled off.

We had been driving just a few minutes when Yusef turned to explain the evening's event. "The work that we do was called Restoring the Neighbor Back to the Hood," he said. "We organize around black liberation weekend. So we'll be introducing the whole concept of black liberation, what it is, but from a historical standpoint. It's not this thing in space without no substance. It's not like it just fell out of the sky," he said.

Black liberation had a history, and that history was connected by the people who lived and died for it—old organizers and new ones. This was why the elder was there. He was a member of the Black Panther Party, and he was one of the founders of his city's branch. He'd earned his stripes years before. Yusef would introduce the elder at the banquet. His presence and Yusef's connected the older and younger generations of the black power movement, which did grassroots organizing in cities like Detroit, Philadelphia, Oakland, and Chicago.

"We'll be honoring people in the community that is taking initiative," Yusef said. The elder would give the keynote address, and Yusef would speak after he was done, discussing what black liberation could mean to the people he grew up with on the west side of Detroit. He would give an award to an organizer from the younger generation of black power activists.

Yusef spent years mentoring kids and twenty- and thirty-somethings from his neighborhood. It had always been this way. He was a cofounder of Zone 8, a gang named after its Detroit zip code, and he did nine years of a fifteen-year bid for a robbery he says he didn't commit. Nine years is a long time. It wasn't inevitable. No one deserves it, according to Yusef, but to him, the bid wasn't surprising.

His mother was fifteen when she had him. The men in her life were abusive. He watched them beat her, and they would sometimes beat him. He learned to fight early. He told me once he looked up to his father. "He was cool," he said. "All boys want to be like their dads. And he was real good at martial arts." But Yusef didn't know the man, not really. He only knew his father lived a few blocks away.

Yusef was nineteen when he was convicted for a robbery, but he had been in and out of juvenile detention, like almost everyone else I met during the course of my work. By that time, his father had been in prison for years on a murder charge. When Yusef was transferred to an adult facility, after a fight and a few close calls, he wrote his father a letter.

"Dear Dad," the letter opened. "By seeing the adress on the envelop, you can see Im down the road from you. I have been in prison for about three months now. I came to prison for assault with a attempt to rob un-arm." He explained that he was convicted of a crime he did not commit. "The fucking black judge talking about he was going to send a message back to my hood," he said. He had not written his father before because "I didn't want to hear one of those I-told-you-so speeches," he wrote.

And he got into a fight with his bunkie. "The coward nigga call himself trying to act hard." But Yusef, who was then Jo-Jo, "was not having none of that." He was sent to the hole, and he told his father that "these fake religious guys trying to kick knowlege to me," ones who "be messing with fags or in to all type shit," were trying to convince him to join their group. Yusef declined, saying he could get into trouble alone. "My attitude is I'ma be a nigga 4 life," he wrote and signed off, "Love U. Jo-Jo."

His father wrote back: "Peace be upon you my beloved Son." He told him he'd received his letter. That he was sorry to see his son in the "belly of the beast." That the prison was a concentration camp and that he was sorry that Yusef had been convicted of a crime he did not commit. He said Yusef must file his appeal within fifty-six days and that he must study the law. He told his son to make his own decision about religion, though he himself had become a Muslim. He said Yusef was more than a nigga and ended the letter by saying he loved him. He left a curious postscript. "Joseph," he wrote, "you misspelled knowledge, religion, envelope, address, message and religious." He urged him to get a dictionary, which he said Malcolm X studied from beginning to end when he was in prison. "Words are powerful," his father wrote, "because they convey who we are. Use your mind to free yourself or somebody will use your mind to keep you a slave."

This began decades of correspondence and mentorship between father and son. An event, perhaps less bizarre than it seemed to me at the time, brought the men together in a way that even their affectionate letters never could have. Yusef was transferred to his father's prison. They even did time on the same wing. This was their opportunity to grow close, and they took it. They studied and prayed and exercised and walked the yard together in the mornings. Yusef grew as a man. He changed his name. He was no longer Jo-Jo from Zone 8. He changed his religion and became Muslim like his father. Yusef has since walked away from organized religion. He steeped himself in the works and words of black revolutionaries, the same people he calls heroes today. He said, "It was like going away to college."

After six short months with his father, he was transferred again, but even this was, in his words, a blessing. "It gave me the opportunity to try out what I learned," he said. Yusef started study groups and a chess club. He organized men inside the prison. He once organized against the guards because they'd used racial slurs. This was itself striking. Yusef used to say he was a "nigga for life." He writes about this time in each of the four books he's published since walking off the yard at the Lakeland Correctional Facility in Coldwater, Michigan. We met a decade and a half later.

Yusef had long since returned to Detroit. He broke up fights and counseled men and did what he could to help them meet their needs. This was all on the same blocks where he cofounded Zone 8. "When the resources left our community, we turned on each other," he once said in an interview. "Crime is a part of a larger system. It forces people into doing illegal things as a result of survival."

Yusef did political education and opened a bookstore and a café. He started rehabbing a vacant building in 2011 that would eventually become a community center, and he started the Restoring the Neighbor Back to the Hood initiative, which included an annual book-bag drive, a block party, and the banquet where the elder would speak and the young revolutionaries would be recognized, completing what Yusef might call a circle of black liberation.

The elder said he didn't want to be recorded when I asked him. "I'll just stop talking," he said, laughing, when I told him that I was a researcher trying to get my head around Yusef's life and work. "I will say this, though," the elder said, looking over his shoulder to make eye contact with me. "So many of us have been caught and criminalized in the prison system," he said. "Yusef is a role model…in terms of self-transformation. Becoming a people's servant. He represents the new leadership in the twenty-first century. On the ground. Grassroots. You can record me on that," he said before turning back around in his seat.

Ronald was one of the first people to tell me about Yusef. He'd done time with Yusef's father. They respected each other, and they were leading voices in a large and growing coalition of organizers directly affected by mass incarceration. While they took different bites of the apple, they had the same goals. The prison system was unsustainable. Yusef wanted his people to be free and independent. Ronald wanted the same. He had been traveling the country, giving lectures to local and national policy makers about the problem of overreliance on prisons and the possibility for reform. He was pushing to change laws, but more than that, he was advocating for a change in perspective.

Ronald walked out of prison in 2012 to a part-time job at a prisoners' rights–advocacy group. He was selected for a fellowship with a national coalition of formerly incarcerated organizers. They hired him within the year. He worked his way up from program associate to director of alumni relations and civic engagement, facilitating the communication with a national network of formerly incarcerated activists. He went from organizing lifers inside the "belly of the beast" to persuading public officials to change law and policy in the halls of power. He's met with judges and state and federal legislators and he's given public lectures at universities, churches, and community-based organizations.

I remember the first time I saw him give a public address. It was 2015. We had been working together for a year and a half. He was invited to Washington University in St. Louis to give the keynote speech at a conference on criminal justice reform. The moment was surreal. His boss, Glenn Martin, was leading the first in a series of fireside chats. He sat on stage with Ronald. Joining them was John Chisholm, a "progressive prosecutor" and the district attorney of Milwaukee County. All you could see of them in that packed auditorium was the men sitting on a stage with a coffee table, three mugs, and their microphones; on a large screen behind them were the words REIMAGINING JUSTICE in red letters on a mostly black background with faded images of city life.

The prosecutor was between Glenn, who sat cross-legged in a sleek gray suit with his MacBook Pro open in front of him, and Ronald, who wore a crisp black jacket, tie, and freshly pressed white shirt. Ronald was comfortable, sitting most of the time with his hands folded in front of him, while Glenn walked the men through the discussion. The audience learned of Ronald's wrongful conviction and the prosecutorial misconduct that had put him in a cage for twenty-seven years. We learned about the importance of reform and the steps the prosecutor took to demonstrate he was open to change. Ronald talked about the tragedy he carried—his son's murder on Father's Day after Ronald had spent a decade locked away for a crime he did not commit.

This was the first time I heard him tell that story to anyone else. There were a couple of hundred people in that auditorium, all hanging on his every word. This man who had been wrong-fully convicted sat on the stage with a prosecutor, both of them trying to bring about change.

Ronald explained that he advocated on behalf of his child's killer. "I did not want that child in an adult prison," he said. "It would not bring back my son."

Ronald, in what I've learned is standard after he gives a public lecture, received a standing ovation. These days I find it hard not to think about the contrast between Yusef's life and Ronald's. Yusef found his father in prison. Ronald lost his only son. The prison shaped their families, pushing each man into political action in ways that I find profound.

I've now heard Ronald's story dozens of times. Each time there's a similar reaction. Gasps. Then silence, as people try to make sense of the boy's death. Sometimes someone cries. The audience is always receptive. It is what comes next that used to bother me.

Ronald would talk about the need for reform, the fact that everyone deserves a second chance. But then he'd say something like, "If we really want change that's lasting, we have to change people's hearts and minds." He would offer a measurement of people who could be swayed: "I may not be able to reach the ones and twos or the nines and tens," he'd say, "but the fours or fives or sixes—those are the people I'm concerned about." I've always found this jarring. Nine hundred thousand black people would still be in cages even if Ronald convinced all the fours, fives, and sixes that they deserved a second chance. Yes, racism and disdain for the poor led us to mass incarceration, but I believed, and still believe, that the law is its engine.

The problem, I thought, wasn't hearts or minds. It was the rules that keep a woman with children from being able to rent an apartment because she has a criminal record. It's the policies that push a landlord to evict a grandmother because her formerly incarcerated grandson slept on her couch. Imprisonment and being viewed as a criminal by the larger society create material conditions that must be dismantled if we're serious about making change. The problem is policy, not people's hearts. It is action, not intention—at least, that's what I believe. But Ronald would follow that statement with a sentiment that challenged my presumptions.

"If you don't change hearts and minds," he'd say, "with the stroke of a pen, when someone new comes into power, they can wipe away all your progress." This is true. History isn't linear. Time passes from year to year, but we don't move from one victory to another until we get closer to some version of the truth or some great new world where our problems have all disappeared. We don't perfect the union, not in the ways we typically talk about. To borrow words from Angela Davis, freedom is a constant struggle.[1] In this case, the struggle is about making a world in which everyone belongs, even the people you're afraid of. The problem of mass incarceration is really a problem of citizenship. This is because citizenship isn't just about whether or not someone has a set of legal rights. Citizenship is something each of us practices in everyday life. It is made through everyday exchanges and between people at every level, because citizenship is about belonging.

The phone rang. I recognized the number. It was the digital woman from the Michigan Department of Corrections telling me that Jeremiah was on the line. It had been nearly a year and he was up for parole. This meant it was time to think of an exit plan. Where would he live? Where would he work? How much would all of this cost? I pressed 0 to accept the call.

Jeremiah and I talked for the next fifteen minutes about plans we'd discussed a dozen times. He would live in my friend Bradley's building, a three-flat with a basement apartment. The basement was in rough shape. The rug was mildewed. It was cold in the winter. The radiator pipes dripped. But the apartment was cheap and there were heaters. It was pretty easy to fix leaking radiator pipes; there's a putty you can buy at Ace Hardware. We could remove the rugs together and clean the basement. I could buy throw rugs for the living spaces, and with insulation and a little drywall, the unit wouldn't get so cold. Add fresh paint and new appliances, and the basement would feel like someone's home.

I would pay Bradley four hundred dollars each month. He would allow my brother to live there for as long as he needed. Jeremiah caught his case in my house, so he couldn't live with me. Besides, we didn't have the room. And if you live with someone on parole, you are subject to the things that person is subject to—random checks at ungodly hours, phone calls, the threat of a raid. This was not only a point of discomfort. There were videos floating around the internet of police shooting the wrong person or raiding the wrong house or killing black people every day going about their normal routines. We are a black family. I have a young black son who answered the door the last time Jeremiah got our house raided. On top of that, my landlord wouldn't permit it. We lived in university housing. They did background checks. If I allowed Jeremiah to live with me, my family could be evicted. Renting the unit from my homeowner friend was the only real option.

I wrapped up the conversation with Jeremiah and left a voice mail for the woman who handles parolee placement at the Michigan Department of Corrections headquarters. She called back a few days later. We went over an application for a parole transfer. He would have to be transported to Chicago. She cleared the plan for Jeremiah's release. A parole officer would contact me within a few days, she said, to inspect the unit where he would live.

A month went by before I heard from the officer. He left a cryptic voice mail, but I was used to this by now. I remembered the awful communication I had with the police when Jeremiah was arrested the year before. They didn't believe that I was a faculty member at the University of Michigan even though they called me at work.

The parole officer said, via text message for some reason, that he would come by in two days to inspect the unit. Should it be approved, he would put in the paperwork to have Jeremiah transported to Chicago on the day of his release. I was nervous about the inspection, but we had a plan. Sometime before he was released, I would grab remodeling supplies and start preparing the drafty basement apartment.

Unfortunately, Bradley had rented the apartment without telling me. He met another man who had been to prison—a white handyman who did electrical and drywall work for Bradley from time to time. The handyman needed a place to stay. He asked Bradley if he could live in the basement in exchange for work on the building. He'd lived in the basement for months. Bradley never said a word.

I learned that Bradley had already rented the apartment when I called to set up the parole inspection. I was stunned and sad and frustrated and angry but I couldn't afford to grieve.

There was so much to do. Where would Jeremiah parole? How would I find a place in just two days? How would I get it approved? Did this mean he would have to stay in prison longer?

Bradley asked me if Jeremiah could sleep in one of the rooms in the basement apartment. Of course he couldn't. I knew what his release papers would say, if he ever got out of prison. Perhaps it would be item six or seven, right after "You may not leave the state," but before "You may not own a firearm" and "You may not drink alcohol": "You may not associate with known offenders; that is, you may not spend time with anyone who has a criminal record." He certainly could not live with a man who was on parole. Besides, the handyman also had a parole officer and conditions of release that he had to follow. He could not afford to have Jeremiah live there any more than Jeremiah could afford to live with him. Associating with a known offender could get both of them sent back to prison. And they would each be responsible for what happened in the unit. If one of them got caught with a gun or with drugs or if he kept alcohol in the apartment, they could both be arrested. And two parole officers would likely be assigned to that one basement apartment, doubling the chance that the unit would be randomly checked or subject to a raid.

This normally would have been the end of things. It almost ended our friendship, though Bradley never knew it. I had no time to argue. Now there was nowhere for Jeremiah to parole. How would I explain this to my brother? What would I say to the parole board? This was the plan the woman at the MDOC headquarters approved, and this was the plan I'd laid out in my letter of support. I'd leveraged my career in that letter.

TO: Michigan Parole Board
Lansing, MI
FROM: Dr. Reuben Miller
Chicago, IL
RE: The Parole of Jeremiah, Inmate Number 1234567

To whom it may concern,

My name is Reuben Miller, the younger brother of the prisoner and an Assistant Professor of Social Work at the University of Chicago. I write this letter in full support of Jeremiah's parole.

As members of Jeremiah's primary support network, our family will do everything we can to help him make a successful transition home from prison. I would like to tell you a bit about my family and background, and then discuss how we will help support Jeremiah upon his release.

I talked about my experiences working with men in the Cook County Jail and my research with people on parole in the state of Michigan. I told them that I understood the nature and severity of his crime and that I would do all that I could to help "hold him accountable," knowing how much parole boards got off on the language of responsibility. I told them that I'd served my country as a hospital corpsman in the U.S. Navy and that my family had a history of service; my maternal grandfather was an infantryman in the army during World War II. I told them that I'd become a religious volunteer after getting out of the service, and I told them about the support system we'd built to help Jeremiah transition to life back home. I wrote my brother Joseph's letter too. He would provide moral support. And I wrote my friend Bradley's letter, discussing, in great detail, Jeremiah's living arrangement. I would cover his rent until he found a job, but not a month longer. He had to be accountable—though I knew I would likely be paying his rent for the long term. Jeremiah had had a drug problem before he went to prison. He would have the same drug problem now, and he'd have a felony on his record. Who would hire him? Who would rent him an apartment? There was no time to think of these things. We had to get him home.

How would I explain to the woman who handled parole placements that Jeremiah's living arrangement had changed? What would I say to my brother? I avoided his phone calls and all calls from a Michigan area code for the next three days. I needed to clear my head. I couldn't think of anywhere else for him to parole. This meant he would have to wait in prison until a place opened. I had just started to make peace with this idea when I got a call from Bradley.

I understood why he'd rented the apartment. Bradley was facing foreclosure. He needed work done in the building. He didn't apologize. I'm not even sure he thought he'd done any-thing wrong. I'm not sure that he knows this even now. But before he got off the phone, my friend offered to let Jeremiah sleep in an extra bedroom in his apartment. I hated the idea. My brother was older than me and needed his own space, and my friend was no-nonsense. I could imagine more than one circumstance that would lead Bradley to put Jeremiah outdoors. But he insisted. Bradley had known Jeremiah for as long as he had known me. We were like family. He would let Jeremiah sleep in his spare bedroom, which was generous, and when the handyman moved out, Jeremiah could rent the basement unit. We had a new plan. I called the woman in Lansing.

I was glad to have a new arrangement for Jeremiah and grateful that Bradley would allow him to sleep in his extra room. But even though he would just be upstairs, it was technically a different address, and that address had to be approved.

Two weeks went by. A parole officer eventually called to set up an inspection, a process he said should take thirty to forty-five minutes. The officer walked in the door, his hair cropped close in a military flattop, his hand gripping his belt just close enough to his gun holster for me to feel uncomfortable. He seemed overly serious when he wasn't cracking some childish joke, but his face was friendly enough for me to overlook it—at least at first. It took just a few minutes to figure out how the visit would go.

The pudgy man enjoyed the power of his position. First, there were the seemingly random comments. "This is who will be leading our country," he said as he glanced at the muted TV. The news was on in the background. The Parkland shooting had happened a few weeks before, and student activists were leading the first of many large rallies. He made some passing reference to Black Lives Matter, doing his best to draw me into a long conversation about why police kill black civilians. He knew I was a professor. He seemed to like something about starting and, perhaps in his mind, winning an argument.

"Did they fight?" he asked me when confronted with the fact of police murder. Young unarmed black men were killed at twenty-one times the rate of young unarmed white men. Native Americans were killed at an even higher rate, but no one paid attention.[2]

Bradley's two large German shepherds were curious, peering out of the bedroom. The agent told my friend to call them in. They trotted out, happy to get their heads rubbed. I was worried that this would be a problem, but the officer said he loved dogs. He cracked some bad joke about shooting a rottweiler during a raid.

"I'm just kidding," he said, noticing the mood drop in the room. "I would never shoot one of these beautiful creatures." But he would kill a black man if he fought back, I thought.

"You'll put in my phone line," the officer said to Bradley and me while he nodded his head up and down signaling that we should say yes, like we were children. He needed to reach Jeremiah and, by extension, Bradley at any time of the day or night. And he promised to call at two or three o'clock in the morning. He also joked that he'd conduct a few raids at around the same time. It was the strangest conversation. In one moment, he would tell some off-color joke like he wanted to be friends. In another, he would make a threat. "You know, when we search a house, we search your things too," he said. "You don't have a gun in here, do you?" He was shaking his head from side to side to indicate that Bradley should say no.

About three hours into the visit I told him I had to leave and he cracked another bad joke. "Your wife has your balls," he said. A three-hour parole inspection, almost none of it about Jeremiah—I should have told him to leave after the half an hour the visit should have taken, but how could I. I needed him to approve the unit.

I didn't know it then, because I didn't have the words, but I was drawn into the economy of favors. I had to overlook my friend renting the basement to that handyman; there was nowhere else I could turn for help. I had to leverage my reputation to get the parole board to believe in the plan or Jeremiah would spend more time in prison. I had to indulge the parole officer, sitting through ridicule, so that he would approve the placement. All of these arrangements could dissolve on a whim. Any of the people I turned to for help could have said no without so much as an explanation.

I didn't hear from the parole officer or the woman from headquarters for nearly three weeks. Jeremiah called and told me the news: after a three-hour visit, and after I'd endured bad jokes and threats for more time than I spend with most people, the officer denied the placement. I called the officer to find out why. I got his voice mail. He replied with a text message a few days later. I suppose this was his way.

Yeah, the unit had dogs, he texted. *That's what the boss said.* This was section 12 of Illinois Criminal Statute 720 at work: "Possession of unsterilized or vicious dogs by felons prohibited."

I was giving a lecture at a university in Georgia about citizenship in the carceral age. I talked about the economy of favors, doing my best to lay out what it's like to live with a criminal record. And I talked about what it meant for everyday activities that were legal for everyone else, like drinking or crossing state lines or spending time with whomever you wanted, to be illegal for you. I discussed how demands that can't be legally required of others, like peeing in a cup or attending an anger-management class, can be required of you. I discussed how the laws and policies that made you dependent on others also made you among the least desirable candidates for help, that the people you turned to in your time of need could be punished if they helped you. And I talked about the lengths that a formerly incarcerated person had to go to in order to convince others to do him the "favor" of offering him a job or renting him an apartment or providing the social services that he needed. I called this "carceral citizenship" and said the emergence of an economy of favors changed how people relate to one another in this new supervised society. It introduced a new power dynamic. Relationships, for formerly incarcerated people, now began from a position of need. You *need* the apartment or the job with the boss who mistreats you or the relationship with the lover you no longer care for because you have nowhere else to go.

I met Sabrina at that event. She was a well-known organizer from Georgia who worked on the campaign in Florida to restore voting rights for people with felony records. She had been featured in a documentary, had won an international fellowship, and had just returned from a tour of prisons in Norway. She happened to be in town when I gave my lecture. We became fast friends.

"Reuben," she said on a phone call a few months later, "I couldn't even get a fucking apartment. This was just last year!" She was gainfully employed. She had strong credit and was well respected in her community. But none of that mattered. She had a criminal record. Her applications were denied. "I got a state representative to write me a letter of recommendation," she said. "You know they still wouldn't rent me an apartment?"

Sabrina eventually found a landlord willing to rent her a place, a woman she described as a fan. "She would come to all my talks and say, 'Let me know if I can ever help you out.' But the more people know your struggles, the weaker your position," she said.

The woman offered Sabrina a lease, and Sabrina moved out of the two-bedroom apartment she shared with her mother, her younger brother, and her two children. She was happy to be out on her own and grateful that the landlord was willing to do the "favor" of leasing her the unit.

"The place had fleas," Sabrina said. "I'm there on the floor with my kids, and the apartment had fucking fleas," she said. Sabrina told the landlord about the fleas and the other problems in the apartment, including mice. "Do you know that she said I was lucky someone was willing to rent to me?"

Sabrina moved out and tried to rent an apartment elsewhere, but when other landlords in their small city called the woman for a reference, she told them that Sabrina was a "difficult tenant." No one in Sabrina's hometown was willing to lease her a decent apartment, one that was clean and in a safe neighborhood.

"People see all these accolades," Sabrina told me, "but I'm still a formerly incarcerated woman."

I've thought a lot about the people I've met over the years, especially in light of caring for Jeremiah, and I've thought a lot about what it would take to improve the lives of people with criminal records. Ronald's words have haunted me. What does it mean to "change hearts and minds"? It seems Pollyannaish, but it requires a radical kind of politics if we take the idea to its limits. It didn't matter if white people or judges or elected officials were afraid of Sabrina or not. It didn't matter that she'd gone above and beyond paying her so-called debt to society. It certainly didn't matter that she'd changed her life. She was still a formerly incarcerated woman. Jeremiah might never land the kind of job that could lift him out of poverty. He still has an X on his back. It didn't matter that I was a professor who had worked in the nation's most prestigious universities. There was nothing I could do to ensure my brother had a place to live. It didn't even matter that Ronald didn't commit the crime for which he was convicted. He still spent twenty-seven years in a cage. They were drawn into a mesh through a history of incarceration, whether they committed crimes or not and whether they changed their lives or not.

The change that Ronald calls for goes far beyond a feeling. You can change all the laws and policies you want, he would say, but if hearts and minds don't change, the victory just won't last. We see this all the time if we care to pay attention. Sabrina helped restore voting rights in Florida for some people with felony records. People convicted of murder would not get their rights restored, nor would people convicted of sex offenses, because these people are feared and loathed. But what does a felony record have to do with the right to vote? How and why are they connected? The legislation restored the franchise to 1.4 million people, a historic victory by any measure despite its limitations. But in less than six months, a newly elected governor signed a bill into law stating that people with criminal records could not vote until they'd paid all of their fines and legal fees. With the stroke of a pen, in Ronald's words, a symbolic debt to society was transformed into an actual bill.

Changing hearts and minds is about recognizing the full humanity of people, even when they've caused you harm and whether you're afraid of them or not. Ronald advocated for his son's killer, because no matter how he felt about that boy, he knew that he needed all the same things that every other boy in this country needed. He needed a community to belong to and a place in that community where he was made to feel as if he belonged. And he was entitled to this community whether he changed his ways or not, just because he was fully human.

Changing hearts and minds, in the way Ronald means it, isn't about how people feel at all. It doesn't even require forgiveness. "Forgiveness is a platitude. But forgiveness without works is dead," he often said. It takes work to make a place for someone who has harmed you. Ronald did not love his son's murderer. "I advocated for him because it was the right thing to do," Ronald said, "and I thought it could be an example to help others move on with their lives." Ronald did the work required of his ethical commitment. Changing hearts and minds has little to do with changing the way people feel. It is a commitment to a radical politics of community and hospitality that would take us far beyond the limits of a moral calculus based on public safety or fear or retribution.

It was 2015. I was back in the passenger seat of the 1996 Caprice, riding with Yusef as he prepared to throw his annual celebration. Restoring the Neighbor Back to the Hood was in its eleventh year. We were on our way to meet with an organization that had pledged backpacks for the event, and we were stopping along the way to pick up donations.

"Thank you, Auntie," he said to a woman who handed him a twenty-dollar bill.

"Thanks, good brother," he said to a man who donated fifty dollars.

We stopped at least six times on what would have been a twenty-minute drive. "Good brothers" and "good sisters" and "aunties" and "mas" all handed Yusef what they could. When we got to the organization, we saw a few of his comrades in line. One brother, a food-justice activist whose name I knew from his reputation in the city, turned to me after giving Yusef dap.

"This brother was wild," he said. "It's a blessing what he's been able to do."

We got to the front of the line. The woman behind the counter greeted Yusef, smiling. She had good news. The organization promised to deliver one thousand book bags. Yusef walked out the door proudly. It felt like a reunion. His comrades spoke on his behalf, but so did the donation. This was twice as many book bags as the organization had donated the year before. We jumped back in the car and made our way to Yusef's place in Zone 8.

We spent the ride catching up on recent events. I had been following Yusef now for six months. He told me about the progress on the community center and the artists who would perform the next day. We were making small talk when Yusef hit the brakes. He pulled over and said, "Come on, good brother," as he hopped out of the car. There was a white man with a clipboard and two white women having a conversation in front of a building. They were real estate developers.

"What's going on?" Yusef said. The man looked surprised. Yusef introduced himself to the group and reached out to shake their hands. "You know who I am?" he asked, smiling just a bit. "Yeah, I know who you are," the man said. He seemed nervous. "Your name kept coming up in our planning meetings," he said.

"Who's on the committee?" Yusef asked.

The man said something about there being community representation. Yusef told the man that his company, a development group, kept inviting the "same old people. You can't do no development unless the community approves, you know that," he said. The man gave Yusef a card and said he would be delighted if he came to a meeting. He said something about the economic benefit to the neighborhood.

We talked for a few more minutes, waiting for the man and his two partners to pull off. "Ain't gonna be no development unless community is meaningfully involved," he said, "and not just some token on an advisory group." We walked back to the car, drove to Yusef's block, and parted ways for the evening.

A thousand children descended on the block the next day, drawn by a bouncy house, food, and free haircuts. The whole operation felt like a family affair. Yusef's mother cooked most of the food. Old friends barbecued hot dogs and set out trays filled with macaroni, corn on the cob, green beans, baked chicken, and cornbread. Men served the guests, which one of the attendees found strange. He asked Yusef, "Where are the women?"

Later Yusef told me, "The comment was sexist and misogynistic. It was important to have men serve as a way of fighting patriarchy."

Yusef's aunts and uncles beamed from the porch of their family home, taking time to talk with strangers. In between performances by local musicians, Yusef's comrade Javon went to the back of a cargo van, returning every few minutes to unveil a surprise for the dozens of screaming kids who gathered by two wooden picnic tables. The first time, the surprise was a full-grown turkey. The next time it was a fifteen-foot python that slithered from his shoulder bag onto the asphalt. My son, Jonathan, was with me. He was ten and happy to be among the kids rubbing the snake's yellow scales. A brave toddler squatted in front of the next surprise, a ninety-pound tortoise, giggling and patting its shell.

I left Jonathan at the booth where Javon, who ran the Detroit Exotic Zoo, quizzed the kids on animal trivia, and I walked over to the community center. About half the work had been completed. There were still exposed walls, but Yusef had put in new windows and a ceiling and done most of the electrical and plumbing work. The architectural plans were on display at the door, and throughout the first floor, there were exhibits portraying black Detroit activists and organizers from the past fifty or so years. One of the walls was papered with Crayola-colored superheroes, each named after a child who completed a worksheet on the project. Their characters were in a fight against gentrification, thwarting the plans of evil "John Corrupto," who plotted to steal their parents' homes at a tax auction.

Right outside the center, local authors read books about time-traveling brown girls who were among the world's leading scientists to children sitting in a circle. Volunteers painted faces and passed out clothes and condoms. Musicians took turns performing on the stage set up down the block. With soul music blaring, Javon brought out the next surprise. He had the crowd make a wide circle. The kids screamed as a kangaroo on a leash hopped out of the van and down the street, shadowboxing from time to time with one of Javon's colleagues.

I walked over to the booth where Yusef was giving an interview to a local reporter. He stood there beaming with one of his good brothers, both of them wearing sunglasses and dashikis.

"What's up with the zoo?" I asked when the chance came up.

He shot me a glance, smirking. "When was the last time you saw a kangaroo in the hood?"

CHAPTER 9

AMERICA, GODDAMN!

It's not the world that was my oppressor, because what the world does to you, if the world does it to you long enough and effectively enough, you begin to do to yourself. You become a collaborator, an accomplice of your own murderers, because you believe the same things they do.

—James Baldwin, *A Dialogue*

The phone rang. Was this the call I had been waiting for?

"Hello," said the digital woman from the Michigan Department of Corrections, letting me know Jeremiah was on the other end of the line. I pressed 0 to accept the call right after she finished her warning about his potential for extortion and right before she gave me the option to block numbers from the facility.

"What's up, Ruber Scoober," he said. I could tell that he was smiling. It was August of 2018. He should have come home in June, but his release date had been pushed back after the parole placement failed. I was still in faculty housing, so he couldn't live with me. Jeremiah and his wife had divorced by then, so he couldn't parole to her house. My friend still had two German shepherds, and there was still a man with a felony record living in his basement apartment. With no family to parole to in Chicago, he had to stay in prison until the MDOC found a place for him to live. But we were in luck. A bed had opened at a transitional-housing facility in Ypsilanti. It was already two months beyond his scheduled release date, and he would not be coming home to Chicago anytime soon. He had two years of probation to serve, and felons can't cross state lines. But Jeremiah had a place to live, at least for ninety days.

We spent the next fourteen and a half minutes going over new plans. I would reach out to friends to see if they knew someone willing to hire Jeremiah. I would call around to find a landlord willing to do us the favor of renting him a room. I would pay his rent until he got back on his feet, and I would pick him up from the Gus Harrison Correctional Facility in Jackson, Michigan, where he had been transferred. He would be out in seven days. I had to get to the prison by seven a.m., which was when they opened the gate for visitors.

His counselor said he would give us extra time since I was coming "all the way from Chicago." After I picked him up, the plan was for us to grab breakfast, then check in at the parole office in Ypsilanti, buy a cell phone, grab lunch, and get Jeremiah an ID. We would catch a movie if there was time, and then have a big dinner in celebration of Jeremiah's almost freedom. I was always so worried about him being hungry. Prison food was never enough for him. On holidays, when we were little, my brother would eat dinner rolls until his back hurt. First he would stuff the rolls with turkey and macaroni and cranberry sauce and Ma Ma's oyster dressing and drizzle the top with her famous gravy, the one with giblets and onions that sat in the special dish. The boy would eat maybe five of those, then he would lie on the floor, holding his back, complaining. When we were grown, he would come by and eat all the groceries in our house, even after I'd made a Costco run. Well, at least he'd eat all the Oreos. And he'd drink all the liquor when we went out, even the bottle of scotch I got from Glasgow on my first trip to Europe.

I was happy he was coming home. I also had appointments the day before and deadlines to make that evening. I left home at two a.m. on the day of his release. Chicago is on central time. I was dead tired, but if I slept any longer, we would be late to meet his parole officer. Besides, Jeremiah was getting out of prison. This was really no time to sleep.

He was released on August 13, 2018, from the Gus Harrison Correctional Facility. There were two families picking up their loved ones when I arrived: A woman in a black hoodie and pajama pants sat in the center aisle. An elderly couple came in and sat not far from her on the left. The guard was friendly, like last time, a nice man with a boyish face. There was some info-mercial on the television suspended over the change machine in the center of the waiting room. The couple's son came out first. Next, Jeremiah and the woman's loved one were buzzed out from behind the Plexiglas-and-steel doors, cracking jokes with each other as they left. Jeremiah was wearing oversize khakis, those awful boots, and a white button-down shirt, but he looked good. He might have gained or lost weight, I wasn't sure, but he had a freshly shaved head and face. We gave each other dap, left, jumped in the car, and headed out.

He showed me his ankle bracelet, and we made small talk

about I can't quite remember what. I was just happy to see him, and I was tired and hungry, and I had to use the bathroom. We didn't stop for breakfast because he told me his prison counselor had insisted he go straight to the parole office. We needed to be there by seven thirty when his agent showed up. The office was forty-five minutes away. We did stop to get gas and use the bathroom and pick up a pack of cigarettes. I was worried we were late, knowing that parole officers can be irrational. But Jeremiah had just gotten out of prison. Nothing would ruin our day.

We pulled up earlier than expected. He hopped out of the car and walked inside while I found a space in the parking lot. There were already ten or so men in the waiting room, and other men trickled in and out, most in jeans or tracksuits, for the next few hours. Some had better haircuts than others. Some had on clothes that looked like giveaways: blue or white button-down shirts tucked into their jeans, the kind of shirts you see in recovery homes. They greeted each other and cracked jokes. A few talked about their jobs. A group of them worked at a nearby factory. A big, friendly, and talkative man in his fifties came in, saw Jeremiah in his "fresh fish" khakis, and started a conversation.

"What's up, big bro," my brother said, looking relaxed but in a way that seemed to me intentional. I could tell he was watching the man. The man had been home a few years, gotten married, and figured out how to "live for God." He had clothes and job leads that he was willing to share. He gave Jeremiah a card and told him to come by his house.

When the religious man got in the back of the line, none of the other men in line acknowledged his presence. Jeremiah glanced at me in a way that said all he needed to. "Fuck outta here," he said under his breath as the man walked behind the door to give his urine sample.

We had been sitting in the hard plastic chairs in that waiting area for an hour and a half when Jeremiah's parole agent came in. He didn't look our way, but we could tell it was him. I waited while Jeremiah got in line with the fifteen or so other men. He walked through the door when he got to the front. Five minutes later he walked out of the door, quickly.

"I had to pee, Ruber Scoober," he said as he walked to the bathroom around the corner in a different section of the building. I wondered why he didn't pee in the cup like the other men. I let it go.

He got back in the line to go meet with his parole officer again. Fifteen minutes later he was back out the door.

"Mr. Asshole heard you were here," he said. "He wants to talk to you, but fuck that," he said. Jeremiah got back in the line and was called to the back, again. Another twenty minutes went by. He came back out the door.

"This asshole," he said quietly, exasperated. "He wants you to come to the back."

I walked with Jeremiah to the cubicles behind the door in the waiting room. His parole officer was sitting at a desk. He was staring at what looked like a map on his computer screen. He asked if I had questions; I didn't. He asked if we had plans for the day; we did. I asked about Jeremiah's curfew. The agent said on normal days he would need to be back by three o'clock, but he would let him stay out today until six since I had driven all the way from Chicago. He asked if I had any more questions. Jeremiah cut in, asking if he could use the bathroom again. The parole officer, annoyed, waved for him to go and said, "You know, I can make this last all day."

He asked about my occupation while Jeremiah was in the bathroom. I told him that I worked at the University of Chicago but that I used to work at the University of Michigan. He told me he knew that from my letter. I wondered why he'd asked. He talked about his goals for Jeremiah. He had to go to treatment. He had to get a job.

"We know that people fail," he said, but he wanted to see Jeremiah succeed. Then the agent showed me his computer screen. No fewer than three people would be monitoring Jeremiah's movements. The agent would be watching, someone from MDOC headquarters in Lansing would be watching through a GPS satellite, and someone from the private company that MDOC contracted to provide the satellite images would be watching.

"We can tell which direction he's facing in the car," he said, then gave some obscure example of how knowing which direction a man with an ankle bracelet sat could somehow keep him out of prison.

Jeremiah came back from the bathroom and looked annoyed that we were still talking. He gave me the signal that I've known since we were kids that it was time for us to leave. I walked back out to the waiting room and sat there for an additional hour. Jeremiah finished his appointments. In the car on the way to breakfast, he told me what bothered him. He had gotten a warning after just one encounter with his parole agent. Other men told Jeremiah that his agent gave violations for the "pettiest shit." "I got the worst fucking agent," he said.

My family calls Jeremiah the grill master. This man, the one with an iron stomach who ate three chicken breasts, two lamb chops, and nearly a plate of mashed potatoes the last time he visited our house, couldn't eat for the rest of the day. We went to

Zingerman's Delicatessen for breakfast. He ordered but didn't touch his food. We went to a fancy diner for lunch. He ordered, but ate only a few bites. We stopped at Outback Steakhouse for dinner. He ordered but couldn't finish his burger.

"I'm supposed to be happy. I'm free, and he got me fucked up," he said as I drove him to the transitional-housing facility where he'd stay for the next ninety days.

The phone rang and my stomach sank. The digital woman was calling me again.

"Hello," she said, "you've got a collect call from"—there was no sound, or at least no one gave a name—"an inmate at the Washtenaw County Jail." I pressed 0 and grabbed my wallet, hoping this was some kind of mistake.

"Ruber Scoober," Jeremiah said, "just did a quick ten days. I was calling to let you know what's going on."

Shit, I thought. He had been arrested again.

"Mr. Asshole was on some bullshit," he said. Jeremiah had been late for an appointment and he violated him, sending my brother to jail to teach him a lesson.

It had been four months since he got out. I'd thought he was doing well. He had gotten a job at a diner up the street from the transitional-housing facility and had worked there for two months. I remember the first time I visited him there. He'd always been proud of me, but this time he was proud of himself. I took a picture of him that I look at from time to time to remind me of when he was happy. He smiled this goofy wide smile as he posed in front of the grill with his spatula raised in his right hand. He made me a milkshake. It was a surprise and took him ten minutes. He worked the back usually but convinced the cashier to let him make me the shake.

Jeremiah got a grant for a vocational-training program. He asked his parole agent and mandated reentry-program case manager if he could go to truck-driving school. The case manager was kind. She found him a bike and arranged for him to have a bus pass to get around the city. She was responsible for coordinating his classes—anger management, workforce development, drug-relapse prevention. And this had been his dream. He'd gotten a CDL a few years prior, right before he went to prison, but Jeremiah was a drunk. He got a DUI, and his license was immediately suspended. Now he had an opportunity to start over. He imagined that he would make more money driving trucks than he'd made at any other job in his entire life. We talked almost every night. He stayed in a hotel by the Detroit Airport, the grant covering his food and lodging for the three-week program. He checked in with me after every test to celebrate on the phone. He graduated easily. There wasn't a ceremony for me to go to, but I sent him money and told him I would drive up to see him in a few weeks.

He had a good relationship with the job coordinator at the trucking company. They found him a job right away, but then I got a call from him one night, late. He was hot. He told me he couldn't take the job as a driver because felons couldn't cross state lines. Even if he got a job as a local driver, he had a curfew and his travel had to be approved. There was no way the parole supervisor would sign off on the new job, even if his parole agent went to bat for him. I'd worried about this when he signed up for the program, but if they knew this would be a problem, why did they send him to truck-driving school? What did they think would happen? A man who had been homeless. A man who just got out of prison. A man who would have a terrible time finding work otherwise. What good would a truck driver's license do?

After ten days, his parole agent picked him up from the jail. He had a surprise for him.

"He felt sorry for me," Jeremiah said. The agent found him a job working the second shift at a tortilla factory. Jeremiah would have to ride his bike across town, but it paid ten dollars an hour, more than he'd made at the diner he left but less than he would have made driving a truck. For some reason they approved the hours. Working nights, or even sporadic hours, apparently wasn't the problem; the parole department just couldn't imagine letting a man with a felony record only a few months home from prison have access to a truck. I suppose it was too much freedom.

He took the job at the tortilla factory but hated every minute of every day. He said he'd thought he had to take it. "I'm too old for this manual-labor shit, Scoober," he said on more than one occasion. He was fired a few weeks later. The job was too demanding. "They changed my shift, and I couldn't keep up," he said.

This too is the afterlife of mass incarceration—to be separated from your hopes and any real idea of freedom. Millions of people are unable to decide for themselves where they will work or live or spend time. Millions more can't find a job or housing at all. There is no place for them to go because no place has been made for them, not even in the public's imagination.

The problem of mass incarceration has never really been about crime. It's that the people who Americans are afraid of are subject to a separate set of rules. They live in a separate and altogether different social world, because they belong to a different political community. No social-service agency, no matter how well funded, can bridge the divide between these two worlds, nor can any of our criminal justice–policy reforms. We have not yet come to grips with our problems or imagined an adequate response because our assumptions about the extent and causes of crime have been wrong from the beginning. You cannot treat or arrest or, perhaps, even reform your way out of mass incarceration because mass incarceration is about citizenship, not criminal behavior, and citizenship is about belonging.

I was on a date with my wife, maybe six months later. Robert Glasper was in town to play at the Jazz Showcase in Chicago. I was walking to an Indian restaurant to grab dinner for the event. (The showcase lets you bring a meal.) We had gotten there early enough to get a table in front of the stage and had a glass of wine. I was walking back with our meal when I got a call. It was the digital woman again. I pressed 0 to accept the call.

"Scoober," Jeremiah said, sounding panicked. "I've never been in trouble like this. I've been in jail more times in this shitty town than in my whole criminal career."

He was serious, and he was worried, and he was telling me the truth. He had already been re-arrested four times. Once he'd stayed in jail for three days. Twice for ten. Once for thirty. This time he was being sent to a ninety-day residential drug-treatment program in a small town in western Michigan. (They didn't tell him it was ninety days. They never told him how long he would have to stay. And he didn't know this at the time either, but his two-year parole would start all over when he was eventually released.)

I live in a paradox. I am privileged. I've worked in elite institutions. I have a wife and a loving family. We've somehow managed to break into the middle class. But I was born poor and black in the age of mass incarceration. Prison follows me, just like it does the people I've written about. It doesn't matter that I haven't been convicted of a crime. I'm as close to the subject of this book as I am to any member of my own family. Jeremiah has been to many prisons, just like the brothers, sisters, fathers, daughters, lovers, and sons I've followed for the past fifteen years. I write this book living like they do, hoping and bracing myself and preparing for the day that I can welcome my loved one home.

Jeremiah was arrested twice more over the next four months. He was sent to another drug-treatment program, this time in Detroit. He did ninety days there, telling me he thought he'd gotten something out of the program.

"Hello," said the digital woman. "You've got a phone call from a prisoner at the Michigan Department of Corrections." *Goddamn,* I thought, then I pressed 0 to accept the call.

Author's Note

This is a work of narrative nonfiction. It is rooted in my study of the lives of incarcerated and formerly incarcerated people that began in 2008 and continues through today, and it draws from my work in social services, which began in 1997 when I was a counselor for foster children accused of sexual assault and ended in 2008 after I'd spent five years as a volunteer chaplain at the Cook County Jail during the height of mass incarceration.

The people in the book are real. I tell their stories as they told them to me and with the consent of each living research participant. Almost all of the dialogue that appears was taken verbatim from interview transcripts. There were times when it was not possible to record conversations, and in those cases, I took notes and re-created the essence of those discussions. I have done my best to confirm with each person that I am depicting the details of his or her experiences accurately. With the exception of public figures', I have changed all names to maintain confidentiality. I have also changed the names of most organizations and, in some cases, the names of streets and neighborhoods.

My research began in Chicago, where between 2008 and 2013 I spent a total of three and a half years in halfway houses throughout the city. That work continued in Detroit, where between 2014 and 2016 I followed sixty men and thirty women starting on the day of their release from Michigan prisons and a police station's lockup facility. During that time, I was introduced to a national network of activists who had collectively spent a couple of centuries behind bars. For the past few years I've been following that group closely across cities throughout the United States.

I've interviewed nearly two hundred and fifty people in the past decade and a half and closely observed the everyday experiences of a few dozen men and women as they returned home and attempted to put their lives back together. But I was also born black and poor in the age of mass incarceration; like every black person I know, I was stopped by the police a number of times and I am well acquainted with the many cages intended for the men and women whose lives I document.

I knew about foster homes and group homes and juvenile detention centers and jails and prisons because everyone I grew up with had been to at least one of these facilities or had a brother, cousin, mother, aunt, or uncle who had been incarcerated. My brother was sent to prison while I was writing this book. He followed another one of our brothers and the father we barely knew. These experiences helped me understand what life is like for the people most affected by mass incarceration and lets me relay what it means to care for a loved one who is locked away.

Acknowledgments

I'm thankful for so much and to so many. My heart is so full. I'm sure I will miss names.

I'm grateful to my God, who would not reject me. Thank You for all You've done. And to the men and women in Detroit, New York, Chicago, and all the towns across the country that are too small for me to name without giving away your secrets, thank you. You shared your stories with me. They are precious in my eyes. Thank you to Ronald Simpson-Bey for our many late-night talks and the pints of Hennessy we have yet to drink. To Hazelette, for the blessing you are. To TJ—may many blessings be upon his loved ones. To Yusef—salute, good brother. To Amanda Alexander and Finn Bell (Finn!), Jhody Polk, and the wonderful Susan Burton: I'm fortunate to have crossed your paths and blessed to call you friends.

Thanks to a wonderful crew of research assistants and project volunteers, especially Emily, Nicole, Adrianna, Kyle, T'Kara, Demetrius, and Judy. Thanks also to Lester Kern, Durrell Washington, and Alize Hill, who gave me critical feedback on the book.

To Joe Summers, who was my pastor and is my friend, and to Donna Ainsworth, the Summers' fam, and the good folks at the Episcopal Church of the Incarnation, especially Billy Joe and Adye Bell Evans, who fed us and loved us and adopted

Jonathan, Adé, Janice, and me (I think in that order). We love you. I look forward to our next meal. And thank you to Jerry Walden and Peter Linebaugh (who I will say more about in a bit) for their constant friendship and support.

Speaking of friends, I'm blessed to have many. To my brother Keith — man, look how far we've come. Did we imagine any of this? God is good. And Harrison Williams, who has been A1 since day 1. I love you, brother. The esteemed gestalt psychologist Jelena Zeleskov Djoric taught me how to "meet the other at the contact boundary." Thank you, my dear sister, and hug my brother Predrag, Isi and Sophie, and your aunt for that delicious meal. Janice and I were convinced after our trip that there was no warmer place than Belgrade. To Fergus McNeill, who is also my brother (I have the tartan to prove it!): there will be a reading in Glasgow for sure, and we'll toast a Bowmore Single Malt, at least an eighteen (maybe one day a sixty-six!).

Speaking of brothers, shout-out to my clique ('cause ain't nobody fresher), listed here in alphabetical order by first name: Desmond Patton, John Eason, Luke Shaefer, Michael Walker, Shaun Ossei Owusu, and Waverly Duck. The scripture says a friend sticks closer than a brother. We've read one another's work. We've shared one another's pain. We've broken bread together. You've blessed me. Megan Comfort is my dear sister who took me as a brother years ago. She's been reading my work and writing way too many letters of support on my behalf for years. Megan, you're incredible and deserve all the good that life has to offer.

Thank you to the great Peter Linebaugh (who will hate that I called him great, but that's how I see him), a brilliant historian who is my comrade and friend. To Bruce Western, who showed up often and brought his sharp mind. Thanks again to Michael Walker and Megan Comfort, who play many roles in my life, and the brilliant Julian Thompson, Lester Kern, Matt Epperson, and Nicole Marwell (who I will say more about). My book workshop couldn't have gone better. Thanks for helping me walk down these chapters; they got away on more than one occasion. And thank you to the sociologist and social theorist Loïc Wacquant, who has been a mentor from a distance and one of the people I've looked to as an example of a scholar who does theoretically rich sociological analyses.

I've been fortunate to have great support at the University of Michigan, where I did much of the research for this book, and at the Institute for Advanced Study, where I wrote the book proposal. My colleagues at the University of Michigan School of Social Work helped launch my professional journey. There are too many people to name, but thanks especially to Laura Lein, my first dean, and Robert Taylor, who introduced me to the Michigan Center for Urban African American Aging Research, which, with the Ford School, the Curtis Center, and the Antipode Foundation, funded my research in Detroit. Heather Ann Thompson, the incomparable historian of urban life and the carceral state, encouraged me to write the book I wanted to write. She also provided real insight on how to navigate writing for the public. And Luke Shaefer (who wears many hats!) not only introduced me to my book agent, the wonderful (and patient) Lisa Adams, but broke bread with me many times, helping to make the University of Michigan a lovely place to work. So did my colleagues and friends at SSW, especially my homeboys Desmond Patton (the clique!), David Cordova, and the entire faculty and staff, including Karen Staller, who was my faculty mentor, and my colleagues Kristen Seefeldt, Beth Glover Reed, Letha Chadiha, Leslie Hollingsworth, Lorraine Gutiérrez, Rosemary Sarri, and Larry Gant for entertaining my ideas. Thank you to my dear friend in Anthropology, the brilliant Damani Partridge, and his lovely family, Sunita, Jasmine, and his equally brilliant and warm mother, for the dinners, brunches, and Zoom connections during COVID, and for letting me crash in Berlin, and thank you to the entire faculty and staff in the Department of Afroamerican and African Studies. Big hugs to Alex Murphy, Sarah Fenstermaker, and Ashley Lucas for your constant warmth and support, and a great big thank-you to the incredible teams at the Institute for Research on Women and Gender and the Prison Creative Arts Program, where I was honored to spend some time. Thanks really to the entire "Michigan mob," including Martha Jones (now at Johns Hopkins), Heather Ann Thompson (again!), and Ruby Tapia, and the good folks at the Carceral State Project and the Institute for Social Research. I appreciate your support.

A shout-out to my crew at the Institute for Advanced Study, especially Lalaie Ameeriar, Andrew Dilts, and David Kazanjian (aka the Brooklyn pub-crawl crew), Ruha and Shawn Benjamin and the late Lee Ann Fuji (#blackexcellence), and Fadi Barda-will, Lori Allen (and Yezid!), Céline Bessière, Nick Cheesman, Karen Engle (my running buddy), Pascal Marichalar, Jonathan Morduch, Amy Borovoy, Ayşe Parla, Massimiliano Tomba, Emily Zackin, Linda Zerilli, Peter Redfield, and Elizabeth Mertz for breaking bread. Thanks to the entire 2016–2017 cohort in the School of Social Science for engaging with my work and to Didier Fassin, Ann-Claire Defossez, Bernard Harcourt, Joan Scott, Donne Petito, and Laura McCune who steered that beautiful ship. You all ate and drank and laughed with me way too late into the night and still managed to produce cutting-edge work and show off your dance moves at nerd prom. Plus, another shout-out to David Kazanjian because he read the entire book!

Thank you also to the good people at the American Bar Foundation, especially my dear sister, the brilliant Bernadette Atuahene, and the "wine and cheese crew," Shaun Ossei-Owusu (thanks again, dear brother; I love watching you shine), Spencer Headworth, Rhaisa Williams, and John Robinson, and the good people at the Populations Research Center at the University of Texas at Austin, especially Sarah Brayne and Becky Pettit, and my crew at Touro University, Dierdra Wilson, Nemesia Kelly, and Gayle Cummings for hearing out and pushing my work.

My colleagues at the School of Social Service Administration at the University of Chicago, some of whom have already been named, have been a constant source of inspiration and friendship since I arrived in 2017.

My dean, Deb Gorman Smith, has provided nothing but support, as has the entire faculty and staff at SSA. And the incomparable Eve Ewing, Yanilda Gonzalez, and Nicole Marwell showed me so much love and support. They each read chapters and gave incredible feedback (Eve and Nicole read the entire book). So did Matt Epperson and Robert Vargas. I can't thank you enough. And to my dear brother Julian Thompson, whose incredible work on drug courts is about to change the game. You are my friends, and you are precious to me. Speaking of friends, a shout-out to the friend lab, with Eve Ewing, Yanilda Gonzales, Robert Vargas, Aresha Martinez-Cordoza, and Nia Heard-Garris, who read my work, and Angela Garcia, Shanta Robinson, and my dear friend Gina Fedock, who have all been so good to me. And speaking of colleagues and friends, Joyce Bell! Waldo Johnson! Gina Samuels! All exclamation points. Fierce supporters and incredible colleagues. So much support from so many people. But this project has benefited from the support of many more.

Thank you to the fellows and fellowship team at New America, especially Sarah Jackson, Melissa Segura, Clara Fitzpatrick, Kevin Sack, and Rachel Aviv, who read and gave really good feedback on chapter 2, and to Awista Ayub, for her continued support and for running the fellows program so well. Thank you to the entire 2018–2019 New America cohort, whose work I so admire, and to Anne-Marie Slaughter and Tyra Mariani, for encouraging us all while putting in such excellent work to move our country forward.

What can I say about the mighty-mighty cohort of the Racial Democracy Crime and Justice Network and the rest of the RDCJN? We've been cracking the ground since 2014. Thank you especially to Michael Walker (so many hats, dear brother!), my sister Nicole Gonzales Van Cleve, Patrick Lopez-Aguado, Danny Gascón, Evelyn Patterson, Lallen Johnson, and Valerie Wright. And to the incomparable Ruth Peterson and Laurie Krivo, for starting it all, and Jody Miller and Rod Brunson, for keeping the party going.

I had such a deep crew of support at Loyola University Chicago, especially in the School of Social Work, at the Center for Urban Research and Learning, and in the Sociology Department, where I studied for six years. Thank you to the esteemed Maria Vidal de Haymes, who wrote so many letters of recommendation for me and listened to my ideas. She and Stephen Haymes gave me my first opportunity to publish and have been real friends over the years; I developed many of the ideas in this book during that time. Stephanie Chapman hired me to work as an adjunct professor and later a full-time instructor. That's how I fed my family. Thank you, thank you, thank you. The entire Social Work Department gets as many heart emojis as I can muster. So does CURL, especially my mentor and dissertation chair

Acknowledgments

Phil Nyden, and my friends at CURL, especially Gwendolyn Purifoye and my boy Joel Ritsema, without whom I wouldn't have survived stats or graduate school or any one of those CURL projects. Along with the late, great dean Samuel Atto, Phil made sure my fellowships were funded and provided space for me to develop how I think. Thank you to Kellie Moore, my brilliant dissertation cochair, and to Rhys Williams and Robert Fairbanks for their work on my committee. My dear brother and mentor David Embrick was on my committee too. We spent many late nights at conferences chopping up social theory and religion and white supremacy, all the stuff that animates this book. I couldn't have afforded those conferences had you not made a place for me to sleep on your floor. A shout-out to Phil Hong too!

To Pastor Mary Trout-Carr, whom I can't thank enough. You've been a mother to me, a motherless child, and you helped dig me out of many a cold and dark place (a slimy pit, says the psalm). Thanks also to my brothers and sisters at the Christian Heritage Training Center Community Church—that new building looks real good! Thanks also to my brother Milano Harden, who has been a real friend to Janice and me—thank you for being a brother. Thank you, especially, to my dear friend and brother Melvin—I love you, man, and I'm proud of you. And to my brother Meridith Johnson, who has shown himself friendly on so many occasions. To my mother, Michele, and mother-in-law, Hyacinth, one who gave me life and one who made my life all the more rich. Thank you for being my family. I love you.

Thank you to my incredible literary agent, Lisa Adams. I don't know how you worked the magic you did. I certainly did not send you a real book proposal when we met. I appreciate all you've done. And to Vanessa Mobley, my brilliant, impressive, and incredibly talented editor. You made this book so much better than I thought it could be. Thank you for believing in my project. I prayed for the right place to publish this book. You and your whole team are wonderful. Thank you to the entire team at Little, Brown and Co. for the work you do every day. Thank you for helping me bring this ship to harbor.

To my blood brothers and sisters, the ones I grew up with and ones I did not know so well. I cannot name you, to protect you. I love you, Skip and Ragala; it's impossible to say what you mean to me—I just don't have the words. To Laura and Donna (my sisters!) and my loves Mira and Ayanna. Props to Ellie and Michael. To Kyle, who went to sleep. I love you as I do your father. My heart is as full with your memory as it is sad that you are gone.

To my Jonathan, who brings so much light into my world, and to my Adé, who chose me and whom I chose. You bring me the kind of joy that's hard to explain. To Rueben. To Jalen. To Jayla. To Amber (wow! Look where we are). I love you and I'm grateful for who you are and who you have become. Finally, to Janice: I would be lost without you. You accepted me for reasons I never quite understood. I was sleeping on couches and sometimes outdoors when we met at that little church. I didn't know what to dream. You taught me to write. You told me things my grandmother told me, although you two never got the chance to meet. You believed in me. There is so much to say. I hope to tell you every day.

I'm blessed and grateful that so many people loved and supported me along the way. Many gave feedback on my ideas, but I didn't always listen. The mistakes are proof of that, and they are mine alone. I'll stop here by saying I love you to my God, my family, and my friends. You've made a cold world much warmer.

APPENDIX:

The Gift of Proximity

There are things that our bodies know but that we ignore far too often. They know that while we each have a soul—which is to say that we each possess what some philosophers call a mind, with its thoughts and emotions that connect us to the broader world of human experience—that soul is wrapped in flesh. And our bodies know that the soul and the flesh are inseparable. They tell us through our frailties. Everything we come to know, we learn through our bodies. Even our relationship with time, a concept that seems abstract, is tracked by our bodies as we age and ache, our flesh logging different kinds of pain and the different sets of feelings associated with them.

In a 1969 address at the West Indian Student Center in London, James Baldwin offered a reflection on the centrality of the flesh.[1] In response to a question on the future of the black personality, Baldwin said, "I think that black people, [and] it seems to me the black personality has a kind of vigor, a kind of vitality and a kind of sense of life. Something which does not come from here." He pointed to his head. "It comes from a much deeper region." In what he called a "severe judgment...if not an indictment of [white] Christianity," Baldwin compared the "not so compartmentalized...African personality" with the "European personality," what philosophers and scientists might call a mind-body dualism, meaning the view that the mind (the fount of the rational cognitive enterprise) and the body (passions, emotions, and unobjective feelings of all kinds) are and should be kept separate. "I think they are terribly worried about the flesh, the senses," Baldwin said. "I think they live in checks and balances which are really, very nearly, pathological."

In this dualistic tradition, rational actors discipline their passions and hold their feelings at bay to engage in what is presumed to be the higher practice of reason. This expresses itself in the "checks and balances" of a world that pretends to distance itself from its passions and in a scientific tradition and a set of social policy positions where the separation of the mind (i.e., the scholarly enterprise) from the body (i.e., the passions of the researcher and the shifting political winds of a given moment) is maintained through scientific methods designed to keep the "truth" of one's discovery free from the taint of bias. The mind and the body—and, by extension, scientific and partisan thought—are considered different things, and social scientists take steps to ensure distance from their own passions and the passions of the people they study. Baldwin considered these kinds of practices pathological because this version of knowledge production is disembodied and necessarily asocial.

The researcher may pretend to be unmoved by shifting political winds or the trials of life that come to us all, but our bodies know that the soul and the flesh cannot be separated. The brain is but one of many organs, and the mind may be nothing more than philosophical abstractions. Our thoughts and actions are mitigated by our feelings and our experiences at a given moment and in relationship with others. Thinking, even scientific thought, is social and occurs within the social worlds that we inhabit, be they the worlds of science and the academy, the worlds of the street, or the worlds of arts and letters. Our thinking reflects our passions and desires and pains at specific moments. We might encounter these things as curiosities and classify them as scientific endeavors rather than, say, causes, and we may subject them to the rigor of our methods to minimize our footprint in the knowledge that we produce, but our passions are the very things that draw us to the questions we ask. Put differently, our *desires,* which is to say our flesh, drive our science and lead us to processes of scientific discovery, and they do so even when we fail to account for them.

This reads like the many critiques of objectivity offered by hundreds of scholars, but Baldwin takes the critique further. The extraordinary measures of separation required to keep the presumptions of the European personality intact are more than difficult to achieve—they are racist and dehumanizing. "In America," Baldwin says, "I, precisely, am the flesh which the Christians must mortify." It is a flesh that they crucify and whip and lynch and work until it dies in the fields. But killing black flesh is a mistake. It is a failure of imagination and a loss of the kind of knowledge we could generate if we allowed our minds proximity to our bodies and to the bodies (that is, the passions and experiences) of the people we're interested in learning about. In other words, we lose the ability to learn how the world works and, just as important, how that same world works within us when we erect a wall between our soul (read as the spirit in the long religious tradition that bleeds into our science, law, public policy, and social relations) and our flesh, and the flesh of the people whose lives we follow. The reason for this is simple. Science hinges on observation, and observation takes place in the body. In Baldwin's words, "Everything you find out, you find out through your senses. Everything awful that happens to you, and everything marvelous that happens to you, happens to you in this frame, this tenement, this mortal envelope...If you mortify that," Baldwin warns, "there's no hope for you," because, he says, "the flesh is all we have."

We need to understand our own lives as perceived through our bodies in order to understand the lives of the people we care for. This is the benchmark of a decades-long black feminist tradition that methodologically and analytically explores what it means to live in a raced and gendered body under a specific set of class relations in a given historical moment.[2] This tradition sees value in the insights that can only be garnered by taking bodily experiences and threats to bodily autonomy seriously and specifically attending to the structural vulnerability of women, especially black and poor women, to the almost always unaccountable harms rendered by the larger white world. It takes for granted that the black body and black being are valuable. Similarly, feminist scholars outside of the black feminist tradition have challenged the kinds of dualism and presumptions of normality and objectivity that suffuse the domains of science, law, and public policy.[3]

The extent to which we understand our lives and the conditions in which we live allows us to better understand the lives of other people. Taking this insight into the realm of practice, if we were, in the words of Bryan Stevenson, to allow ourselves to get proximate, we might learn, in a much deeper way, about the lives of others. This is not the same as autoethnography, although I have no problem with that approach. (In the autoethnographic tradition, scholars use their biographies and experiences to connect to the broader social and cultural world.)

Rather, this is closer to what the sociologist Loïc Wacquant calls a "carnal sociology"—that is, a sociology "of the flesh."

Wacquant asks us to get our bodies in tune with the onslaughts of life. He calls this an "enactive ethnography," one in which ethnographers learn through their bodies by accomplishing everyday tasks. Wacquant became a boxer, which allowed him to get close to the people whose lives he wished to understand and to learn, from his flesh, what it meant to practice this craft in a place like the South Side of Chicago. My fieldwork experience was different. I did not *become* a "ghetto resident" or a prisoner in order to understand what it meant to live through mass incarceration; I didn't have to. I was born black and poor in a world where poor black people are disdained and blamed for their problems. Ethnographers (and, I would argue, other kinds of methodologists as well) have pushed us for years to think about our bodies as sentient and situated in a social world, but Wacquant pushes us further. He asks us to think of the ways that we suffer and the skills that we acquire to get through our pain.[4] This is because suffering is a fact of life, but suffering is also experienced differentially, meaning the burden of pain is not shared in the same ways, and some people, through social arrangements and their actions, experience more pain than others. This is a simple statement with profound implications. The burden of pain separates us, clouding our understanding of one another when we presume our experiences are universal, but it has the potential to facilitate connection. It may do this for the scholars who seek to become like the people they study, and it does this for those of us whose biographies connect us to our research participants in an equally profound way.

In a 1974 address on fieldwork to the Pacific Sociological

Association, Erving Goffman, perhaps the most cited sociologist to work in the American Academy, described the practice of ethnography in a way that bears quoting at length. For Goffman, fieldwork is about

> subjecting yourself, your own body and your own personality, and your own social situation, to the set of contingencies that play upon a set of individuals, so that you can physically and ecologically penetrate their circle of response to their social situation... That "tunes your body up" and with your "tuned-up" body and with the ecological right to be close to them (which you've obtained by one sneaky means or another), you are in a position to note their... response to what's going on around them and you're empathetic enough—because you've been taking the same crap they've been taking—to sense what it is they're responding to.[5]

Goffman called this the "core of observation"—to be close and empathetic enough to understand what is happening in and to the bodies of the people you study. If you cannot accomplish this task—the task of a shared experience—Goffman said, "I don't think you can do a piece of serious work."

While ethnographers, following the feminist tradition and Wacquant, have attempted to capture the "carnal aspects" of their craft, criticisms of "me search" and the presumed need for critical distance has led to particular kinds of ethnographies in which scholars emphasize "differences," "blind spots," and insights that are "stumbled upon." This work is important—we all have blind spots and biases that must be addressed, and many insights come about in unexpected ways—but there is an opportunity to think carefully about proximity, or what Goffman calls "getting close," as a goal and a gift.

Scholars who manage to get proximate through "one sneaky means or another" are likely to see things that scholars who have not achieved this proximity cannot. But there is an unaccounted-for problem to this approach that gets in the way of real proximity, and it may obscure the knowledge produced by even the best ethnographers. We might call this the problem of empathy and the limits of the empathetic imagination.

The problem of empathy, in this case, presumes that once you've suffered the same things as the people whose lives you study, you will develop an understanding of why they act the way they do. Empathy requires that we walk a mile in the shoes of others. We project ourselves into their skin to understand the hows and whys of their actions.[6] But the limits of what we can call the "empathetic imagination" begin and end with our own experiences. We must first "take the crap they take" in order to understand why they respond in specific ways. But the ways we experience our fieldwork are mitigated by our lives and the positions in the social world we've occupied. Our social positions matter; our race, class, gender, sexual orientation, ability status, religion, the regions in which we live, our politics, and all the other axes of social difference we occupy contribute to how we experience the world. The reason for this is simple: Our identities shape how others treat us and how we understand ourselves, and there are entire systems of identity-based benefits and burdens. But beyond the trap of our identities, which are constructions, abstractions (for example, no one is *actually* white or black, and our understandings of gender or religion or what it means to be from, say, "the South" mischaracterize and overlook the sum of our experiences), our training may matter just as much.

Scientists, journalists, and commentators on the world's social problems have largely been taught to operate from the mind-body duality. The questions we ask are governed by the very conditions that make those questions necessary. And even when we've been trained in the carnal aspects of our craft, our writing is rewarded when it does the work of separation. It doesn't matter how well they know the people they've come to study, or the extent to which they care about their well-being, there is a currency in *explaining* the social worlds of "others," which presumes that the audience is necessarily different from the people with whom the scholar has spent their time. This is why a scholar can spend years in the field and *still* write about their research participants as if they were from a different planet when their field sites may be just a few miles from their home or they may have moved to their field sites for years at a time. This subtle trick of positioning, where the researcher is the foreign, authoritative, and disembodied voice narrating the lives of people different from them, prevents us from getting close and makes it difficult to describe those worlds in ways that resonate with the lives of the people with whom we've spent so much time. Put differently, the empathetic imagination centers the needs and experiences of the researcher, who has ventured into "foreign territory" to explain the lives of "others" to the "general reader," or the generalist scholar, or even the specialist in their field—that is, to so-called normal people. It doesn't matter if you're black or poor or someone who does not conform to sexual or gendered expectations studying people who are presumed to be "like you," that is to say, if you're an "insider." If you write about your work or the people you follow with the distance and scholarly posture we're rewarded to assume, you may replicate the power dynamics you attempt to uncover, even if you're hoping to generate empathy among your readers.

The point is not *just* to empathize. Empathy alone has too many limits. The point is to walk alongside the people you spend time with and to do your best to learn from and communicate something about their lives with all the tools that you have. I may never experience the loss of a loved one to a drunk driver, but I understand my own pain and joys and the ways I accomplish the routines of my life. If I invest the time to pay attention to the specificities of my pain as I walk aside and attend to the experiences of others, I may be able to connect with them in more than a surface way. I will see things people who are not close fail to see, and I may be able to relay what I see in ways that resonate with their lives. We need a sociology of being, a sociology of "being together," to challenge the limits of empathy, which at the end of the day centers on the researchers and not the people whom those researchers follow.

I may never know what it means to be deported, but paying attention to the specificities of my pain offers connection to the people I hope to learn from.

RESEARCH METHODS

This book is my attempt at a sociology of being together. I wanted to know how poor people—more specifically, poor black people—experienced the transformation of their social world in the wake of mass incarceration and what the nation's history of punishment might tell us about the state of social life under these conditions.

My research began in Chicago, where I spent a year and a half conducting interviews with people who lived in homeless shelters, over a third of whom were formerly incarcerated, and three and a half years observing and conducting interviews at halfway houses throughout the city. I conducted more than one hundred interviews with the formerly incarcerated residents of those halfway houses and shelters, with local politicians, and with reentry program staff, and I did historical analyses of criminal justice and social welfare policy. I learned a great deal about the reentry program as an organizational form and the expression of the evidence-based practices that scholars, policy makers, and program planners hope ward off deviance and economic dependence. Most of that work is covered in chapter 7 of this book, but some of it is dispersed throughout. For example, I met Zo from chapter 2 during this time.

I found that studying the evidence-based treatment group provided me with a vehicle to understand how criminal justice and social welfare policies were experienced and how the most marginalized among us interpret those policies. While findings from this work led to well-cited and (I believe) influential publications, I couldn't quite capture how social policies were "lived out." That is, I knew what men experienced in treatment and what they told me about their lives, but I couldn't capture how the policies that cleared the way for these programs shaped their lives at home. I didn't learn much about their families or friends beyond what they told me. My work was bounded by the treatment group. I knew I needed to break out of the halfway house in much the same way that most criminologists needed to break out of the prison if I hoped to understand the broader impacts of mass incarceration.

Shortly after I took my first faculty job at the University of Michigan, I was awarded funding through an NIH pilot grant to launch the Detroit Reentry Project, a qualitative study of the reentry experiences of ninety men and women released from jails, prisons, and police station lockup facilities into Detroit. I sampled men and women from the Detroit Detention Center, the city's centralized lockup facility, and the Detroit Reentry Center, a residential treatment program. I also interviewed thirty-six "important people," those relatives, friends, and community members that research participants said were most influential in their lives. Finally, I conducted fieldwork, following twelve men and ten women, which allowed me access to their daily routines. This is how I met Jimmy and Yusef and how I eventually came to hire Ronald, Yvette, and Daniel. I documented their experiences as they attempted to find work and stable housing, provide for their families, and make a place for themselves in their home communities.

I learned that formal criminal justice mechanisms—like probation, parole, and the forty-eight thousand laws, policies, and administrative sanctions that target formerly incarcerated people—constrained their lives in obvious and demonstrable ways, but informal sanctions mattered just as much. By this I mean *local practices* mattered as much as formal laws and policies in the daily lives of formerly incarcerated people and their families. I found that the people closest to them shared the burden of their incarceration, and their everyday, mundane encounters could change their experiences and trajectories. Put differently, pastors, aunts, girlfriends, and grandmothers were as important to their reentry experience as the probation and parole officers they reported to and the employers and landlords who would not hire them or grant them a lease. This interplay between formal and informal systems of coercion and control became a central thread in my research. I had to know how, under these conditions, someone might find a way out.

In the spring of 2016, I got a grant from the Antipode Foundation to study the resistance strategies of formerly in-carcerated people and was awarded membership in the School of Social Science at the Institute for Advanced Study, in Princeton, New Jersey. I spent the next year following activists and social service providers, taking part in their campaigns to reverse the fallout from mass incarceration. This work led me to follow a national network of activists on their campaigns in LA, Ypsilanti, Chicago, Gainesville, Philadelphia, Flint, and New York City. These activists pushed for policy reforms, engaged in peaceful protests, and worked to build for-profit and nonprofit companies to hire formerly incarcerated people. These three independent studies formed the basis of *Halfway Home*.

There were some important analytic decisions. Like other qualitative scholars, I reviewed and reread my field notes and interview transcripts over and over again, highlighting impor-tant themes that emerged across cases. The experiences I've chosen to narrate best represent the sets of experiences the two hundred and fifty people I interviewed and dozens of people that I followed shared. Each of the book's chapters represent a major theme from the data, and the literature I present is meant to contextualize what I found within the broader universe of ideas that I hope to capture, what I've come to call the "Afterlife of Mass Incarceration."

PROXIMITY IS A GIFT

I employ proximity as a method, drawing close to the people I've encountered through my biography, experiences, education, and training to understand their social situations, leaning into the proximity that I hoped to achieve in the way that I analyzed and presented the data. Put simply, my social locations as an ethnographer, a sociologist, a professor, a black man who grew up poor in Chicago, a former chaplain at the Cook County Jail, and a social worker supporting at-risk youth helped me understand, through my body, my fieldwork, and the lives of the people who occupied my field sites. My education and training may have differed considerably from those people whose lives I studied (though this was not always the case) and I have never gone to prison, meaning I wasn't exactly an "insider,"[7] but I knew what it was like to have incarcerated family members, and I've had my own brushes with the law. I may not have experienced waiting for a spouse or child to come home after a long sentence, but I understood, in a visceral and emotional way, what it meant to pay for overpriced snacks from a vending machine or drive four hours to a prison on a day when the unit is on lockdown. I know how it feels to watch someone you care about marched away in chains, and I understand, from my body, the burdens and benefits of caring for a prisoner. I've done my best to examine my own pain and use it to relate to the very different pains of the people I've come to study. These experiences have helped me do more than just empathize with my research participants—empathy would center me and limit my analytic abilities to the sets of experiences that I've had and my ability to project those experiences into the lives of other people. They allow me to ask new questions and design, implement, and analyze data from my studies from the peculiar insight that my flesh provides.

But there is another analytic decision that's important to highlight. In the spirit of proximity, I've chosen to include the experiences of people who are close to me, including some members of my family. The reason for this is simple. The subject/object divide that animates much of our social scientific inquiry is artificial. It reflects the very mind-body dualism and the limits of empathy that my sociological practice of being there hopes to challenge. To be close, analytically and meth-odologically, means to wrestle with the many different ways that one's biography and experiences shape and are shaped by the object of their examination. Many scholars do this work in a positionality statement that they provide in the intro-ductions to their books or that they save for a methodological appendix. I've chosen to do this work throughout the book because my proximity has helped me better understand the lives of the people I followed. Furthermore, I was born poor and black in a racially segregated neighborhood in the era of mass incarceration; I couldn't have avoided the prison if I tried. For these reasons, I have chosen to communicate how a social situation *feels* as a technique of data presentation that provides readers, who may not be proximate to those experiences, access to the data they need to assess the veracity of my claims. Put differently, it is my position that my expressing the joy, fear, or weight of a given social situation helps the reader more objectively assess my interpretation of the data. This is not just a descriptive technique but an analytic approach.

Being close to a social situation allows the ethnographer (or researcher who employs any method) and the reader to under-stand, through what they see and feel, the social situation of others. This is a goal of ethnographic practice: to understand what it means to accomplish the daily routines and experience the regular onslaughts of life associated with a given social position at a specific moment in time. A sociology of being together takes proximity as a method and an analysis, because, to the careful social scientist, proximity is a gift.

Notes

INTRODUCTION

1 See Henry Louis Gates Jr. and Evelyn Brooks Higginbotham, eds., *African American Lives* (New York: Oxford University Press, 2004). See also Henry Louis Gates Jr., "The First White Man in Chicago Was a Negro?," *Root,* September 30, 2013.

2 City of Chicago, "Chicago History," https://www.chicago.gov/city/en/about/history.html.

3 The historical record indicates that du Sable had deep, positive ties with the Potawatomie. While this is likely the case, it should be noted that the relationships between black people, free or enslaved, and the indigenous people who lived on the lands they came to occupy were long and complicated. In some cases, black people were owned by native people as slaves. Tiya Miles's work, for example, recounts the slaveholding relationships between black slaves and the Cherokee plantation owners who bought and sold them. See Tiya Miles, *Ties That Bind: The Story of an Afro-Cherokee Family in Slavery and Freedom* (Berkeley: University of California Press, 2005). In other cases, black people were soldiers fighting alongside or against American Indians as colonists from France, Britain, and eventually the fledgling United States expanded their landholdings; see Justin Leroy, "Black History in Occupied Territory: On the Entanglements of Slavery and Settler Colonialism," *Theory and Event* 19, no. 4 (2016). In still other cases, black people joined with First Nations people, forming maroon societies. See Richard Price, ed., *Maroon Societies: Rebel Slave Communities in the Americas* (Baltimore: Johns Hopkins University Press, 1996).

4 The Total Emancipation Act was not ordered in the British colonies until 1834 and applied only to the international trade of slaves within the British empire, and while slavery was abolished in France in 1794, two decades after du Sable settled at the mouth of the Chicago River, the slave trade was reinstated by

299

Napoleon in 1802 and would not be ended in the French colonies until 1848. It would take a civil war and the passage of the Thirteenth Amendment to abolish the practice of slavery in the United States, but that wasn't until 1863. The theft of land, through settlement and colonial expansion, and the theft of black and Indian people to cultivate that land are bound together. See Tiya Miles, *Dawn of Detroit: A Chronicle of Bondage and Freedom in the City of the Straits* (New York: New Press, 2017).

5   The Emancipation Proclamation freed enslaved people in the Confederate states on January 1, 1863, but it would take the Union army to enforce black freedom. In Confederate states with little Union presence and few people paying attention to the health and well-being of black people, emancipation was delayed. Black freedom wasn't announced in Texas until June 19, 1865, two and a half years after slavery officially ended there. While this was the basis for the Juneteenth holiday, which commemorates the abolition of slavery in the United States, slavery was still legal in two border states, Delaware and Kentucky, until the ratification of the Thirteenth Amendment, on December 6, 1865. And while the practice of slavery had been formally illegal since the end of the Civil War, recent accounts place black slaves on plantations and in homes in Arkansas, Florida, Louisiana, and Mississippi well into the 1960s. See Henry Louis Gates Jr., "What Is Juneteenth?," PBS.org, January 16, 2013, and Antoinette Harrell, "Black People in the U.S. Were Enslaved Well into the 1960s," Vice.com, February 28, 2018, https://www.vice.com/en_us/article /437573/blacks-were-enslaved-well-into-the-1960s.

6   Du Sable was the first nonindigenous settler. The Potawatomie, Ojibwa, Odawa, Menominee, Miami, and Ho-Chunk were already well established in the area when du Sable and his wife, Kittahawa, built their home and trading post. See Odette Yusef, "Do Descendants of Chicago's Native American Tribes Live in the City Today?," WBEZ.org, July 11, 2012, https://www.wbez.org/shows/curious-city/ do-descendants-of-chicagos-native-american-tribes-live-in-the-city-today/42633 cd1-325e-4ee2-a254-ecf36c555cc0.

7   *Quadroon*, a racial classification in popular use during the eighteenth and nine-teenth centuries, designated free people of African descent and slaves who may have "passed" for white but had one-quarter "black blood"—that is, they had one black grandparent. Like the terms *mulatto* and *octoroon*, *quadroon* is a crude expression of the pseudoscientific one-drop rule, which extended the classification of "black" to any person of African descent born within or brought to the United States. These kinds of racial practices did the work of distinguishing so-called white from so-called black Americans, consolidating blackness and whiteness as racial categories in the U.S. racial hierarchy. See John Hope Franklin and Evelyn Brooks Higginbotham, *From Slavery to Freedom* (New York: Knopf, 2000).

8   Arent Schuyler de Peyster, *Miscellanies* (New York: A. E. Chasmer, 1813).

9   Ibid.

10   See Gates and Higginbotham, *African American Lives*, and Gates, "First White Man."

11   Du Sable sold his estate in 1800 to a fur trader and interpreter, Jean La Lime. Among his possessions were his forty-by-twenty-two-foot wooden house complete with walnut furniture; a horse mill; a smokehouse; a stable; a barn; thirty-eight head of cattle; thirty hogs; two mules; and forty-four hens—considerable holdings for the time. At one point du Sable bought four hundred acres of land from the U.S. government. See Milo Milton Quaife, "Property of Jean Baptiste Point Sable," *Mississippi Valley Historical Review* (1928): 89–96, and Gates, "First White Man."

12   John Kinzie, a white trader from Quebec who bought du Sable's home from a man he later stabbed to death, would be remembered as the city's founder. The historian Milo Milton Quaife, in "Property of Jean Baptiste Point Sable," wrote, "Point Sable preceded Kinzie by at least fourteen years…. Unless the fact of negro blood be deemed to bar his claim, Point Sable, rather than Kinzie, must be regarded as the first settler at Chicago" (page 89). And Kinzie had something of a sordid past. He was a prominent trader who moved to the city around 1804, when he bought the home from his trading partner Jean La Lime. He was appointed justice of the peace by William Henry Harrison, then the governor of the Indiana territory (which included Chicago) and future president of the United States, but in 1812 he killed La Lime, who, according to some accounts, suspected him of corruption in his trade with the British. Word spread of the killing, which was labeled "Chicago's first murder," causing Kinzie to flee for a time to Milwaukee. He moved again to Detroit, where he was accused by the British of treason, arrested, and put on a ship to England. By 1816, he'd escaped and returned to Chicago, where he lived out the rest of his life. Historical accounts from as early as 1912 identify Kinzie as the founder of the city. There is a street named after John Kinzie, but there is still no street named after du Sable, the city's black founder. See Gates, "First White Man"; "Chicago's First Murder," *Chicago Daily Tribune*, November 27, 1942, and Bessie Louise Pierce, *A History of Chicago, Vol. 1: The Beginning of a City 1673–1848* (Chicago: University of Chicago Press, 1937), 21.

13   Melanie Newport, "When a Psychologist Was in Charge of Jail," Marshall Project, May 21, 2015. Jails are almost always unpopular, but Cook County was notorious for its abuse. There was the barn-boss system, where well-known prisoners were given unofficial authority to run the wings of the jail, and reports called the county a "veritable jungle of sexual perversion, dope traffic, extortion and bestial violence—the worst institution of its kind in the annals of penology"; see Hans Massaquoi, "The Warden Who Reformed 'the World's Worst Jail,'" *Ebony* (July 1969): 61.

14 For a history of the Cook County Jail and the fascinating role that Winston Moore played in changing the landscape of jails in the United States, see Melanie D. Newport, "Jail America: The Reformist Origins of the Carceral State" (PhD diss., Temple University, 2016).

15 Winston E. Moore, "Stop Coddling Hoodlums: Going Easy on Criminals Encourages Crime," *Ebony* (August 1979): 118–22.

16 Vernon Jarrett, "Dunk the Darkie Returns to Town," *Chicago Tribune,* July 27, 1975.

17 Formerly incarcerated activists would object to the use of terms like *convict, offender,* and *prisoner,* arguing for the use of person-centered language when referring to people who've had any manner of experiences, including experiences with the law. I agree; I use the term *ex-convict* here to capture the spirit of the move, and I use *convict* and *offender* in other places only when they are a part of a quote or refer to names of specific organizations. There are times when I use the word *prisoner* to reflect the social condition of people behind bars—that is, the condition of being in jail or prison. Otherwise, I refer to those with criminal records and those who have been to jail and prison as *people.*

18 In a study of people's incomes before and after incarceration, 52 percent of the sample reported having no income in the three years prior to their incarceration. Another 32 percent reported earning between five hundred dollars and fifteen thousand dollars in one or more years within the same period. See Adam Looney and Nicholas Turner, "Work and Opportunity Before and After Incarceration," Brookings Institution, March 14, 2018. For more recent statistics on the U.S. jail and prison population, see Wendy Sawyer and Peter Wagner, "Mass Incarceration: The Whole Pie 2019," *Prison Policy Initiative* 19 (2019).

19 The National Registry of Exonerations collects data on all known wrongful convictions in the United States. It's important to note the limitations of the data. The process of securing an exoneration is a long and complicated one.

20 I take instruction from Ruth Wilson Gilmore's thesis in *Golden Gulag* (Berkeley: University of California Press, 2007). For Gilmore, the prison is a geographic solution to social problems—that is, the prison is used to house surplus populations (people who serve little economic use in a given society) and address questions of what to do with surplus land and capital (both political and financial). Relatedly, I'm taking a note from Angela Davis, who argues that prisons hide American poverty by "disappearing vast numbers of people from poor, immigrant, and racially marginalized communities." Since the targets of carceral expansion are historically marginalized groups (poor black people and, increasingly, people from poor Latinx, immigrant, and white urban and rural communities), and since the prison produces or extracts wealth through government contracts, Gilmore and Davis would argue that the "prison industrial

complex" masks American racism. There's a real debate about the extent to which a prison industrial complex, as Davis and Gilmore formulate it, exists. Prisons are largely public. Aside from contracting for ancillary services and renting beds to the state and federal governments to house immigrant detainees, prisons are not privately run. But while disagreeing with Davis and Gilmore in a number of important ways, sociologists of punishment, like Loïc Wacquant, whose work is key to my thinking on these issues, similarly finds that "hyper incarceration," or the targeting of poor black men for punishment, resulted from shifts in economic, social welfare, and criminal justice policy. In Wacquant's formulation, prisons house unskilled black workers made "redundant" by deindustrialization, financial deregulation, and a shrinking and increasingly punitive welfare state. Under what critics have termed *neoliberalism,* or the market-driven economy, the government no longer regulates financial markets in ways that provide a sense of social security for most people. Instead, it produces and manages "social insecurity," or people's fears of crime and violence and the populations they presume are its cause. Following this line of thought, I've greatly benefited from John Eason's prescient work on prison placement. Prisons, Eason argues, serve an economic, political, and cultural role, certainly in prison towns but also in the broader social landscape of the United States, by raising the per capita income of prison-town residents, employing a fairly diverse prison-guard work-force, and, most provocatively, offering a way for towns and local governments with bad reputations to "rehabilitate their spoiled identities." Whatever theories we embrace in our critiques of the penal state, there's fairly broad agreement in at least two domains. First, incarceration is used as a solution to social problems that extend far beyond the criminal legal system, including inadequate access to physical- and mental-health care, poor education, systemic poverty, and racial resentment. And second, criminal justice policy overwhelmingly targets black people and the poor. For data on racial disparities in wrongful convictions, see Samuel R. Gross, Maurice Possley, and Klara Stephens, "Race and Wrongful Convictions in the United States," National Registry of Exonerations, Newkirk Center for Science and Society (2017). For work on the prison as a solution to social problems, see Angela Davis, "Masked Racism: Reflections on the Prison Industrial Complex," *Colorlines* (September 1998); John Eason, *Big House on the Prairie: Rise of the Rural Ghetto and Prison Proliferation* (Chicago: University of Chicago Press, 2017); Loïc Wacquant, *Punishing the Poor: The Neoliberal Government of Social Insecurity* (Durham, NC: Duke University Press, 2009), and Gilmore, *Golden Gulag.*

21   Roy Walmsley, "World Prison Population List," eleventh edition, Institute for Criminal Policy Research, 2016, https://www.prisonstudies.org/sites/default/files/resources/downloads/world_prison_population_list_11th_edition_0.pdf.

22   There have been a few remarkable books on the Cook County Jail. Nicole Gonzalez Van Cleve's *Crook County: Racism and Injustice in America's Largest Criminal Court* (Stanford, CA: Stanford University Press, 2016) offers a careful ethnography of the Cook County court system. Melanie Newport's *Community of the Condemned: Chicago and the Transformation of the American Jail* (Philadelphia: University of Pennsylvania Press, forthcoming) offers a definitive history of jail reform in Cook County, noting that the impulse to reform jails is a key driver of mass incarceration.

23   Four Illinois governors have been sentenced to prison in the past forty years: Otto Kerner (governor from 1961 to 1968) was convicted of bribery; Dan Walker (governor from 1973 to 1977) was convicted of bank fraud; George Ryan (governor from 1999 to 2003) was convicted of racketeering; and Rod Blagojevich (governor from 2002 to 2009), the first Illinois governor to be impeached, was convicted on corruption charges. See Associated Press, "4 of Illinois' Last 7 Governors Went to Prison," *Daily Journal*, January 30, 2013.

24   "Charges Claim Illinois Governor Blagojevich Sought to Sell Obama's Senate Seat," *Chicago Sun-Times*, December 9, 2008.

25   Sarah Shannon and her colleagues were the first to estimate the number of people with felony records in a widely cited paper published on the Social Science Research Network in 2010 and then as a peer-reviewed article in the journal *Demography* in 2016. See Shannon et al., "The Growth, Scope, and Spatial Distribution of People with Felony Records in the United States, 1948–2010," *Demography* 54 (2016): 1795–1818.

26   For the concentration of people released from prisons in Illinois, see Nancy G. La Vigne, Christy Visher, and Jennifer Castro, "Chicago Prisoners' Experiences Returning Home," Urban Institute, December 2004. For the demographic profiles of each Chicago neighborhood, see the Chicago data portal at https://data.cityofchicago.org. I've drawn on this data to make similar claims about the racial geography of prisoner reentry in Reuben Jonathan Miller, "Devolving the Carceral State: Race, Prisoner Reentry, and the Micro-Politics of Urban Poverty Management," *Punishment and Society* 16, no. 3 (2014): 305–35.

27   Nancy La Vigne et al., "A Portrait of Reentry in Illinois," Urban Institute, April 17, 2003; Miller, "Devolving the Carceral State."

28   Class and place matter quite a bit to this story. We were both born poor in poor neighborhoods where neither of us could avoid brushes with the law. But we were also born black, and the research is clear that the protections of class don't extend equally across racial lines. In a recent study, Raj Chetty and colleagues found that when comparing families in the top 1 percent of the parental-income distribution, 2.2 percent of black boys were incarcerated compared with just .02 percent of white boys, an eleven-to-one racial disparity. Put differently, black

boys from millionaire households were as likely to be incarcerated as white boys raised in families with an annual income of just thirty-six thousand dollars. See Raj Chetty et al., "Race and Economic Opportunity in the United States: An Intergenerational Perspective," *Quarterly Journal of Economics* 135, no. 2 (2020): 711–83.

CHAPTER 1: CONFESSION

1   Loïc Wacquant pushes us to learn from our flesh, and by this he means that ethnographers get proficient in the daily activities of the people they study because it allows them to learn from their bodies and through their bodies about the experiences of others. See Wacquant, "For a Sociology of Flesh and Blood," *Qualitative Sociology* 38, no. 1 (2015): 1–11.

2   See "The 10 Most Dangerous Cities in America," *Market Watch*, June 24, 2013, https://www.marketwatch.com/story/the-10-most-dangerous-cities-in-america-2013-06-22; Kristin Longley, "Flint Lawmaker Requests Settlement Money to Pay for More Police as Flint Tops Nation's Violent Crime List," Michigan Live, June 18, 2012, https://www.mlive.com/news/flint/2012/06/flint_lawmaker_requests_forecl.html; Lori Jane Gliha, "Growing Up in America's Most Dangerous City, Flint," Aljazeera America, October 24, 2013, http://america.aljazeera.com/watch/shows/america-tonight/america-tonight-blog/2013/10/24/growing-up-in-americasmostdangerouscityflint.html.

3   Twelve Michigan officials were charged with crimes ranging from misconduct to manslaughter for their role in the Flint water crisis. Seven took plea deals. By 2016, Darnell Early and Gerald Ambrose, the two emergency managers who presided over the crisis, were each charged with two felony counts, one on false pretenses and another on misconduct in office. By 2018, Nick Lyon, the former director of the Michigan Department of Health and Human Services, along with Early, Ambrose, and two other state officials, was charged with manslaughter. This was due in part to an outbreak of Legionnaires' disease linked to the contaminated water that claimed the lives of at least twelve people, but the water crisis may have contributed to many more deaths, given that deaths from pneumonia increased by 43 percent in 2014. These charges were dropped in 2019 when a new administration took office and a new district attorney took the helm of the prosecution. For a discussion of the initial charges filed against the emergency managers, see Merit Kennedy, "Two Former Emergency Managers, Two Others Face Felony Charges Over Water Crisis," NPR.org, December 20, 2016, https://www.npr.org/sections/thetwo-way/2016/12/20/506314203/2former-flint-emergency-managers-face-felony-charges-over-water-crisis. For deaths

related to the water crisis, see Kayla Ruble et al., "Flint Water Crisis Deaths Likely Surpass Official Toll," *Frontline,* July 24, 2018, https://www.pbs.org/wgbh/frontline/article/flint-water-crisis-deaths-likely-surpass-official-toll/.

4   In 1980, people classified as black represented 50.9 percent of Michigan's prison admissions despite black people making up just 13 percent of the state's population. People classified as white made up 84 percent of the state's population but just 39 percent of state prison admissions. These trends have been remarkably consistent even with the explosive growth and relatively modest decline of Michigan's prison population, which increased from 15,168 people in 1980 to 38,761 people in 2018. Today, black Americans are 6.2 times more likely to be sent to prison than those classified as white; black people represent 53 percent of the state's prison population and 37 percent of all people held in jail, despite being just 14 percent of the state's population. In addition to these egregious racial disparities, the Pew Center on the States found in 2012 that the Michigan Department of Corrections led the nation in sentencing length and the amount of time served, which increased a staggering 79 percent between 1990 and 2010. Since the publication of the Pew study, the sentence length in Michigan has continued to grow, as does the number of people serving life sentences and the racial disparities in legal outcomes among them; a staggering 68 percent of all people serving a life sentence today are classified as black. Put differently, not only are there long-standing racial disparities in Michigan prisons, but the people incarcerated serve more time than almost everyone else in the country. For a discussion of the length of prison sentences by state, see Adam Gelb, Ryan King, and Felicity Rose, "Time Served: The High Cost, Low Return of Longer Prison Terms," Pew Center on the States (June 2012). For statistics on Michigan jails and prisons by race, see Christian Henrichson, Eital Schattner-Elmaleh, and Jacob Kang-Brown, "Incarceration Trends in Michigan: Incarceration in Local Jails and State Prisons," Vera Institute of Justice (2019), https://www.vera.org/downloads/pdfdownloads/state-incarceration-trends-michigan.pdf. For historic trends in incarceration by race in the state of Michigan, see Patrick A. Langan, "Race of Prisoners Admitted to State and Federal Institutions, 1926–1986," U.S. Bureau of Justice Statistics, 1991.

5   In *History of Sexuality,* Foucault wrote that confession "plays a part in justice, medicine, education, family relationships, and love relations, in the most ordinary affairs of everyday life, and in the most solemn rites; one confesses one's crimes, one's sins, one's thoughts and desires, one's illnesses and troubles; one goes about telling, with the greatest precision, whatever is most difficult to tell." Michel Foucault, *History of Sexuality,* vol. 1 (New York: Pantheon, 1978), 59.

6   See Peter Brook, *Troubling Confessions: Speaking Guilt in Law and Literature* (Chicago: University of Chicago Press, 2001).

7   Contrition is a condition of the heart, a "sorrow of soul and a hatred of sin committed, with a firm purpose of not sinning in the future." St. Thomas Aquinas wrote, "The act which obtains forgiveness is termed by a figure of speech called contrition." See John Joseph Wynne, *The Catholic Encyclopedia: An International Work of Reference on the Constitution, Doctrine, Discipline, and History of the Catholic Church*, vol. 4 (New York: Universal Knowledge Foundation, 1913).

8   The text of the Fifth Amendment reads, "No person...shall be compelled in any criminal case to be a witness against himself, nor be deprived of life, liberty, or property, without due process of law."

9   See Neil R. McMillen, *Dark Journey: Black Mississippians in the Age of Jim Crow* (Chicago: University of Illinois Press, 1990).

10   *Brown v. Mississippi*, 297 U.S. 278 (1936), https://supreme.justia.com/cases/federal/us/297/278/.

11   See McMillen, *Dark Journey*, 198.

12   *Brown v. Mississippi*.

13   The court record shows that Mr. Ellington could not sit the day after his torture and that he had trouble sitting during the trial. See McMillen, *Dark Journey*.

14   Ibid., 199.

15   Ibid.

16   Ibid.; *Brown v. Mississippi*.

17   *Brown v. Mississippi*.

18   As the first Supreme Court decision to reverse a criminal conviction based on a coerced confession, *Brown v. Mississippi* "triggered the development of an entire area of constitutional law," according to law professor Morgan Cloud, and helped establish legal precedent for a number of landmark decisions, including *Miranda v. Arizona*, which requires police officers to advise suspects of their right to remain silent and have an attorney during interrogations. See Morgan Cloud, "Torture and Truth," *Texas Law Review* 74 (1995): 1211.

19   Stennis sent three men to the death chamber even though he knew their confessions were procured by torture, but he opposed the criminal prosecution of Richard Nixon in 1974, saying his impeachment was punishment enough. He was named the eighty-fifth president pro tempore of the Senate in 1987, an honorary position acknowledging his seniority and esteem within the chamber. President Ronald Reagan named a naval super-carrier in his honor when he retired in 1989, the USS *John C. Stennis*. He took a job as a lecturer at Mississippi State University and taught there until his death in 1995 at the age of ninety-three. See David Rosenbaum, "John C. Stennis, 93, Longtime Chairman of Powerful Committee in the Senate, Dies," *New York Times*, April 24, 1995; Matthew Yglesias, "The White Supremacist Caucus," *Atlantic*, November

26, 2007; John M. Crewdson, "Scott Says Capital Leaders Oppose Nixon Prosecution," *New York Times,* August 12, 1974.

20   McMillen, *Dark Journey,* 200.

21   Matthew R. Durose and Patrick A. Langan, "State Court Sentencing of Convicted Felons 2004: Statistical Tables," *Bureau of Justice Statistics Bulletin* (August 3, 2007).

22   This is what Sarah Lageson has called digital punishment and part of what Susila Gurusami calls the "carceral web." See Sarah Esther Lageson, "Digital Punishment's Tangled Web," *Contexts* 15, no. 1 (2016): 22–27, and Susila Gurusami, "The Carceral Web We Weave: Carceral Citizens' Experiences of Digital Punishment and Solidarity," *Punishment and Society* 21, no. 4 (2019): 435–53.

23   See Gina Fedock, "Life Before 'I Killed the Man That Raped Me': Pre-Prison Life Experiences of Incarcerated Women with Life Sentences and Subsequent Treatment Needs," *Women and Criminal Justice* 28, no. 1 (2018): 63–80.

24   In Michigan, state court judges are appointed through a nonpartisan election, meaning any citizen in the state can vote on the appointment of a judge.

25   See Gelb, King, and Rose, "Time Served."

26   See Ashley Nellis, "Still Life: America's Increasing Use of Life and Long-Term Sentences," Sentencing Project, May 3, 2017.

27   This is part of a larger pattern. In Chicago, a white police officer, Jason Van Dyke, was found guilty of second-degree murder after shooting a black boy, seventeen-year-old Laquan McDonald, sixteen times from behind. People breathed a sigh of relief when he was convicted, thinking the guilty verdict meant justice had been served. This was the first time in fifty years, perhaps the first time in all of U.S. history, that an on-duty officer had been found guilty of murder in the killing of a black boy. This was the city where police detective Jon Burge was accused of torturing over two hundred black men, and although the city paid millions of dollars to their families for the torture, essentially admitting Burge was guilty of the crimes, no one had gone to prison. It was the same city in which police reportedly ran a "black site" in one of the city's poorest neighborhoods, frequently disappearing young black men and then returning them days later to stand trial. If sentencing guidelines were followed, Van Dyke would have spent the rest of his life in prison. He was guilty on sixteen counts of aggravated assault, each carrying a four- to twenty-year sentence, and of second-degree murder, which in Illinois carries a sentence of between four and twenty-six years. The prosecutors requested that Van Dyke spend at least eighteen years behind bars. The judge didn't follow the prosecutors' request, instead sentencing Van Dyke based on the second-degree murder charge alone. Van Dyke got less than seven years. For a discussion of Jon Burge and his legacy, see Laurence Ralph, *The Torture Letters: Reckoning*

with *Police Violence* (Chicago: University of Chicago Press, 2020), and his equally compelling article on the collective memory of torture on Chicago's South and West Sides, "The Qualia of Pain: How Police Torture Shapes Historical Consciousness," *Anthropological Theory* 13, nos. 1–2 (2013): 104–18. For reporting on the black site in Chicago's Homan Square neighborhood, see Spencer Ackerman, "The Disappeared: Chicago Police Detain Americans at Abuse-Laden 'Black Site,'" *Guardian,* February 24, 2015. For reporting on the background and outcomes of the Laquan McDonald shooting and the trial of Jason Van Dyke, listen to Jenn White's podcast episode "The Police Killing of Laquan McDonald," *Sixteen Shots,* https://www.wbez.org/stories/ep-30-81-months/00af24cd-fc27-4063-9e13-6401e5826982. See also Nausheen Husain, "Laquan McDonald Timeline: The Shooting, the Video, the Verdict, and the Sentencing," *Chicago Tribune,* January 18, 2019.

28   See Ariel Levy, "Dirty Old Women," *New York*, May 18, 2006.

29   See Chanel Miller, *Know My Name: A Memoir* (New York: Viking, 2019). See also Claire Cohen, "Judge Who Gave Stanford Sex Attacker Brock Turner 6 Month Jail Sentence Is Recalled from the Bench," *Guardian,* June 6, 2018.

30   See Michael Walker, *Jailing* (New York: Oxford University Press, forthcoming).

CHAPTER 2: GUILT

1   For the video, see https://www.youtube.com/watch?v=_ONict5F3w4.

2   There were many stories of fatal encounters between police officers and black children circulating in 2017. A grand jury failed to indict Officer Timothy Loehmann, who shot and killed twelve-year-old Tamir Rice within two seconds of arriving on the scene. Tamir, another black boy thought to have a weapon, was playing with a toy gun in the park of a Cleveland community center. The officers described him as a twenty-year-old man in their report. Police analysts on cable news referred to the boy as "the male." The video of his murder has circulated for years. In Detroit, seven-year-old Aiyana Stanley-Jones was shot in the head by Officer Joseph Weekley while she was sleeping on her grandmother's couch. Weekley had stormed in during a botched SWAT team raid—botched because they raided the wrong home. Officers had thrown a flash-bang grenade into an open window and knocked the door in. The police first reported that Aiyana's grandmother reached for Weekley's gun. Weekley's defense attorney said she slapped the gun in her attempt to grab it. His weapon discharged "accidentally," piercing the child's skull and exiting through her neck. But the grandmother said that she was reaching for Aiyana because the grenade had burned the poor child's blanket and that the couch where the child slept was on the opposite side

of the room. Weekley sobbed on the front lawn, while a crew from the A&E network's hit TV show *The First 48* filmed the debacle. They were already following Weekley's exploits for a different show, *Detroit Homicide.* Investigators did not find the grandmother's fingerprints on the weapon, and the actual suspect the SWAT team was looking for, a person who lived in an upstairs unit, was arrested without further incident. Despite the evidence—a raid on the wrong apartment, a dead child, an officer who admitted he shot her—the trial of the Detroit SWAT team officer Joseph Weekley ended in a hung jury, twice. The two mistrials ensured a conviction would never be secured. The DA dropped all charges before a third trial could commence and dashed all hopes for any real sense of justice for Aiyana Stanley-Jones or her family. Protesters have since been arrested for chaining themselves to the police station. For reporting on the police killing of Aiyana Stanley-Jones, see Charlie LeDuff, "What Killed Aiyana Stanley-Jones?," *Mother Jones* 6 (2010). For a discussion of the courtroom dynamics in Officer Weekley's trial and an examination of grief and black motherhood, see Rhaisa Kameela Williams, "Toward a Theorization of Black Maternal Grief as Analytic," *Transforming Anthropology* 24, no. 1 (2016): 17–30.

3   In another set of videos released around the same time, three different unarmed black children were subjected to the treatment the five unarmed boys received. In one video, an officer stopped two eleven-year-old black boys and made them walk backward at gunpoint with their hands over their heads. Their crime? Walking in the same direction as a seventeen-year-old who matched the description of another boy with a gun. But this doesn't just happen to boys. Eleven-year-old Honestie Hodges was held at gunpoint by the Grand Rapids police. Like the boys, she was made to walk backward, but in her case it was from the doorway of her home while her mother pleaded, "She's only a child." The police were searching for her aunt Carrie Manning, a forty-two-year-old white woman wanted for stabbing her little sister. The child screamed, "No!" as they put her in handcuffs. For coverage of the chilling encounter between Honestie and the Grand Rapids Police, see Matthew Haag, "Handcuffing 11-Year-Old Girl Was a Mistake, Police Chief Says," *New York Times,* December 15, 2017.

4   John Lamberth and Jerry Clayton, "Grand Rapids Police Department Traffic Stop Data Analysis: Report for the City of Grand Rapids." Lamberth Consulting, April 2017. https://www.grandrapidsmi.gov/Government/Departments/Police-Department/Traffic-Stop-Study.

5   Karen E. Fields and Barbara Jeanne Fields, *Racecraft: The Soul of Inequality in American Life* (London: Verso, 2012).

6   Saidiya Hartman, *Lose Your Mother: A Journey Along the Atlantic Slave Route* (New York: Farrar, Straus and Giroux, 2007), 6.

7   Ibid. See also Ibram X. Kendi, *Stamped from the Beginning: The Definitive History of Racist Ideas in America* (New York: Nation Books, 2016).

8   See Kendi, *Stamped,* 23.

9   Ibid., 22. The chronicle was commissioned by the king's heir, King Alfonso V, and written by Gomes Eanes de Zurara.

10 African societies have rebelled against the Atlantic slave trade since it began in the sixteenth century. For example, Queen Nzinga Mbandi (circa 1583–1663) of Ndongo, known today as Angola, fought against the Portuguese for three full decades. And while the rebellion on the *Amistad* is among the most famous insurrections that took place during the "middle passage," by some estimates there were revolts during no fewer than one in ten Atlantic crossings. Finally, there were hundreds of documented revolts in North America, on plantations, in the barracoons, and anywhere slaves were held. See Linda M. Heywood, *Njinga of Angola* (Cambridge, MA: Harvard University Press, 2019), and David Richardson, "Shipboard Revolts, African Authority, and the Atlantic Slave Trade," *William and Mary Quarterly* 58, no. 1 (2001): 69–92.

11 Indentured servants were more populous than slaves in the American colonies through the middle of the seventeenth century.

12 The colonists knew the female indentured servants to be fallen women, accused of prostitution or worse, "wayward children" plucked by constables from city streets, or drunkards, thieves, or petty criminals who had escaped the hangman's noose. Others were dirt poor, fleeing the hunger resulting from an expanding British Empire.

13 See Peter Linebaugh and Marcus Rediker, *The Many-Headed Hydra: Sailors, Slaves, Commoners, and the Hidden History of the Revolutionary Atlantic* (Boston: Beacon Press, 2013); Peter Linebaugh, *Red Round Globe Hot Burning: A Tale at the Crossroads of Commons and Closure, of Love and Terror, of Race and Class, and of Kate and Ned Despard* (Berkeley: University of California Press, 2019).

14 The English Civil War was far from a distant memory, and rebellion was a chief concern. There were many slave rebellions and just as many rebellions of indigenous people. The most infamous at the time may have been King Philip's War, the rebellion of the Wampanoag people led by Chief Metacomet. The war ended with the death of the chief, his body hacked to pieces, but by that point, some six hundred colonists and three thousand American Indians were dead. Local economies were decimated, and colonists' lands were burned to the ground or left in ruins. See Jill Lepore, *The Name of War: King Philip's War and the Origins of American Identity* (New York: Vintage, 2009). See also Kendi, *Stamped.*

15 See Andrew Dilts, *Punishment and Inclusion: Race, Membership and the Limits of American Liberalism* (New York: Fordham University Press, 2016), 191–92.

16 According to the *Oxford English Dictionary* of 1671, a white man was "a person

of a race distinguished by a light complexion." From this point forward, colonial charters referred to European immigrants as white.

17 The innovations listed were in the law. In everyday life, trinkets, stage plays, and advertisements depicted black children happy and free from pain in their bondage, and the political campaigns of labor reformers depicted white child laborers in agony, identifying white children as innocent and in need of protection—a consideration black children were not afforded. See Robin Bernstein, *Racial Innocence: Performing American Childhood from Slavery to Civil Rights* (New York: New York University Press, 2011).

18 See "Racist Images and Messages" in *The African Americans: Many Rivers to Cross.* "Extra" from 2013 PBS documentary, episode 4. https://www.pbs.org/show/african-americans-many-rivers-cross/.

19 David M. Oshinsky, *"Worse Than Slavery": Parchman Farm and the Ordeal of Jim Crow Justice* (New York: Free Press, 1996). See also Reuben Jonathan Miller, "Race, Hyper-Incarceration, and U.S. Poverty Policy in Historic Perspective," *Sociology Compass* 7, no. 7 (2013): 573–89.

20 Du Bois noted overincarceration in free Philadelphia as early as 1619. Black people were 4 percent of the general population but 30 percent of the jail population; Beaumont and Tocqueville also noted this in their travels. But between 1865 and 1900, black people were overrepresented in the jails and prisons of all major U.S. cities. See William Edward Burghardt Du Bois, "The Philadelphia Negro: A Social Study," *Series in Political Economy and Public Law* 14 (1899), and Gustave de Beaumont and Alexis de Tocqueville, *On the Penitentiary System in the United States and Its Application in France* (Philadelphia: Carey, Lea, and Blanchard, 1833). For work on the great migration, see Isabel Wilkerson, *The Warmth of Other Suns: The Epic Story of America's Great Migration* (New York: Vintage, 2011).

21 Khalil Gibran Muhammad, *The Condemnation of Blackness: Race, Crime, and the Making of Modern Urban America* (Cambridge, MA: Harvard University Press, 2019); Elizabeth Kay Hinton, *From the War on Poverty to the War on Crime* (Cambridge, MA: Harvard University Press, 2015); Miller, "Race, Hyper-Incarceration, and U.S. Poverty Policy."

22 Phillip Atiba Goff et al., "The Essence of Innocence: Consequences of Dehumanizing Black Children," *Journal of Personality and Social Psychology* 106, no. 4 (2014): 526.

23 Rebecca C. Hetey and Jennifer L. Eberhardt, "Racial Disparities in Incarceration Increase Acceptance of Punitive Policies," *Psychological Science* 25, no. 10 (2014): 1949–54.

24 See Robert Brame et al., "Demographic Patterns of Cumulative Arrest Prevalence by Ages 18 and 23," *Crime and Delinquency* 60, no. 3 (2014): 471–86.

25 Ibid. This is racism at work. The study found that 39 percent of white men will be arrested by their twenty-third birthday for a "non-traffic violation," meaning for an actual crime. This makes sense given what criminologists know about deviance and the life course. Most crimes will be committed by people between the ages of sixteen and twenty-five, and white people are no exception. Nine hundred thousand white men are held behind bars on any given day, one in eight white women has a currently incarcerated loved one, and 48 percent of white people in this country have a family member who has spent time in jail or prison, but mass incarceration is nonetheless largely viewed as a black problem, hiding the fundamental transformation of how we govern and its pernicious effects on an entire nation within a discourse of black deviance. For a fascinating discussion of how white criminality was written out of official crime reports during the progressive era, see Muhammad, *The Condemnation of Blackness*. For research on American families with incarcerated loved ones, see Hedwig Lee et al., "Racial Inequalities in Connectedness to Imprisoned Individuals in the United States," *Du Bois Review* 12, no. 2 (2015): 269–82. See also Peter K. Enns et al., "What Percentage of Americans Have Ever Had a Family Member Incarcerated? Evidence from the Family History of Incarceration Survey (FamHIS)," *Socius* 5 (2019): 1–45.

26 Loïc Wacquant, "For a Sociology of Flesh and Blood," *Qualitative Sociology* 38, no. 1 (2015): 1–11.

27 The sociologist Loïc Wacquant writes about this in his article "Deadly Symbiosis: When Ghetto and Prison Meet and Mesh," *Punishment and Society* 3, no. 1 (2001): 95–133.

28 The rapper Common, also a Chicagoan from the South Side, has a verse about this in the song "Sixth Sense" on the album *Like Water for Chocolate*: "In front of two-inch glass and Arabs I order fries / Inspiration when I write, I see my daughter's eyes."

29 See Becky Pettit and Bruce Western, "Mass Imprisonment and the Life Course: Race and Class Inequality in U.S. Incarceration," *American Sociological Review* 69 (2004): 151–69.

30 The "sons of Ham" comes from a misinterpretation of a biblical passage in which Noah gets drunk after a day's work in his vineyard and falls asleep with no clothes on. Ham "saw the nakedness" of his drunken father. He told his brothers, Shem and Japheth, who took a garment and placed it over their father, having "walked backward, their eyes covered" without "seeing their father's nakedness." Noah wakes up to discover what Ham has done and curses Ham's son Canaan to be a "servant of servants...unto his brethren." While there has been dispute over the nature of the immoral act Ham committed and who the "sons of Ham" were historically, this passage has been used as part of an ideological

justification for slavery—the curse was presumed to produce black skin—and was referred to often by Christian slaveholders in the United States. See Kendi, *Stamped.*

31 "Every other black person" is quite literal. One in two black women has a currently incarcerated loved one, while one in two black U.S. adults has had a family member spend at least one night in an American jail or prison. See Lee et al., "Racial Inequalities," and Brian Elderbroom et al., "Every Second: The Impact of the Incarceration Crisis on America's Families," FWD.us, December 2018.

32 James Baldwin, "The American Dream and the American Negro," *New York Times,* March 7, 1965.

33 Carl Bailik, "Detroit Police Response Times No Guide to Effectiveness: Figures Are Clouded by Lack of Standardization," *Wall Street Journal,* August 2, 2013.

34 Annie Sweeney and Jeremy Gorner, "Chicago Police Solve One in Every 20 Shootings. Here Are Some Reasons Why That's So Low," *Chicago Tribune.* August 8, 2018.

35 The 911 response times in Detroit have gotten much better. As of 2019, police took fourteen minutes on average to respond to an emergency call of any kind, and Chicago's homicide clearance rate improved to 53 percent by 2020.

36 Social scientists talk about this as reaching the point of data saturation. This is the point that findings from your data look similar across people and social contexts, and you've heard all the responses that may be possible from a particular source of data.

37 Zo was sentenced before truth-in-sentencing laws were passed in the state of Illinois. He was eligible for "good time," meaning that for every day he served without a major infraction of prison rules, he would be given credit for one day off his sentence. After 1998, people convicted of most crimes in the state of Illinois would serve between 60 and 100 percent of their time. For the crimes Zo committed, which were violent, most people serve 85 percent of their time. Zo would have served at least seventeen years under today's rules. We would likely never have met.

38 This is the famous question W.E.B. Du Bois raises in *The Souls of Black Folk: Essays and Sketches* (Chicago: A. C. McClurg, 1903).

CHAPTER 3: SINNERMAN

1 There were six killings in Birmingham that day. Fourteen-year-old Virgil Ware was killed by a boy returning from a white supremacist rally, and sixteen-year-old Johnny Robinson was shot in the back by a police officer. See Karyn Miller-Medzon, Robin Young, and Ciku Theuri, "4 Little Girls Died in the

16th Street Church Bombing in 1963. A 5th Survived," WBUR.org, April 30, 2019, https://www.wbur.org/hereandnow/2019/04/30/16th-street-baptist -church-bombing-survivor; Tim Padgett and Frank Sikora, "The Legacy of Virgil Ware," *Time* 162, no. 12 (2003): 52–54; and Samuel Momodu, "Johnny Robinson (1947–1963)," Blackpast.org, November 1, 2017.

2   Here I take a note from Saidiya Hartman's writing on "wayward" black girls and women. In Hartman's book *Wayward Lives, Beautiful Experiments: Intimate Histories of Social Upheaval* (New York: W. W. Norton, 2019), the sociologists and social reformers descending on the city to do good or study the Negro problem miss the "beautiful experiments" that so-called wayward black girls, like Ida B. Wells, engage in because they are too busy looking for social disorganization. "She escapes unnoticed on the trellis," Hartman writes, while the interlopers take pictures of clotheslines, toilets, and tenements. This is because the social reformers, the journalists, and the social scientists of the progressive era could not imagine a world in which unnamed black girls could make a city in their own image, where they could find a precious if precarious life despite their social condition.

3   See Geraldine Downey and Scott I. Feldman, "Implications of Rejection Sensitivity for Intimate Relationships," *Journal of Personality and Social Psychology* 70, no. 6 (1996): 1327. See also Geraldine Downey et al., "The Self-Fulfilling Prophecy in Close Relationships: Rejection Sensitivity and Rejection by Romantic Partners," *Journal of Personality and Social Psychology* 75, no. 2 (1998): 545.

4   Echoing this wisdom, sociologists of culture and black life in urban America Marcus Hunter and Zandria Robinson write of a "black map of America," areas where black people, through their sweat and play and creativity, make "chocolate cities"; sociologists call this "place making." See Marcus Anthony Hunter and Zandria Robinson, *Chocolate Cities: The Black Map of American Life* (Oakland: University of California Press, 2018).

5   Detroit has had black residents since French colonists "settled" the land. The historian Tiya Miles tells us that black slaves were made to finish the pelts that were traded in the region, the same pelts that drew Jean Baptiste Point du Sable, the black founder of Chicago, to the area. And Detroit was one of the last stops along the Underground Railroad. The town of Ypsilanti, Michigan, a refuge founded by escaped slaves and black freedmen, was just a day's journey west. The black population exploded after emancipation and again during the first waves of the great migration. About four thousand black people lived in Detroit in 1920. That number swelled to one hundred and twenty thousand by 1930, a 611 percent increase in just a decade. On the heels of the war effort, some four hundred thousand black and white migrants fleeing the South made their way to the city and competed for work on the factory floor. Race riots ensued, the first

major one taking place in 1943. The most famous was the Detroit riot of 1967. The city never quite recovered. See Tiya Miles, *Dawn of Detroit: A Chronicle of Bondage and Freedom in the City of the Straits* (New York: New Press, 2017), and Thomas Sugrue, *The Origins of the Urban Crisis* (Princeton, NJ: Princeton University Press, 2005).

6   "Detroit's Black Bottom, See It Then and Now," *Detroit Free Press,* February 26, 2017, https://www.freep.com/story/news/local/michigan/detroit/2017/02/26/black-bottom-detroit-photos/98421140/.

7   See *United States of America v. City of Detroit, Detroit Police Department,* https://www.clearinghouse.net/chDocs/public/PN-MI-0001-0003.pdf. The Department of Justice, led by Attorney General John Ashcroft, found the Detroit Police Department: (1) used excessive force against Detroit residents; (2) subjected Detroit residents to false arrests; (3) "fail[ed] to protect detainees in DPD holding cells from undue risks of harm by, inter alia, failing to ensure fire safety, failing to provide adequate medical and mental health care, failing to provide adequate supervision, and failing to ensure adequate environmental health and safety conditions"; and (4) deprived residents "of rights, privileges, and immunities secured or protected by the Constitution."

8   Ibid.

9   Ibid.

10   Ibid. The DOJ report found that some officers didn't wash their hands or use gloves when preparing meals for the people they detained, which consisted of a slice of bologna and two pieces of white bread. In one district, officers fed the people they detained just twice in thirty-three hours because the station ran out of bologna.

11   Ibid.

12   In the United States, jails are typically shorter-term facilities for people who are awaiting trial or who have been convicted of less serious offenses. Prisons are generally for people convicted of serious crimes. Detention centers are not prisons, and they are usually different from jails in that the people held there have not yet had their day in court. But there are many exceptions in all of these cases. Jails house mostly pretrial detainees, but trials and court cases can last years. I met people in county jails who had been incarcerated for up to five years. Kalief Browder, for example, was incarcerated on Rikers Island for three years. This is a fairly regular occurrence. I've also met dozens of people who spent just months in prison. Finally, detention centers are supposed to release detainees after a few hours to a few days, but part of the reason for the consent decree was that police lockup facilities held people for days to weeks at a time.

13   Ruth Wilson Gilmore, author of *Golden Gulag* (Berkeley: University of California Press, 2007), would call this a "prison fix." While some may think it's unfair to

term the Detroit Detention Center a prison—people are, after all, held there for forty-eight hours or less—it's a detention center located on a prison compound, situated next door to a prison repurposed to train people for their reentry back into Detroit city limits (the Detroit Reentry program), and it is run under the auspices of the state's prison administration by a prison warden, prison guards, and prison administrators. Thus, one in seven Detroit residents are effectively sent to prison each year. The prison is quite literally being used to address a social problem—in this case, the problem of police abuse.

14   The people who cycle in and out of prisons and, especially, those who cycle in and out of jails are vulnerable by any measure. We've known since 1996 that something like two-thirds of the previously jailed population live on less than six hundred dollars a month, and 80 percent are considered indigent for the purposes of legal defense. This is a very hard group to keep track of. To follow people in this situation over the long term, we took their names and contact information as well as the contact information of two people who could get in touch with them. People ran out of minutes on their cell phone plans often or their phones would be disconnected when we called them. This meant we had to rely on their mothers, spouses, siblings, boyfriends, girlfriends, and children to get in touch with them. The sociologist Bruce Western lays out the difficulties and benefits of tracking formerly incarcerated people over time. See Bruce Western, *Homeward: Life in the Year After Prison* (New York: Russell Sage Foundation, 2018). Similarly, the sociologist Becky Pettit wrote a book, *Invisible Men,* in part as a corrective to the systematic undercounting of incarcerated and formerly incarcerated people by federal agencies and social scientists. Pettit writes in the foreword of her book, "Even after leaving prison and jail, ex-inmates commonly fall outside of the purview of policymakers or the microscope of social science research. Tangential connections to households, curtailed political rights, and weak attachments to the labor market relegate ex-inmates to a liminal status in which they are rarely counted." See Becky Pettit, *Invisible Men: Mass Incarceration and the Myth of Black Progress* (New York: Russell Sage Foundation, 2012).

15   The CDC has been conducting research on father involvement since 2002. It reveals that, while black fathers are less likely than white fathers to be married to the mothers of their children, they are more likely to be involved in routine activities associated with parenting. See Jo Jones and William D. Mosher, "Fathers' Involvement with Their Children: United States, 2006–2010," *National Health Statistics Report* 71 (December 20, 2013), https://www.cdc.gov/nchs/data/nhsr/nhsr071.pdf. See also G. M. Martinez et al., "Fertility, Contraception, and Fatherhood: Data on Men and Women from Cycle 6 (2002) of the National Survey of Family Growth," *Vital and Health Statistics* 23, no. 26 (2006), http://www.cdc.gov/nchs/data/ series/sr_23/sr23_026.pdf.

16   Jones and Mosher, "Fathers' Involvement with Their Children."

17   Epidemiological studies since the 1980s show that many autoworkers died of various forms of cancer. See Josiah Rector, "Environmental Justice at Work: The UAW, the War on Cancer, and the Right to Equal Protection from Toxic Hazards in Postwar America," *Journal of American History* 101, no. 2 (2014): 480–502.

18   Despite findings from studies that confirmed the hunches of the workers who slowly died, there would be no cancer-related settlements for another two decades.

19   The presidents of those companies went to Washington during the great recession, hat in hand, looking for relief. They left the capital with checks while Jimmy sat in prison.

20   I take *economy* to mean the social domain of production, exchange, distribution, and consumption. I'm concerned with how goods and services, including money and resources, flow toward and among people who've been accused of a crime and the people they come in contact with. For formerly incarcerated people, who are excluded from the social, economic, and civic life of the city, the favor is the engine of distribution—that is, goods and services flow in the direction of formerly incarcerated people based on the extent to which they can convince others who have resources to help them. It is a favor because the interested parties put themselves at risk, going above and beyond the expectations of daily life to provide support. They can be sued. They can suffer reputation loss. The people they choose to help can re-offend, or they may have abused their trust in the past. This is a distinct condition for formerly incarcerated people because of the thousands of laws and policies that make it nearly impossible for them to meet their basic human needs without the help of others. Since their criminal records do this work across the domain of social life, they cannot know from whom they will need favors later, raising the stakes of their interactions and changing the nature of their relationships. I've worked with colleagues to elucidate this theory; see Reuben Jonathan Miller and Amanda Alexander, "The Price of Carceral Citizenship: Punishment, Surveillance, and Social Welfare Policy in an Age of Carceral Expansion," *Michigan Journal of Race and Law* 21 (2015): 291, and Reuben Jonathan Miller and Forrest Stuart, "Carceral Citizenship: Race, Rights and Responsibility in the Age of Mass Supervision," *Theoretical Criminology* 21, no. 4 (2017): 532–48.

21   See Rose Hackman, "What Happens When Detroit Shuts Off the Water of 100,000 People," *Atlantic,* July 17, 2014.

22   See Bernadette Atuahene and Christopher R. Berry, "Taxed Out: Illegal Property Tax Assessments and the Epidemic of Tax Foreclosures in Detroit," SSRN.com, June 26, 2018.

23   Jonathan Sherry, "A Data-Driven Look at Diversity in Venture Capital Start-ups," CBInsights.com, June 15, 2015, https://www.cbinsights.com/research/team-blog/venture-capital-diversity-data/.

24   Tracy Jan, "Minority-Owned Firms Report Tougher Time Accessing Credit Than White Firms," *Washington Post,* November 8, 2017, https://www.washingtonpost.com/news/wonk/wp/2017/11/08/minority-owned-firms-report-tougher-time-accessing-credit-than-white-firms/?utm_term=.95697209576b.

CHAPTER 4: MILLIONS OF DETAILS

1   See Olga Grinstead et al., "The Financial Cost of Maintaining Relationships with Incarcerated African American Men: A Survey of Women Prison Visitors," *Journal of African American Men* 6, no. 1 (2001): 59–70. See also Saneta de Vuono-Powell et al., "Who Pays? The True Cost of Incarceration on Families," Ella Baker Center for Human Rights, Forward Together, and Research Action Design, September 2015.

2   There's a beautiful passage in the now famous debate between James Baldwin and William F. Buckley that makes a similar claim. Baldwin speaks of the "millions of details 24 hours of every day which spell out to you that you are a worthless human being." But what's worse, he continues, "nothing you have done, and...nothing you *can* do, will save your son or your daughter from having the same disaster." See James Baldwin, "The American Dream and the American Negro," *New York Times,* March 7, 1965. For an empirical demonstration of the fallout of mass incarceration on children's lives, see Sara Wakefield and Christopher Wildeman, *Children of the Prison Boom: Mass Incarceration and the Future of American Inequality* (New York: Oxford University Press, 2013). See also Sarah Shannon et al., "The Growth, Scope, and Spatial Distribution of People with Felony Records in the United States, 1948–2010," *Demography* 54 (2016): 1795–1818, and Bruce Western and Christopher Wildeman, "The Black Family and Mass Incarceration," *Annals of the American Academy of Political and Social Science* 621, no. 1 (2009): 221–42.

3   These kinds of insights are largely missing from discussions in the social sciences about "reflexivity," which scholars typically use to mean an analysis that accounts for one's subject position and training in the production of scientific knowledge. Many reflexivity statements list researchers' social positions and draw some causal relationship between who the researchers presume they are and what they've found. These kinds of analyses miss the fact that there's a peculiar insight that one may gain from experience with a given social situation because those experiences are viewed as bias, something to control for in a scientific model. I have instead

tried to embrace that experience in hopes of demonstrating what closeness to a social situation might reveal.

4   Supporting an incarcerated loved one is complicated. There are so many different rules, written and unwritten, that you have to follow and so many different people you have to take orders from—the arresting officer, the litigation special-ist, the defense attorney, the bail bondsman, the judge, the guard at the gate, the parking-lot attendant, the guard in the visiting room, the government employee at the desk. Some have had bad days. Some are pleasant. Some are just there to do their jobs. Some raise their voices or fail to acknowledge that you are stand-ing there in front of them, annoyed, as they continue reading their papers or finishing their bagels or drinking their coffee or having their conversation. Any of them can ruin your day. And there's so much to keep track of. Times. Dates. So many different fees. Not to mention your own bills and responsibilities. You have to arrange childcare or take a day off or work extra hours to earn the cash to make the visit. And after you've made a thousand plans to anticipate the one hundred problems you'll most likely encounter, you can still get turned away.

5   See Megan Comfort's beautiful ethnography *Doing Time Together* for a discussion of what she calls "secondary prisonization," or the ways that visiting loved ones are brought into the control and management strategies of prisons. Megan Comfort, *Doing Time Together: Love and Family in the Shadow of the Prisons* (Chicago: University of Chicago Press, 2008).

6   See Hedwig Lee et al., "Racial Inequalities in Connectedness to Imprisoned Individuals in the United States," *Du Bois Review* 12, no. 2 (2015): 269–82; Peter K. Enns et al., "What Percentage of Americans Have Ever Had a Family Member Incarcerated? Evidence from the Family History of Incarceration Survey (FamHIS)," *Socius* 5 (2019): 1–45; and Wakefield and Wildeman, *Children of the Prison Boom.*

7   The anthropologist Michel-Rolph Trouillot writes in *Silencing the Past: Power and the Production of History* (Boston: Beacon Press, 1995), "That U.S. slavery has both officially ended, yet continues in many complex forms—most notably institutionalized racism and the cultural denigration of blackness—makes its representation particularly burdensome in the United States. Slavery here is a ghost, both the past and a living presence; and the problem of historical representation is how to represent that ghost, something that is and yet is not." The specter of black criminality works in similar ways, playing a role in shaping everyday life that's sometimes subtle and sometimes much more forceful. For a fuller discussion, see Reuben Jonathan Miller and Amanda Alexander, "The Price of Carceral Citizenship: Punishment, Surveillance, and Social Welfare Policy in an Age of Carceral Expansion," *Michigan Journal of Race and Law* 21 (2015): 291.

8   In 2018, Ann Arbor was ranked number one on the website Livability's list of best American cities. Its median income, low poverty and crime rates, and high rates of education place it in the top 10 percent of all cities in the country; see https://livability.com/best-places/top-100-best-places-to-live/2018/mi/ann-arbor.

9   See Elizabeth Swavola, Kristine Riley, and Ram Subramanian, *Overlooked: Women and Jails in an Era of Reform* (New York: Vera Institute of Justice, 2016).

10   For an eloquent and concise discussion of the War on Drugs and its fallout, see chapter 4 of Carol Anderson's *White Rage: The Unspoken Truth of Our Racial Divide* (New York: Bloomsbury, 2016).

11   See David Thacher, "The Rise of Criminal Background Screening in Rental Housing," *Law and Social Inquiry* 33, no. 1 (2008): 5–30.

12   This is what legal theorist David Thacher calls "institutional exclusion." The box requiring applicants to disclose their convictions was added to almost all rental applications. This was a serious and unprecedented change. Reviewing the legal record prior to 1971, Thacher writes, "Historically, the common law imposed almost no duties on apartment owners for the condition of their property. Viewing tenants as no different from consumers, it echoed the maxim caveat emptor in the maxim caveat lessee, and it refused to hold landlords liable for disruptive conditions under public nuisance doctrine on the assumption that rental leases conveyed both the rights and the responsibilities for a property's use to the tenant." In addition, Thacher finds that prior to these shifts in the 1990s, housing law protected landlords from crimes tenants committed while on their premises.

13   See Martin Gilens, *Why Americans Hate Welfare: Race, Media, and the Politics of Antipoverty Policy* (Chicago: University of Chicago Press, 2009). For a discussion of the relationship between the development of tough-on-crime policy and the retrenchment of social-welfare policy, see Loïc Wacquant, *Punishing the Poor: The Neoliberal Government of Social Insecurity* (Durham, NC: Duke University Press, 2009). See also Reuben Jonathan Miller, "Race, Hyper-Incarceration, and U.S. Poverty Policy in Historic Perspective," *Sociology Compass* 7, no. 7 (2013): 573–89.

14   This new risk paradigm is most often discussed in regard to treatment. Types of so-called offenders are grouped by their risk profiles and triaged into services. But aside from locking them up, exclusion is a central way to avoid the risks posed by potential criminals. Law professors Malcolm Feeley and Jonathan Simon describe this as the "new penology"; see Feeley and Simon, "The New Penology."

15   This new form of risk management, what Jonathan Simon and Malcolm Feeley call "actuarial justice," moved into employment, family law, and licensing law, when criminal history became a major consideration in establishing "good moral character." A number of state and federal licenses hinge on the moral-character clause, including sitting for the bar exam, getting a license to sell real estate,

cutting hair in a barbershop, joining the board of a nonprofit organization, running a day care, grooming dogs, voting, signing up for food stamps, adopting a child, and getting a student loan. These restrictions vary from state to state but the outcomes are almost always the same. The thousands of laws that regulate the lives of people with criminal records make it nearly impossible for them to live independently—that is, to meet their basic human needs. See Malcolm M. Feeley, "Actuarial Justice and the Modern State," in Gerben Bruinsma, Henk Elffers, and Jan De Keijser, eds., *Punishment, Places and Perpetrators* (London: Routledge, 2012), 78–93. See also Reuben Jonathan Miller and Amanda Alexander, "The Price of Carceral Citizenship: Punishment, Surveillance, and Social Welfare Policy in an Age of Carceral Expansion," *Michigan Journal of Race and Law* 21 (2015): 291.

16 This statement is truer for some people than for others. Martha Stewart's stock seems to have rebounded after her famous stint in a federal penitentiary, and Sheriff Joe Arpaio became more of a celebrity after a judge found him in contempt of court for refusing to stop racially profiling Latino immigrants. He was issued a pardon in 2017 by President Trump, who praised the sheriff for his "more than fifty years of admirable service." That same year, Crystal Mason was sentenced to five years in a state penitentiary. Her crime? Voting in a federal election while on community supervision with a felony record. When she started her sentence, she left three children at home.

CHAPTER 5: IN VICTORY AND SPECTACULAR DEFEAT

1 James Baldwin, "A Report from Occupied Territory," *Nation* 203, no. 2 (1966): 39–43.

2 Roughly two thousand migrant children are held in immigrant detention centers; a staggering seventy thousand migrant children were held in custody at some point in 2019. See Wendy Sawyer and Peter Wagner, "Mass Incarceration: The Whole Pie 2019," *Prison Policy Initiative* 19 (2019).

3 In 2007, 52 percent of state inmates and 63 percent of federal inmates had minor children. See Lauren E. Glaze and Laura Maruschak, "Parents in Prison and Their Minor Children," *Bureau of Justice Statistics Special Report*, August 2008.

4 See Sara Wakefield and Christopher Wildeman, *Children of the Prison Boom: Mass Incarceration and the Future of American Inequality* (New York: Oxford University Press, 2013).

5 This is a conservative estimate; it doesn't include nonresidential parents. See David Murphey and P. Mae Cooper, "Parents Behind Bars: What Happens to Their Children," *Child Trends* 42 (2015): 1–22.

6   See Eli Hagar, "How Incarcerated Parents Are Losing Their Children Forever," Marshall Project, December 3, 2018, https://www.themarshallproject.org/2018 /12/03/how-incarcerated-parents-are-losing-their-children-forever.

7   Ibid. See also Dorothy Roberts, *Shattered Bonds: The Color of Child Welfare* (New York: Basic Books, 2002).

8   Black people are twice as likely to be arrested and five times more likely to be incarcerated than their white counterparts. They serve longer sentences—20 percent longer, on average—and do their time under harsher prison conditions.

9   Summarizing three decades of research, the legal scholar Dorothy Roberts and legal advocate Lisa Sangoi write, "Black families are more likely to be reported to the child abuse hotline and investigated for child abuse and neglect. They are more likely to have cases against them substantiated and to have their children removed from their care... In places like New York City and Chicago, Black and brown families compose virtually all families under supervision and virtually all the children in foster care. Once in foster care, Black children generally receive inferior services and are kept out of their homes for longer periods of time than their white counterparts. Black parents are also subjected to termination of parental rights at higher rates than white parents." See Dorothy Roberts and Lisa Sangoi, "Black Families Matter: How the Child Welfare System Punishes Poor Families of Color," *Appeal,* March 26, 2019, https://theappeal.org/black-families-matter-how-the-child-welfare-system-punishes-poor-families-of-color-33ad20e2882e/. See also Roberts, *Shattered Bonds.*

10   Rather than offering poor pregnant women the support that they needed, like drug treatment or access to food and stable housing, officials arrested them, and their children were sent to foster care when a doctor, nurse, or well-meaning social worker reported the mothers' addiction. See Dorothy Roberts, *Killing the Black Body: Race, Reproduction and the Meaning of Liberty* (New York: Vintage, 1997).

11   Melinda Atkinson, "Aging Out of Foster Care: Towards a Universal Safety Net for Former Foster Care Youth," *Harvard Civil Rights and Civil Liberties Law Review* 43 (2008): 183.

12   Adoption and Safe Families Act of 1997, Pub. L. No. 105-89, 111 Stat. 2115 (1997), https://www.congress.gov/105/plaws/publ89/PLAW-105publ89.pdf.

13   D. Kaeble, "Time Served in State Prison, 2016," Bureau of Justice Statistics, November 29, 2018.

14   See Hagar, "How Incarcerated Parents Are Losing Their Children Forever."

15   In Illinois there is a "rebuttal assumption" concerning the depravity of a parent once that person has been convicted of three felonies. A rebuttal assumption means that the parent's depravity is established and presumed unless the parent proves otherwise, the same way a court will presume the innocence of a defendant until

he or she is proven guilty. Once a person receives a third felony conviction, the burden of proof is on the defendant to prove to the court he or she is *not* depraved. Those felony offenses could have occurred decades ago as long as the defendant's last felony conviction was within a five-year window of the proceedings. See http://www.ilga.gov/legislation/ilcs/ilcs3.asp?ActID=2098&ChapterID=59. The largest study of returning prisoners to date found that people released from jails and prisons had 4.9 criminal convictions on average. This exceeds the bar to establish depravity, which would make them, per the court's definition, unfit parents. See Matthew R. Durose, Alexia D. Cooper, and Howard N. Snyder, "Recidivism of Prisoners Released in 30 States in 2005: Patterns from 2005 to 2010," *Bureau of Justice Statistics Bulletin,* April 2014.

16   White children represented just 4 percent of all foster-care admissions in New York City in 2018. Black children represented 40 percent. See "2018 Monitoring and Analysis Profiles with Selected Trend Data: 2014–2018," Office of Strategic Planning and Policy Development, New York State, https://ocfs.ny.gov/main/reports/maps/counties/New%20York%20State.pdf.

17   Roberts and Sangoi, "Black Families Matter."

18   A Google search for *adopt a prison baby* yields eleven million hits. There are thousands of online forums where would-be adoptive parents seek legal advice on how best to facilitate the adoption, even when the child's biological parents are unwilling to give the child up. In one forum, a woman lamented being asked to post bail for a pregnant mother. The prisoner's husband, who was also incarcerated and whose child the woman wished to adopt, explained that his wife "won't make it in here." He asked her to post the five-thousand-dollar bail needed to free his pregnant wife. "She thinks she will be found innocent," the would-be adoptive mother wrote on the message board. "I think she will be found guilty."

A different poster in the adoption forum compared the father's bail request to extortion. The would-be parent assured him that she would never "buy a child." Notwithstanding the "thousands of dollars in certain attorney fees" that she was more than willing to pay, paying bail for a pregnant mother whose child she wished to adopt was a bridge too far. "We told them that the best thing for her (meaning the pregnant mother in jail) is to let us adopt the child," the woman wrote. "Child protective services will just take it, like they did her other two." That is, the would-be adoptive mother would not post the bail for the pregnant mother of the child she hoped to adopt. She was happy to pay an attorney, but not "buy a child" by purchasing the mother's freedom. The best thing for the pregnant woman to do would be to let a stranger adopt her "jail baby." She should make this life-altering decision from her cell, the place where her husband said he didn't think that she would make it.

19   A year after the rule's passage, HUD issued a new report. The act, they said, was a success: "Now, an entire household can be evicted or denied housing if a housing authority has reasonably determined that any member or guest of a household is engaging in illegal drug use or criminal or other activities." See "Meeting the Challenge: Public Housing Authorities Respond to the 'One Strike and You're Out' Initiative," U.S. Department of Housing and Urban Development, September 1997.

20   This state of affairs, what the sociologist Waverly Duck, following Erving Goffman, might call an "interaction order," has infiltrated and altered even the most intimate of relationships. For a discussion of interaction orders as they relate to urban drug markets, see Waverly Duck, *No Way Out: Precarious Living in the Shadow of Poverty and Drug Dealing* (Chicago: University of Chicago Press, 2015).

CHAPTER 6: CHAINS AND CORPSES

1   See *Miller v. Alabama,* 567 U.S. 460 (2012).

2   I. A. Binswanger et al., "Release from Prison—a High Risk of Death for Former Inmates," *New England Journal of Medicine* 356 (2007): 157–65.

3   See ibid. and Dora M. Dumont et al., "Public Health and the Epidemic of Incarceration," *Annual Review of Public Health* 33 (2012): 325–39.

4   See Dumont et al., "Public Health and the Epidemic of Incarceration."

5   People who have been incarcerated report worse health outcomes after they leave prison than they reported the year before; see John A. Schnittker, "Enduring Stigma: The Long-Term Effects of Incarceration on Health," *Journal of Health and Social Behavior* 48, no. 2 (2007): 115–30.

6   See Evelyn J. Patterson, "The Dose-Response of Time Served in Prison on Mortality: New York State, 1989–2003," *American Journal of Public Health* 103, no. 3 (2013): 523–28.

7   Dumont et al., "Public Health and the Epidemic of Incarceration."

8   See Ashley Nellis, "Still Life: America's Increasing Use of Life and Long-Term Sentences," Sentencing Project, May 3, 2017.

9   The organization itself was the result of a class-action lawsuit. Prisoners' rights advocates, most of whom were jailhouse lawyers, filed motions against their state Department of Corrections for denying their right to effective legal counsel. The Supreme Court mandated the launch of Prison Legal Services in 1972 as a part of the remedy. The organization worked to support the civil and human rights of prisoners, largely through litigation.

10   See Orlando Patterson, *Slavery and Social Death: A Comparative Study* (Cambridge, MA: Harvard University Press, 1982). For an application in U.S. jails and

prisons, see Joshua M. Price, *Prison and Social Death* (New Brunswick, NJ: Rutgers University Press, 2015).

11   See Patterson, *Slavery and Social Death,* and Price, *Prison and Social Death.*

CHAPTER 7: TREATMENT

1   The national rate of violent crime and the rate of violent crime across Chicago and cities like it dropped substantially in the decade that Zo was in prison, a trend that has continued, but crime rates did not drop in some of the nation's most disadvantaged neighborhoods. In a study of homicide records between 1990 and 2010 in Chicago, Andrew Papachristos and colleagues found that while crime rates dropped in almost all Chicago neighborhoods, the "relative inequality in crime between the city's safest and most dangerous neighborhoods actually increased by 10 percent." This means that while the crime rate generally dropped, the gap between the safest and most dangerous neighborhoods increased, in part because homicides remained concentrated in the city's most dangerous neighborhoods. See Andrew V. Papachristos, Noli Brazil, and Tony Cheng, "Understanding the Crime Gap: Violence and Inequality in an American City," *City and Community* 17, no. 4 (2018): 1051–74.

2   Ibid.

3   See Robert P. Fairbanks, *How It Works: Recovering Citizens in Post-Welfare Philadelphia* (Chicago: University of Chicago Press, 2009).

4   Even without the great recession having exacerbated already disproportionate rates of poverty and unemployment in Chicago's "inner city," the Near West Side and communities like it have remained among the city's most prominent sites of social containment and control through the community-based, federal, and state-administered criminal justice and social welfare organizations enmeshed within its landscape. The innocuously titled Youth Center and the seemingly benign Center for Adult Transitions are in fact a juvenile-detention facility and a work-release program for state detainees, respectively. Mercy's Wings serves the needs of formerly incarcerated women struggling with addiction, unemployment, and family separation, and St. Michael's Way serves drug-addicted men seeking work and stable housing after lengthy prison terms.

5   See President George H. W. Bush's Inaugural Address at https://www.c-span.org /video/?c4294402/president-george-hw-bush-inaugural-address. The unemployment rate was 7.2 percent when President George H. W. Bush left office in 1992, a 30 percent increase from when he took office in 1988.

6   The Second Chance Act reinvigorated the debate over the place of rehabilitation

in criminal justice administration and signaled the ascendance of prisoner-reentry programming as the rehabilitative strategy of choice, renewing a sense of optimism that prisoners could be rehabilitated. This was a significant departure from how we thought about prisons after the 1970s and the advent of the "what works" movement. See Reuben Jonathan Miller, "Devolving the Carceral State: Race, Prisoner Reentry, and the Micro-Politics of Urban Poverty Management," *Punishment and Society* 16, no. 3 (2014): 305–35.

7   Second Chance Act of 2007, Pub. L. No. 110-199 (2007), http://thomas.loc.gov /cgi-bin/bdquery/ z?d110:HR01593:@@@D&summ2=m&.

8   See Devah Pager, *Marked: Race, Crime, and Finding Work in an Era of Mass Incarceration* (Chicago: University of Chicago Press, 2008), and Jeremy Travis, *But They All Come Back: Facing the Challenges of Prisoner Reentry* (Washington, DC: Urban Institute Press, 2005).

9   See Nina Martin, Sandra Morales, and Nik Theodore, "Migrant Worker Centers: Contending with Downgrading in the Low-Wage Labor Market," *GeoJournal* 68, no. 2 (2007): 155–65.

10 For a discussion of the application of human-capital theory to prisoner reentry, see Reuben Jonathan Miller, "Devolving the Carceral State: Race, Prisoner Reentry, and the Micro-Politics of Urban Poverty Management," *Punishment and Society* 16, no. 3 (2014): 305–35. For general discussion of the theory, see J. Heckman, "Doing It Right: Job Training and Education," *National Affairs* 135 (1999): 86–107, and J. Heckman and Y. Rubinstein, "The Importance of Noncognitive Skills: Lessons from the GED Testing Program," *American Economic Review* 91, no. 2 (2001): 145–49.

CHAPTER 8: POWER

1   See Angela Y. Davis, *Freedom Is a Constant Struggle: Ferguson, Palestine, and the Foundations of a Movement* (Chicago: Haymarket, 2016).

2   See Ryan Gabrielson, Ryann Grochowski Jones, and Eric Sagara, "Deadly Force, in Black and White," ProPublica, October 10, 2014.

APPENDIX: THE GIFT OF PROXIMITY

1   See https://www.youtube.com/watch?v=2zkWshZRm-M&t=1467s.

2   See, e.g., Angela Y. Davis, *Women, Race, and Class* (New York: Vintage, 2011); Patricia Hill Collins, *Black Sexual Politics: African Americans, Gender, and the New Racism* (London: Routledge, 1990); and Kimberlé Crenshaw, "Mapping

the Margins: Intersectionality, Identity Politics, and Violence Against Women of Color," *Stanford Law Review* 43 (July 1991): 1241–99.

3   For a challenge to the duality of objectivity and relativism and a discussion of the "good trick" of the presumption of neutrality in the scientific endeavor, see Donna Haraway, "Situated Knowledges: The Science Question in Feminism and the Privilege of Partial Perspective," *Feminist Studies* 14, no. 3 (1988): 575–99.

4   Loïc Wacquant, "For a Sociology of Flesh and Blood," *Qualitative Sociology* 38, no. 1 (2015): 1–11.

5   Erving Goffman, "On Fieldwork," *Journal of Contemporary Ethnography* 18 (1989): 125–26.

6   For a discussion of empathy and its limits, see Saidiya V. Hartman, *Scenes of Subjection: Terror, Slavery, and Self-Making in Nineteenth-Century America* (New York: Oxford University Press, 1997).

7   Randol Contreras might call me an "insider/outsider." See Randol Contreras, "The Need for More 'Carnal,'" *Qualitative Sociology* 38, no. 1 (2015): 27–31.

INDEX

About the Author

REUBEN JONATHAN MILLER is an assistant professor at the University of Chicago in the School of Social Service Administration. Before coming to Chicago, he was an assistant professor of social work at the University of Michigan, a faculty affiliate with the Populations Studies Center, the Program for Research on Black Americans, and the Department of Afroamerican and African Studies. He has been a member of the Institute for Advanced Study in Princeton, New Jersey; a fellow at New America and the Rockefeller Foundation; and a visiting scholar at the University of Texas at Austin and Dartmouth College. A native son of Chicago, he lives with his wife and children on the city's South Side.

@reubenjmiller